1004533863

D0122613

SIN AND SOCIETY

in the seventeenth century

SIN AND SOCIETY
in the seventeenth century

JOHN ADDY

Routledge

London and New York

LEARNING RESOURCE
CENTRE
GRANT MacEWAN
COLLEGE

FOR ANTHONY McLOUGHLIN

First published 1989,
by Routledge
11 New Fetter Lane, London EC4P 4EE
29 West 35th Street, New York, NY 10001

© 1989 John Addy

Set in 10/12 Baskerville by Mayhew Typesetting, Bristol
and printed in Great Britain by
T.J. Press (Padstow) Ltd, Padstow, Cornwall

All rights reserved. No part of this book may be reprinted
or reproduced or utilized in any form or by any electronic,
mechanical, or other means, now known or hereafter
invented, including photocopying and recording, or in any
information storage or retrieval system, without permission
in writing from the publishers.

British Library Cataloguing in Publication Data

Addy, John
Sin and society in the seventeenth century.
1. Church of England. Diocese of Chester.
Consistory Court
I. Title
262'.03'42714

ISBN 0-415-01874-9

Library of Congress Cataloging in Publication Data

Addy, John
Sin and society in the seventeenth century / John Addy.
p. cm.
Bibliography: p.
Includes index.
1. Church of England. Diocese of Chester — History 2. Chester
Region (England) — Moral conditions. 3. Chester Region (England)
— Church history — 17th century. I. Title.
BX5017.C5A4 1989
283'42714 — dc19 88-30369

CONTENTS

CONTENTS

PREFACE

This study is the product of some thirty years of research undertaken during vacation periods and as opportunities arose. My interest in ecclesiastical courts and their records is the direct result of the research I undertook when studying for a higher degree at the University of Leeds.

My first foray was in the surviving records of the archdeaconry of Richmond, now located in the record offices at Preston, Carlisle, Leeds, and Chester, when I discovered that only a very preliminary listing had taken place. It quickly became apparent that proper sorting, classifying, and listing of the records would have to be undertaken, if I and future historians working in this field were to make any sense of what had survived the centuries of neglect, ravages of damp, fungi, mice, and general decay. Theoretically, the boxes containing the court records were supposed to consist simply of such records, but when investigated yielded up some fascinating information on churchwardens' accounts, church plans, and a variety of other official documents.

My interest then began to extend to the whole of the ancient diocese of Chester and by 1987 I had catalogued the whole of the surviving consistory court papers between 1600 and 1730 which in total amounted to some 10,500 files. As a result, it has proved to be a somewhat difficult task to compile a selection of cause papers fully illustrative of the cases, since the available material that was produced is so vast.

One would have wished to include some of the many testamentary causes, for these throw light on the living and social conditions that many testators experienced, at the same time providing useful information for genealogists. But these have been excluded from the study, as has the huge number of tithe disputes. These really involve a study of the economic problems of parish and deanery, and together with the testamentary causes could well be incorporated into a further study.

In the end it was decided to compile a study of causes to illustrate standards of morality and social relationships that were prevalent in this huge diocese during the seventeenth century, and which in some ways are typical of present-day morality.

What has been attempted is a study of the problems that beset those clergy who held livings that were endowed with inadequate stipends, so that only those who were ill-trained and totally unsuited for the life of a parish priest would accept them. Child abuse is another area that has been reviewed, for the abuse of children, especially by schoolmasters, reflects some of the same malaise that hits press headlines today. The disputes concerning title to a seat or pew in church not only reflect the social ambitions of property owners, but provide details of the ownership and tenancy of houses over several generations, so providing family historians with a further source of information. Defamation, sexual slander, and matrimonial problems were as frequent then as they can be at the present day, and would have provided the tabloid press, had it existed, with good material for some entertaining stories. I have attempted to fit the cause papers into the seventeenth-century scene in an effort to penetrate the minds of the middling and poorer sort of people in Stuart England, who never kept diaries.

The consistory court files can be disappointing in that few exist that give the complete sides for both parties. Often there is no record when a cause is concluded, for frequently no sentence survives, implying that the cause was either settled out of court or lapsed because funds were no longer available to continue the cause in court: the consistory act books do not record a sentence in every cause.

What follows in this study is entirely due to the support and encouragement I have received from many friends and colleagues to produce a study of the Chester consistory court which I hope will encourage others to undertake similar studies in other dioceses so that a reliable picture can be constructed of the thoughts and lives of those in seventeenth-century England who comprised the major part of the population.

I am indebted to many friends, but I must especially extend my thanks to Dr A.T. Thacker, Mrs Jenny Kermode, Dr Christopher Hill, Mr G.C.F. Forster, and the archivists at Leeds, Carlisle, Kendal, Preston, and Chester Records Offices for allowing me easy access to the cause papers. Also to Dr W.J. Shiels of the Borthwick Institute of Historical Research, Dr J.A. Sharpe, Dr P.A. Clark, Dr C. Hill, and Mr F.G. Emmison for permission to quote, and the Principal and Governing Body of the College of Ripon and York St John for their unstinting support. Finally I must express my sincere thanks to Mrs Susan Collins for her patience in typing the final text and without whose assistance I should have been sorely tried.

If readers obtain as much pleasure from reading this study as I have had in compiling it, I shall be more than amply rewarded.

College of Ripon and York St John
September 1988

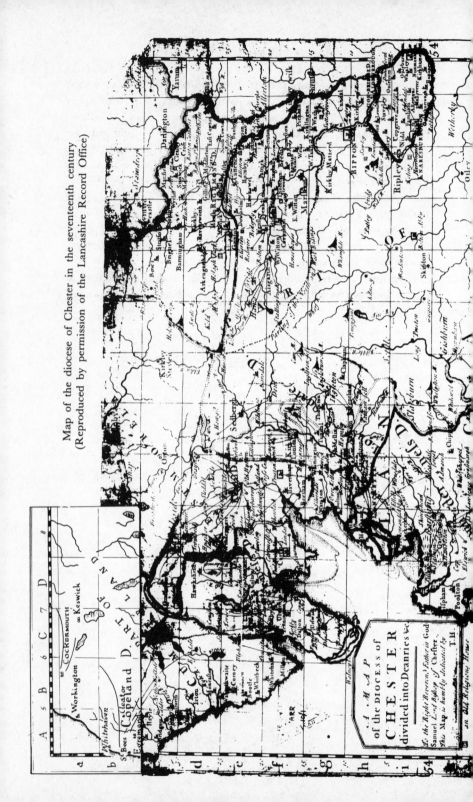

Map of the diocese of Chester in the seventeenth century
(Reproduced by permission of the Lancashire Record Office)

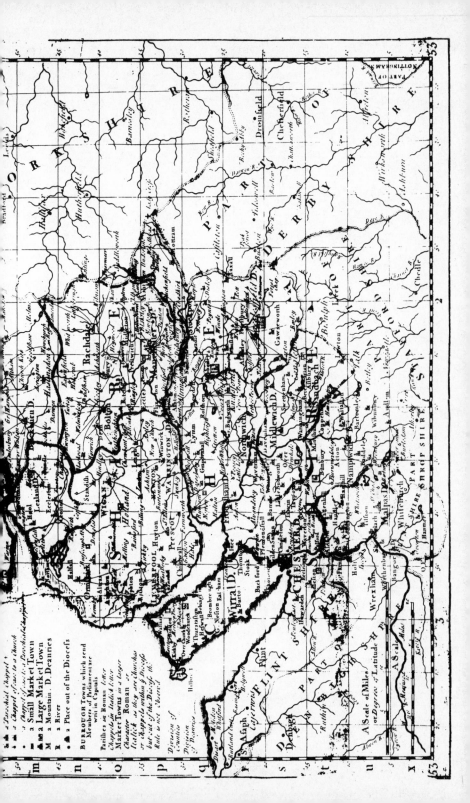

Part 1

THE DIOCESE

Chapter One

THE STRUCTURE OF THE DIOCESE

It is essential, if one is to understand the scope of the cases that came before the consistory court, to comprehend the structure of Chester diocese. In origin it was one of the six dioceses founded by Henry VIII in 1541. The new diocese was created by removing the archdeaconry of Chester from the diocese of Lichfield and Coventry and the archdeaconry of Richmond from the huge diocese of York. The archdeaconry of Chester included within its boundaries the county of Chester and all Lancashire, south of the Ribble, the Welsh counties of Denbigh and Flint, and a few isolated parishes in Carmarthen and Caernarvon.

The archdeaconry of Richmond extended over a vast area of land. It included that portion of Lancashire between the Ribble and the Derwent, plus the southern half of the county of Westmorland and the coastal strip of Cumbria. It extended across the Pennines to take in the rural deaneries of Richmond, Catterick, and Boroughbridge, extending as far south as Nun Monkton some six miles west of York. The boundaries of this archdeaconry indicate a survival of the territorial organization that existed in the north before the county boundaries were clarified.[1] For administrative purposes the archdeaconry of Chester was subdivided into twelve rural deaneries and that of Richmond into eight.

Geographically the new diocese was one of great variety. Cheshire was an area of flat, even country consisting of arable, pasture and meadow land, with large woods and parks all interspersed with tracts of heath and common land. The enclosed farmlands produced wheat, oats, barley, and rye. The breeding and fattening of Irish cattle was an expanding industry while

3

poultry farming was extensively practised. In order to feed the population of the growing and prosperous city of Chester, market gardening was steadily becoming an established part of the rural economy by 1640. Wild fowl of all kinds was in abundant supply and salt was mined at Northwich, Nantwich, and Middlewich. On the whole, the Cheshire area was a prosperous region, and its population was fond of litigation, so providing the consistory court with no small amount of business.

To the north was Lancashire the south-west of this county was a region of forest and moss whose existing woodland was slowly cleared during the seventeenth century and the land divided into enclosed fields. One result arising from enclosure was the number of claims by clergy for tithe on crops from newly enclosed ground. Tithes were part of an incumbent's stipend, and clergy thought it worth going to a certain amount of trouble to claim them.

The peat mosses and marshes formed an obstacle to easy travel and communication. Indeed, the extensive marshlands of Chat Moss, Trafford Moss, and Carrington Moss formed a complete barrier between Lancashire and Cheshire. Until 1805, when these marsh lands were drained, it was extremely dangerous to attempt a crossing of these marshes. Hence there were only three crossing points over the Mersey, at Warrington by a bridge, and at Widnes and Liverpool by ferry boat. The main north–south road was via Warrington, which was the lowest point at which it was possible to bridge the Mersey.[2]

East Lancashire was, for the most part, an area of mountain and moorland where the climate was bleak, and the soil bare and most unpromising, inhabited by a rough, tough society.[3] The land around Euxton and Leyland was chiefly moss, while to the north of Bootle lay the Altcar marshes and sand dunes. To the east were the high Rivington moors, an area almost denuded of population so that the only line of communication from east to west was the highway between Wigan and Bolton. The existence of swift streams of soft water from the moors and supply of local wool enabled the woollen industry to develop around Rochdale, whose society revealed all the moral weakness associated with artisan life in the seventeenth century.

The southern part of Cumbria and Westmorland, including the Lake District, was a wild, rugged, mountainous area composed of fell, moor, and lakes, where copper, iron, slate, and wood abounded; an area whose mineral resources were relatively un-exploited save on a small scale, so that in the seventeenth century this was a relatively poor region. The two ports of Whitehaven and Workington conducted an extensive shipping trade with Ireland and the supply of local wool from the Westmorland fells enabled a small textile industry to flourish at Kendal and Kirby Lonsdale. Until the construction of a system of turnpike roads, in the eighteenth century, the only easy access to the coastal strip of Cumbria, which formed the rural deanery of Copeland, was across the dangerous sands of Morecambe Bay.[4]

Over the Pennines in the three Yorkshire deaneries of Rich-mond, Catterick, and Boroughbridge mixed farming with cattle rearing and sheep breeding predominated. Lead mining flourished in Wensleydale and Nidderdale where the morals of the mining communities were a source of some concern to the incumbents of the Dales parishes.[5]

At the end of the seventeenth century the diocese of Chester was some 120 miles in length and 570 miles round the perimeter, containing within its boundaries some 533 churches and parochial chapels. In common with the other three dioceses of the northern province, the parishes were extensive in area. For instance, the parish of Prestbury comprised some 62,740 acres and included within its boundaries ten parochial chapels of ease, of which that in the growing town of Macclesfield was one. Rochdale, an equally large Lancashire parish, included the remote Pennine villages of Saddleworth, Uppermill, and Todmorden. In north Lancashire the parish of Whalley was twice the size of the old undivided parish of Leeds. The parishes of Cumbria and Westmorland were equally large; that of Crosthwaite extended over seventy square miles and the parish of Kendal included within its boundaries no less than fifty villages and fourteen chapels of ease. Millom, another large parish, extended some eighteen miles up the Duddon valley, so efficient ecclesiastical government was often difficult to enforce.

The diary of Henry Prescott, deputy registrar of the diocese between 1689 and 1719, records the difficulties of travel at this period. He describes the appalling conditions of the main roads through Lancashire, the problems encountered when using the secondary ones, his encounters with storms, floods, and tempests that made each journey an adventure. Little wonder that he records his thanks to God for his safe return home to Chester after each journey; 'arrived safe at my corner. D.O.M.G.' is a frequent entry in his diary.[7]

A good illustration of the problem is presented by the dispute between the vicar of Warton and the inhabitants of Silverdale chapel in 1687 which was not finally resolved until 1695. Thomas Lawson, vicar of Warton, disliked the activities of James Atkinson, the reader and schoolmaster of Silverdale, in holding divine service twice each Sunday. Lawson thought the inhabitants ought to attend their parish church, except in winter, and so reduce the number of services at Silverdale.

John Sparke, vicar of Bolton-le-Sands, wrote to the bishop about the matter in September 1691. In his letter Sparke described the problems of travel between Silverdale and Warton parish church: 'the danger of the way on one hand, the sea on the other, the rocks in the middle, the mosses, all such as prohibit the people of Silverdale to pay a constant attendance at their parish church'. He also rebuked the bishop for his negligence by claiming that, if he had acted earlier, then 'these trifles would never become the blabbing Country's discourse nor give occasion to these wild mountaineers to show their teeth'. Finally, Dr Fenton, vicar of Lancaster, visited Silverdale and described in a letter to the bishop the problems he faced.

> The distance between Warton Church and Silverdale chapel I take to be four miles. The way is plain & open from the sides of two great hills to all the severity of the weather Seawards. In the midst lies a deep Mosse where I thought we must have left our horses & were once in despair of making our way, till Mr. Lawson's clerk broke a hedge & conducted us thro' mens grounds, which might have indicted us for a trespasse.[8]

The problems of communication and travel made it most difficult for any bishop of Chester to have had but a scant knowledge of conditions in the remote parishes of the Lake District and Pennine moorlands until the construction of the turnpike roads in the following century.

Chapter Two

THE ADMINISTRATION OF THE DIOCESE

The machinery for the administration of this difficult and poor diocese was clumsy and involved since it differed in many ways from that operating in other English dioceses. In the Middle Ages, the archdeacons of Chester and Richmond had acquired additional powers. The archdeacon of Richmond, by an agreement arranged with Archbishop William Melton in 1331, was granted quasi-episcopal powers, an agreement that implied that at some date in the future a strong archdeacon, with powerful lay support, would be able to create an independent archdeaconry of Richmond, which could be elevated to diocesan status.[1]

When William Knight was nominated bishop of Bath and Wells in 1540 he was archdeacon of both the archdeaconries, and resigned one to the archbishop of York and the other to the bishop of Lichfield.[2] Henry VIII then united the two archdeaconries to form the new diocese of Chester, with the dissolved monastery of St Werburgh as the cathedral church and administrative centre. The same problems then arose in Chester as had arisen in Exeter where the centre of the diocese was too far removed from those parishes where trouble could and did arise.[3]

Under the new arrangements, the office of archdeacon was vested in the bishop so that from 1541 onwards the two archdeacons were titular officials only with a stipend of £50 per annum, each paid from the revenues of the diocese. This reduction of the powers of the archdeacon was to prevent any future archdeacon creating a semi-autonomous jurisdiction within his archdeaconry. The bishop was entitled, as archdeacon, to appoint one or more commissaries as he thought fit, to act on his behalf in the archdeaconries, which was in effect a virtual continuation of the medieval practice. By this means, the powers of the commissary could be regulated to suit the policy of any bishop at any time. This is well illustrated by analysing the causes that were heard at Chester, rather than at Richmond, during the sixteenth and seventeenth centuries. A succession of very able commissaries of Richmond, after 1660, combined with a number of short episcopates, encouraged the commissaries to attempt to recover some of their lost powers.[4]

The diocesan chancellor, who was also vicar general and official principal, acted as commissary for the Chester archdeaconry with powers to hear and determine contentious causes in the courts.[5] The diocesan officials, including the commissaries and rural deans, were appointed by letters patent which set out their powers in detail.[6]

Since the archidiaconal jurisdiction was vested in the bishop, he required deputies to act for him in the rural deaneries. Therefore the bishop controlled the office of deans rural, who were to exercise their authority, as representatives of the bishop, under the terms of their letters patent and the custom of the archdeaconries. They had the power to hold visitations and correction courts, to prove wills and grant probate for the estates of deceased persons who left personalty below £40 in value. Wills of deceased knights, esquires, and clergy were proved either at Richmond or Chester. Until 1700, the bishop reserved the deanery of Amounderness as preferment for his chaplain, so it was administered from Chester rather than Richmond.[7] By ancient custom, the commissary of Richmond had his own registrar to record his acts, as had rural deans.[8] In order to maintain a watching brief over the activities of the deanery registrars, the diocesan registrar became registrar general, those in the deaneries acting as his deputies.[9]

The peculiarity of the Chester diocese that set it apart from other English dioceses was the existence of not one but two consistory courts. The Chester consistory was presided over by the chancellor, and the Richmond consistory by the commissary who sat in Trinity Chapel, Richmond. It had been the custom, at least since 1331, for the archdeacon to have his own consistory at Richmond, usually presided over by his commissary. This custom was continued after 1541 for geographical reasons, especially the problem of crossing the Pennines in winter. The existence of two identical courts, with proctors competing for business, led to many disputes between the chancellor and the commissary, as appeal causes from Richmond were transferred directly to the chancery court at York and not to Chester.[10]

This orderly diocesan arrangement was disturbed by the existence of a number of peculiar jurisdictions outside the direct control of the bishop. Two of these, Masham and Middleham, were large tracts of territory. The former was dissolved in 1547 when the revenues of the peculiar were granted to Trinity College, Cambridge, and the jurisdiction to Chancellor Wriothesley as a lay fief.[11]

Middleham had been the favourite residence of Richard III as Duke of Gloucester, who converted the parish church into a collegiate church for a dean and six canons to commemorate his marriage to Lady Ann Neville. In 1481, Archbishop Rotherham exempted the church from all ecclesiastical jurisdiction, and this was later confirmed by a bull of Pope Sixtus IV; it continued to be a royal peculiar until it was dissolved in 1857.[12]

The dean and chapter of York had acquired control of the remote parish of Kirby Ireleth and its parochial chapels in the deanery of Copeland.[13] The chapter had also acquired control over the parishes of Aldborough, Boroughbridge, and Burton Leonard with the right to hear and determine contentious causes.[14]

During the seventeenth and eighteenth centuries, the Anglican Church and its organization was regarded as the spiritual expression of the community. Arthur Warne had described it in these words:

> this community was expected to be loyal to the Crown as head not only of the Church but also of the State, and respectful to the laws of man as to those of God. Ideally this community included all Englishmen and those who remained outside, as Roman Catholic or Dissenter, had to be accounted for and their conduct watched for subversive activity.[15]

The methods by which the Church exercised discipline and control, or attempted to, was by the process of visitation. The churchwardens had to complete and return to the visitor – the bishop, commissary, or rural dean – their replies to the questions in the Book of Articles. The questions asked required answers as to the state of the parsonage house, the churchyard, the church fabric and church furnishings, details of services held in the church, and finally reports upon the morals and behaviour of both clergy and laity.[16]

The consciences of many churchwardens must have been severely strained when compiling their returns. Frequently they kept an eye on the next year's elections, so often omitted to present causes that might be prejudicial to their re-election to office. Offenders presented to the visitor were cited to appear at the church appointed for the visitation court. Cases were dealt with by summary justice, there was no jury, and offenders were either convicted and subjected to a humiliating public penance, to be performed in one or more churches or market-places, or cleared by compurgation, a practice that continued in Chester diocese long after it had disappeared elsewhere.[17] Those who ignored the citation and failed to appear were automatically excommunicated.

Serious cases were heard in the consistory court before the bishop or his chancellor, as vicar general, with legal representation. The majority of cases heard in the consistory court involved defamation, fornication, adultery, bastardy, sexual slander, divorce, matrimonial cases, drunkenness, refusal to pay church rates, tithes, to conform to the established church, brawling in church, working on Sundays and holy days, preaching puritan doctrines, or cases transferred from the visitation court; it is this formidable list of subjects that has provided the material for the body of this book.

Criminal or 'office' cases, as they were known, could be initiated by the consistory judge himself of his own 'mere motion' or promoted by another party, while civil or instance cases were always between party and party. Usually the court followed a form known as plenary procedure. This system produced large quantities of documents, of which the principal ones were, first, the full statement of the case known as judge's articles in office cases, or the libel in instance ones, and, second, the allegations or counter-statement of the defence. Then followed a number of statements or numbered questions known as interrogatories used to examine witnesses, and to which both the plaintiff and the defendant responded. The replies of the witnesses were recorded and known as depositions. Other papers could be attached to strengthen the case by either party, such as plans or deeds, to support the articles of either side. The case was concluded by the sentence definitive. An appeal was possible to the chancery court at York and from there to the judges delegate in London.

In the case of office causes, if the accused could prove his innocence by compurgation – that is, by the oaths of a specific number of honest men – he was absolved. If he failed, he had to perform a penance in public in church on Sunday morning, dressed in a white sheet, bare-legged and bare-foot, holding a white wand in his hand. He had to repeat after the incumbent the details of his offence and then obtain a certificate of performance signed by the incumbent and churchwardens. Towards the close of the seventeenth century penances tended to be commuted for money payments. Failure to respond to an order to perform a penance meant excommunication, and the obstinate could also be arrested and imprisoned by the secular arm if requested.[18]

The structure of these courts was medieval with their judges, proctors, registrar, and apparitors (court summoners). There had been an opportunity to modernize the procedure of the courts at the Restoration but, according to Dr A. Whiteman, this opportunity was lost and no changes were made.[19]

The diocesan authorities had problems with those who owed no allegiance to the Church of England. Roman Catholics were very strong in the Lancashire deaneries of Amounderness and Furness, while there were pockets of recusancy in the deaneries of Richmond, Catterick, and Boroughbridge. Puritanism was well established in the textile parishes of Rochdale and Bolton and in the chapels of Manchester, which by 1660 had become parishes where Presbyterians and Independents were present in large numbers. From 1652 onwards the Quakers had established themselves, sometimes exercising considerable influence, in northern parts of the diocese.[20]

It can by no means be asserted that the clumsy ecclesiastical administration effectively handled those who dissented from the Church of England. Nevertheless, quarter-sessions maintained a watchful eye on those groups of wandering people who attended no church. As with the church courts, so the efficiency of quarter-sessions depended upon the keenness or otherwise of the justices of peace in enforcing the law.

Under such circumstances it was essential that both Church and State supported each other. Until 1640 the church courts were supported by the High Commission, based in York for the northern province. Even this royal prerogative court, and the Chester High Commission, faced the same problem as the traditional church courts: the inability to compel defendants to appear. Only a minority of those cited ever appeared, yet for those who did, the High Commission had powers that made it a formidable weapon.[21]

The High Commission was not restored in 1660 but the civil courts continued to support the church courts upon receipt of a writ, *de excommicato capiendo*.[22] Otherwise the only penalty the courts could impose was that of excommunication which was unsupported. Even this was only, 'as effective as a rough, tough, rationalistic, priest despising people were willing to let it be'.[23] For the majority, excommunication presented few problems save for those who had to deal with other bodies when, for example, instigating a case before the Mayor of Chester's court or contesting a will in consistory.

This outline of the diocese and its administration reveals that the communities that made up this huge, rambling diocese were individualistic. Court cases reveal the contrast between the attitudes of those who lived north of the Ribble and those who lived south of it. For the inhabitants of the three deaneries to the east of the Pennines, Chester was remote, a far distant city and, if surviving correspondence is accurate, they showed little interest in the diocesan centre. The greater part of the diocese was a poor region where life was hard and whose population would go to great lengths as well as great expense to defend the honour of their community against those who would deride it. Hence, litigation in the church courts became a proper course to pursue to defend one's honour and that of the local community.[24]

Part 2

SIN AND THE CLERGY AND PARISH OFFICERS

Chapter Three

INTRODUCTION

The Church, from the days of St Paul, has always been concerned with the moral behaviour and conduct of its members, based on the commission given to the apostles, and to that end has framed rules and regulations for church members. Indeed the operation of such controls, implied in the rules, can be traced continuously from New Testament times onwards.[1] It is important to remember that, in the Early Church, discipline was exercised by the whole body of church members. However, the recognition of the Church as a legally constituted organization by the Emperor Constantine led to change. When Christianity became the recognized state religion it was the duty of all members of society to become Christians. Hence, numbers joined the Church whose commitment fell far below the norm accepted by the Early Church.

It quickly became impossible for the body of church members to impose discipline on such large numbers, for the Church expanded rapidly and with the emergence of the papacy a new alternative system had to be created. The exercise of discipline on church members became the function of a number of church courts ranging from the central court, the Roman Curia, down to the correction court of the rural archdeacon, all supervised by clerical officials. The courts encouraged the evolution of a trained body of canonists, especially after 1139 when Gratian produced his *Decretum*, or corpus of canon law. During the Middle Ages later generations of canon lawyers expanded the corpus considerably.[2]

The Reformation, in England as elsewhere in Europe, led to the rejection of medieval canon law in those lands that accepted

the new doctrines of the Reformation. By the close of the sixteenth century, it had become necessary to produce a body of
canon law for the Elizabethan Church as settled in 1559. The
legal basis upon which English canon law operated in the seventeenth century was the work of Archbishop Bancroft, with the
able assistance of Sir Thomas Ridley, John Cowell, and Sir
Edward Stanhope, who were the leading canonists of Doctors'
Commons, the central body of canon lawyers.[3]

To enable this work to be undertaken, James I, as Supreme
Governor of the Church, issued his licence to convocation
empowering the members to codify and revise canon law as practised in England. Parliament, with its vociferous group of Puritan
members, was violently opposed to the move since it was anxious
to protect those clergy who were opposed to the Elizabethan
Church Settlement of 1559 from the penalties imposed by canon
law. A bill was introduced into the Commons to give effect to a
measure that would protect, in some degree, the dissident clergy.
Although the bill was passed by the Commons, it was thrown out
by the Lords, and no relief for those clergy became available.
Convocation quietly and discreetly continued with the work of
revision so that by 26 June 1604 it had produced a body of 137
canons to regulate and give authority to the government of the
Church.[4]

By the seventeenth century the whole concept of punishing
'sin', which had come to mean the violation of the norms of
behaviour, was coming under scrutiny.

The rise of capitalism was accompanied by a moral revolution.
The accepted standards of conduct were no longer regarded as
they had been in the Middle Ages, when they were part of a very
unequal agrarian society at the mercy of famine, plague, and war
which were seen as punishments for sin. The remedy for sin was
by confession and absolution.

Protestantism retained the medieval conception of sin but
without the medieval insurance policy of a confession and absolution. Men now claimed the right to do what they wanted with
their own, so usury, or charging of interest on money loaned,
forbidden by medieval canon law, was now increasingly used in
the new capitalist world. The protestant emphasis on personal
conscience which became the final arbiter as to what was, and
what was not, 'sinful', worked against the imposition of external

codes of behaviour on those whose consciences refused to accept them. In reality the protestants were trying to establish new standards in the face of the disintegration of the old.[6]

Christopher Hill claims that what made the church courts and canon law obnoxious was the continued attempt to enforce such standards of conduct, which were suited for an unequal agrarian society, long after the development of trade had caused large areas of England to leave such a society behind.[7] This was especially true of the prosperous south and east, but the north and west, especially the northern parts of Chester diocese, were still areas where preaching was inadequate despite the Puritans' attempts to supplement it.[8]

While the common law was busy adapting itself to the needs of the growing industrial and trading sectors, the church courts continued to interfere with trade by bringing suits against those who worked on holy days instead of attending church, those who never observed saints' days, and, in the textile areas of Yorkshire and Lancashire, those who operated their fulling mills on Sundays. They also interfered with credit by bringing suits in the consistory courts against those who practised usury. From time to time, ridiculous charges were brought, such as at Askrigg in 1668 when Christopher Autherson was excommunicated for 'hanging his stockings out to dry on Sundays'. Equally foolish was the case against Ann Tomlinson of Leeds for, 'bakeing her household bread on the Sabboath Daie'.[9]

> Like the Justices of Peace, the church courts had the power
> not shared by the ordinary common law courts to order
> some positive action to be taken and insist on notification
> that this had been taken. The church courts were
> administrative as well as judicial bodies where judges and
> prosecution were often closely associated if not identical.[10]

It is apparent from a study of the court files that the chancellor of the diocese tended to identify his interests with those who administered the courts rather than with those of the bishop.[11] A study of the diary of Henry Prescott, deputy registrar of Chester diocese, appears to confirm this, for he and the chancellor worked very closely together.[12]

It is also important to remember that for the 'hot' protestants the Bible was the guide to every action and the source of all truth. Biblical quotations were used to confirm and criticize every situation from politics to social life and biblical texts could be used without reference to their context, past history, or the problems of translation. The Puritans, and later the Dissenters, regarded the observance of Sunday as strictly as Jews the Sabbath, with neither work nor amusement. It was sinful not to observe the Sabbath but no longer sinful to ignore saints' days and feasts since these interfered with daily work. Amusements were regarded as the work of the devil and the theatre as the devil's playhouse. Maypoles and theatres were the haunts of profane youth and doting fools, while cards were a curse. Randolph attacked maypoles and whitsun ales:

> The Morice Idols, Whitsun Ales can be
> But the profane relics of a Jubilee.
> Those in a zeal t'expressed how much they do
> The Organs hate, have silenced Bagpipes too.
> And harmless Maypoles, all are railed upon
> As if they were the Towr's of Babylon.[13]

Puritans had no objection to the consumption of alcohol but rather to the English custom of drinking healths. Henry Jessy attacked the custom in the *Lord's Loud Call to England*, while Samuel Ward in his *Warning Piece to Drunkards and Health Drinkers*, gives 120 examples of God's judgement on drunkards.[14]

William Erbery wrote that Baptist services were occasions of pipe smoking and Thomas Edwards said it was better for Christians to be in an alehouse or brothel than observe a public fast day. Alcohol and tobacco were believed to heighten spiritual vision, while blasphemy, according to Abiezer Coppe, was freedom of expression from moral restraint. Yet to many members of the sects, sin only existed in the imagination and therefore fornication and adultery were not sins.[15]

Dancing was considered to be a sinful and evil habit. Philip Stubbs made a virulent attack upon the custom.

> Dancing, as it is used (or rather abused) in these days, is an introduction to whoredom, a preparative to wantonness, a provocative to uncleanness, and an introite to all kinds of lewdness. . . . For what clipping, what culling, what kissing

and bussing, what smouching and slabbering one of another, what filthy groping and unclean handling is not practised everywhere in these dancings . . . and shewed forth in their bawdy gestures of one to another.[16]

In the light of such propaganda, little wonder that Puritans clung to the doctrine that the nature of man was totally corrupt and that divine vengeance would mete out wrath against all sinners. Hell, therefore, was a reality to be avoided at all costs. For the traditionalists, who believed the State Church was designed not only to keep men in order and subordination on earth but to act as a tutor, to guide them to heaven, to deny the Church and its clergy was to deny good order. Those who denied the Church and its clergy should be punished in the same way as those who despised the moral code in behaviour and sexual relationships.

Chapter Four

SIN AND THE CLERGY

Professor Dickens has argued that the main feature of Elizabethan parish life was that of a small, closely integrated community, which enabled the detection of offenders to be a relatively easy task.[1] However, in the northern province, of which Chester diocese was a part, matters were very different. Overall, the parishes of Lancashire and Cheshire and those in the archdeaconry of Richmond were very large and fragmented, so the task of detection was extremely difficult. A parish in the southern province with some forty or fifty households was easy to control but Lancashire parishes, and those in Cumbria and Westmorland, contained on average some 350 households.

A national survey of parishes in 1603, quoted by Dr C. Haigh, gives an average of 243 communicants to each parish, but the figure for the Chester diocese was 696.[2] The majority of the parishes in the diocese contained parochial chapels that were served by a non-resident incumbent, or had the services of an assistant curate at intermittent intervals, or were served by lay readers: the use of readers was a strong feature of parochial life for two centuries or more in this diocese.

Plurality was rife as at least one-third of the Lancashire rectories were held by pluralist incumbents and this was very marked amongst those who held the wealthy ones. Although the statute of 1535 permitted benefices of less than £8 a year to be held in plurality, incumbents who had livings above this figure could also be pluralists if they were chaplains to the Crown, or to the nobility, or to one of the archbishops, or other specified persons. Canon 41 permitted a graduate with the degree of M.A. to hold two benefices if these were not more than thirty miles apart.

Canon 47 made it obligatory for the incumbent to provide a resident curate for one of his two benefices.[3] By 1690 the maximum stipend of £8 bore no relation to the real value of livings, so the distance of thirty miles as specified to be the maximum distance allowed between two benefices held in plurality was overcome by resorting to the use of the fictitious or 'computed' mile.

If the possession of a wealthy benefice could lead to disorder, then poverty could create very serious problems. Bishop Chadderton was of the opinion that half the benefices in his diocese had 'no other incumbents than very beggarly vicars and curates'. The Chancellor of the Duchy of Lancaster stated that 'on account of the smallness of the church livings there are few or no incumbents of learning or credit among them'.[4] Many livings were worth less than £10 a year and a number in the Lake District were below £5. A not considerable number had no settled endowments, but depended upon voluntary offerings of the congregation. The curate of Wythop in Cumbria was said to 'beg his bread from door to door'.[5]

This unsatisfactory state persisted well into the eighteenth century. In 1743, Stephen Sutton, vicar of Kirby Ireleth (a peculiar of the dean and chapter of York), wrote in his visitation returns to Archbishop Herring:

> I can assure your Grace . . . that a whole Colony of poor
> Raw Boys taken from the home-bred insignificant schools of
> this Country and Ordain'd Deacons on some sorry Titles,
> Mere Readers' Places, by his Lordship of Chester, hath
> (after some small probation here) been transplanted, or sent
> abroad into Your Grace's Diocese . . . to seek their Fortunes
> there, and furnish the Yorkshire Clergy with low pric'd
> Curates.[6]

A study of the biographical details of such ordinands reveals that many came from farming backgrounds or were sons of shopkeepers and artisans; they had little, if any, pastoral training and many remained in deacon's orders for long periods. The well placed men were, in complete contrast, ordained deacon and priest within a few weeks or even days to take a family living which they then held for life.[7] The non-graduate ordinands, who were less well connected, frequently waited several years before advancing to priest's orders while some remained in the diaconate for life.

In a province where many clergy were ill-educated it is not surprising to find that John Cosin, archdeacon of the East Riding of York, asked the following questions concerning the clergy at his visitation:

[Does any] give himself to base and servile labour, vain and idle pastimes, or ryot at the taverne, in resorting to common bowling allies, in playing dyce and cards, in hawking and hunting like a gallant; in sporting and dancing like a wanton person . . . a swearer, a blasphemer of God & his saints, a fighter, a brawler, a fornicator, an usurer, a sower of discord . . . buying of selling like a merchant or misbehave like a gentleman?[8]

The consistory court files contained abundant evidence concerning clergy who committed one or more of the faults listed by Cosin.

Before 1640 the church courts had the support of the High Commission at York in dealing with both offending clergy and laity. The Commission, as a prerogative court, had extensive powers that enabled it to exercise discipline with a strong arm. It could make an offender enter bond for a penal sum, suspend or degrade an incumbent, or confine him in the most unpleasant prison of the Kidcote on Ousebridge, York, or in the castle, an experience the majority of offenders did not wish to repeat.

The case of William Storrs, rector of Hawkswell, illustrates the real power of the High Commission. In 1639 Storrs was presented with a list of ten charges to each of which he entered the plea of guilty, and the charges reveal something of his character. He was accused of excessive drinking 'whereby he hath reeled, staggered and fallen to the ground'. On some Sundays and holy days he was so drunk that he was unable to read divine service in Hawkswell church so no prayers were read on those occasions. Even when he was in residence, he neglected to read prayers on several Sundays and holy days. Although he had given due notice of a celebration of Holy Communion many times and the parishioners attended, alas he was too drunk to celebrate. Christmas appears to have been a season when he indulged in drink to excess:

his omittynge to read prayers upon Xpmas day AD 1634; his

administering of the blessed Communion upon Xpmas day AD 1635 when he was distempered with drink and after the Communion was ended his immediate going to the Alehouse & his abode there for an howre; his Drinkinge all . . . the fornoon upon Newyears day 1635; his Drinkinge several daies and nights before Xpmas AD 1638 and no prayers on 20th January.

When Storrs was drunk he was ready to quarrel and fight, so many of his parishioners avoided his company and ran away if they met him. He was accused of attacking and wounding

Thomas Dickenson with a thick short staffe, John Glasse with a long pole, William Rudd with a great stone, John Maisterman with a hand hammer, Thomas Wynne with a stone, Anne Barker with a battledore and his ungodly speach that he would rather give holy Communion to the Devill than to Cicily Hutchinson.

The Commission then issued the following orders which Storrs had to obey. First he was to make a public declaration of his offences in church before the congregation. Then he was to be suspended from his benefice for seven years. The profits of his rectory were to be sequestrated so that he could draw no income from the benefice. The sentence of excommunication was passed on him for laying violent hands on two clergy. He had to purge himself of adultery with Elizabeth Pearson under the hands of eight beneficed clerks in the Hawkswell area, to enter bond on surety of £100, and to report monthly to the commissioners.[9]

Storrs managed to obtain the support of the incumbents of Catterick, Tanfield, Patrick Brompton, Langton-on-Swale, Kirby Hill, East Witton, Pickhill, and Easby. For some reason, not recorded in the court act book, the hearing was postponed until 12 March 1639. On the appointed day, neither Storrs nor his eight compurgators appeared, so in his absence he was declared to be contumacious and sentence of deprivation from his benefice and degradation from his orders was passed on him.

Some clergy in the Restoration period were little better but the strong arm of the High Commission was never restored so the punishment meted out was not as severe. In 1662 the Crown presented Charles Anthony to the vicarage of Catterick with the chapels of Hipswell, Hudswell, and Bolton-on-Swale. It is evident that Charles Anthony was well connected, for his brother-in-law, Sir Jeremy Lambrook, was deputy governor of the East India Company, and his own brother was governor of Londonderry. The churchwardens were suspicious as to the validity of his institution to the benefice, so in 1664 they presented him to the commissary at the visitation on the grounds that he had obtained the living by simony, but he denied the allegation and the case was dismissed for lack of evidence.[10]

In 1665 the churchwardens again presented the vicar for not instructing youth in the catechism nor going on the Rogation perambulation of the parish bounds. This time the vicar laid the blame on his curate William Bolton who, upon investigation, was found to possess neither licence nor admission to serve the cure of Bolton chapel. As Anthony made no appearance at court he was excommunicated for contumacy.[11]

Matters doe not appear to have improved, for in 1666 the churchwardens once again presented their vicar for neglect of duty. This action so infuriated Charles Anthony that he 'did beat Robert Jacques churchwarden in his own house'. Once again he denied the charge so the commissary of Richmond ordered him to appear before the bishop of Chester at Wigan on 3 September 1666 when he was severely reprimanded.[12] For a time there appeared to be signs of improvement, but within a year Charles Anthony fell foul of the chapelwardens of Hipswell on the grounds that he disobeyed the canons, by

> not administering the Communion three times as ordered by
> the Canon . . . neglecting his Cure in officiating but four
> Lords days from Easter 1666 until Michaelmas then next
> following. And from Michaelmas last for officiating but two
> Lords days every month.[13]

Charles Anthony was then suspended from his benefice for three years but returned to enjoy the fruits of the living until his death at Catterick in 1685.[14]

Another difficult incumbent was Leonard Clayton, the vicar of Blackburn. In 1663 he was presented at the visitation by his churchwardens on the grounds that he was non-resident, that he abused the officers of the consistory court and had threatened both the parish clerk and the churchwardens with violence if they dared to present any attenders at conventicles to the rural dean.[15]

From time to time negligence in providing a curate to serve a parochial chapel, as happened at Hipswell in 1639, led to an appearance before the High Commission at York. In March 1639, a parishioner, John Kitson, promoted a suit against Richard Fawcett, vicar of Catterick, for 'not providing a minister to serve Hipswell Chapel'. Fawcett was ordered to appear at York on 12 March 1640 to explain the reasons why he had failed to comply with the court order. He attended court on 19 March, and was ordered either to do duty himself at the chapel or provide a curate to serve at his own charge so long as he remained vicar of Catterick, and to enter bond of £100 to execute the order.[16]

Fawcett appears to have ignored the order for he found himself once more in court to explain why he had done no duty at Hipswell, 'on Ascension daie and the Sundaie after, nor on any Sundaie since Easter except one . . . and from the 14th May to the 14th June'. At this point, Kitson ceased to pursue the case further, for war with Scotland was now imminent and 'as a trained Soldier [he] was likely to be called northward by his Majesty' on 9 July 1640.[17]

The evils of non-residence continued throughout the century and long after, so many northern parishes suffered from this practice. In 1674, Isaac Simpson, rector of Coppenhall, was presented on the grounds that he, 'doth reside above Thirty miles distant from the parish church . . . without Licence . . . & seldom or not at all officiates there'. There was no resident curate in the parish while the 'pretended' curate lived four miles away at Acton where he was schoolmaster. This meant, according to the libel,

> there is No Curate to visit the sick, baptise the infants, or to
> visit the dying and bury the dead . . . so that many and
> severall parishioners and other persons have within these few
> years last past been interred in the parish church . . .
> without any Christian buriall.

In addition he permitted the parsonage house to become a ruin, a kiln to collapse, and timber to be stolen.[18]

Many clergy in the rural parishes, especially the remote chapels, led a lonely life cut off from intercourse with their fellows and so were driven to seek the company of their parishioners in the tavern. One such was Oswald Wilson, curate of Lund chapel, who confessed, when cited into court that 'he did plaie at cards at certain tymes with honest companions and some tyme at the dyce also which his plaie was for companie sake'.[19] Dr Tindal Hart confirms that the less desirable elements in a parish acquired a favourite pastime of abusing the incumbent[20] so that in many places it degenerated into what was 'clergy baiting'. This allegation can be supported by the evidence that came into the York consistory. The same Oswald Wilson was involved in a dispute with a parishioner named Humfrey Galaway, who

> came to his chamber dore and called him pedlar uttering
> many other opprobrious words against him. Whereupon he
> being so much tried came furth of his chamber haveing a
> key and a bed staple in his hand and gave Galaway a box
> of the ear with his fiste haveing the said keye in the same so
> that it myghte be he broke Galaways head.[21]

This was no isolated case as brutal attacks upon the clergy were frequent in the northern parishes. One good case comes from Burton-in-Kendal in 1674 between Thomas Proctor and the vicar John Ormerode. Thomas Dawson of Old Hutton and William Speight of Bendrigge had been members of the jury at the Appleby assizes in the case of John Ormerode vicar of Burton v. Thomas Proctor for 'Battrey'. Peter Jackson, a witness, had openly stated that Proctor 'was lighted from his horse mending his bridle' when John Ormerode rode up to him, leapt down from his horse, ran to Proctor and took hold of him before he could strike a blow. John Ormerode then threw Proctor to the ground and, 'stroaking up the hair knockt him on the head with a stone and left him lying dead halfe an hour'. The leading witness in the consistory cause, Richard Tompson, said that the evidence Peter Jackson had given was false. The real truth was that Proctor had dismounted; ran before Ormerode's horse and threatened him that

> if Mr. Ormerode would not light down and fight with him
> . . . he the said Thomas would knocke him of his horse.
> And if the Gentlewoman riding behind Mr. Ormerode
> suffered any blow she might blame Mr. Ormerode for a
> cowardly rogue.

Ormerode accordingly dismounted then Proctor hit him with his staff first before Ormerode could take hold of him. When the affray ended Proctor tried to mount his horse but needed assistance. Richard Tompson and his wife Ann had been present from the beginning since they were riding together with John Ormerode and his wife along the road from Milthorpe to Burton-in-Kendal when the incident took place, so Tompson refused to assist Proctor to mount his horse but continued the journey with the Ormerodes. Tompson had seen the whole of the affray but then he had also been in court where he heard Thomas and Francis Proctor prompt Peter Jackson 'what they would have him depose'. It was evident that Jackson had only appeared on the scene when the affray had ceased.[22] Jackson was then punished for committing perjury.

From time to time, clergy were abused by members of the congregation during divine service. One case arose at Doddleston in 1613 when a member of the congregation interrupted the signing of the psalm by calling out, 'Unless we will be his Swyneherds we cannot live by him.'[23] In 1638 the rector of Aldford successfully defended himself against the accusations of Ellin Booth that, 'he was a paltry priest and hath undone my mother', meaning that he had committed adultery with her.[24]

At Witton it was John Walton who slandered Richard Mather, the curate, by saying to him, 'thou art a lying priest and you came thither beggarly and as bare as a louse but set a beggar on horseback and he will ride', implying that in his opinion the curate had done very well for himself since he came to the benefice of Witton.[25] When Robert Leaver attempted to strike Edward Kenion, vicar of Prestwich, and called him 'Stinking Sir' as he attempted to push him into the river, he stated in his defence that he did not recognize the vicar, since he 'wore no gown but only a short coat over his doublet and breeches'.[26] Others could be blunter still in their comments, as was John Cowper to Adam Bolton M.A., vicar of Blackburn, when he said to him, 'I care not a fart for yow'.[27]

It was not only the parochial clergy who suffered from the detractors, but bishops themselves were liable to attack. In 1666, Richard Hincks of Chester was cited into the consistory for slandering Bishop George Hall by stating that 'hee is noe Lord but a bee shitt and I care not for the bawdy court'.[28] Bishop Hall was a hard-line diocesan who interpreted literally the 1662 Act of Uniformity and the measures of the Clarendon Code. Although there are references to the church courts as bawdy courts before

1640, this term becomes increasingly adopted by those who lived in the northern part of the diocese.

Occasionally an incumbent would retaliate only to find himself presented in court by the person whom he had criticized. In 1616, John Bowen, curate of Goostry, was cited to appear in court for having said that 'Henry Mainwaring was neither a just nor an honest man' and that, 'as a magistrate encouraged wrongdoers who trod gods minister underfoot', implying that Mainwaring enforced discipline upon Puritans. He had also stated that Richard Parker 'should have chains about his legg and a rope round his neck' indicating that he was only fit for the gallows. For this slander he was penanced by the court.[29]

Some attacks on the clergy could be quite brutal. In 1628, Thomas and William Greenfield, of Whalley parish, challenged Thomas Warriner, vicar of Clitheroe, to a fight; they threatened to kill him after 'beating him with their fists and a staff and drawing his blood'.[30] A similar case arose at Crosthwaite when James Docker brought a charge against the vicar, Richard Routh, for 'beating him on Sundaie the first of March last, drawing his blood, pulling his hair from his head and burning his hair'. On the same day Routh 'did plai at football with others, he kicked the ball and abused the players by laying violent hands on them'.[31] The incumbent of Crosthwaite was suspended from his benefice but totally ignored the order and openly read prayers in Crosthwaite church on Sunday, 10 May 1640.

Seventeenth-century games of football were by no means the type with which we are accustomed today. They were opportunities for violence of every kind and both bishops and archdeacons made every effort to prevent clergy joining these games. The archdeacon of York faced the same problem in the large and unruly parish of Halifax.[32]

One source of great annoyance to authority was the existence of vicarage alehouses. It appears that basically these were kept partly for profit, and partly to provide refreshment for the congregation who frequently had to travel some distance to church, especially in the archdeaconry of Richmond. At Kirkhammerton, when the vicar was charged with keeping an alehouse, he stated that 'his sister's daughter and her husband do sell ale and beare in the house which he hath by reason he is curate of Kirkhammerton being lycensed by two Justyces of Peace'.[33] This pattern was repeated at Ribchester where the churchwardens stated that Henry Norcrosse, the vicar, was

> an alehouse keeper contrarie to law, keeping in his howse wicked persons upon the Sabboth daie especially xi fidlers upon 3rd July 1614 and keeping gaming in his howse on the Sabboth, having tiplying and drinking in his howse in time of divine service and on the xii February being the Sabboth had thirty four persons playing on three pairs of cards.[34]

Both canon and civil law forbade the opening of alehouses in time of divine service, but in the large northern parishes it was virtually impossible to enforce the law. In several of the northern towns, especially in the textile areas, the law was openly flouted. The clergy were required by canon to read the homily against gluttony and drunkenness at least once in the year, but it is quite clear that many clergy ignored the direction. The vicar of Christleton, George Eccles, was cited to appear in the consistory for excessive drinking of wine, ale, and beer, so that, 'he fell in the street in Chester' and had also failed 'to preach a sermon against drunkenness' after he had been instructed to do so.[35]

The curate of Wilmslow deftly turned the tables on the constable who arrested him for being drunk in 1626. Laurence Leicester was charged with the offence of excessive drinking in the alehouse of Randle Burgess in Moberley. Under the influence of drink he had thrown a black pot at the head of Humphrey Newton, sworn violently at him, and was quite unable to stand on his feet. On 31 October 1626, he had visited one alehouse after another in Wilmslow, where he was arrested and promptly taken before the dean of Chester and a magistrate and bound over. Immediately after this, Leicester took the constable to Randle Burgess' alehouse, where he made, 'the constable so drunk that he fell into a ditch on the way home and you [Leicester] left him there at nine of the clock in the evening'.[36] The constable had to get himself out of the ditch and find his way home.

Not every accusation made against the clergy for drunkenness succeeded. When Thomas Cougher of Tarvin brought a suit against Thomas Lawson, clerk, for being drunk in the pulpit the parishioners produced a testimonial of good character and the cause was dropped.[37]

The existence in the remoter parts of the diocese of a number of ill-educated and barely literate men, who were often ordained by some Irish bishop, gave rise to a serious problem. Stipends for curacies were so low in the northern chapelries that only men of limited ability would accept them. The cause from St Bees is a good example of this. St Bees was a very large parish containing a number of parochial chapels, of which Woodland was one. William Lickbarrow, the vicar, had engaged a curate by the name of William Coates to serve this chapel in 1634. He proved to be so unsatisfactory that a suit was brought against him in the consistory court:

> that you the said William Coats, who of a saylor were made a Minister and ordayned by the late Bp. of Man deceased are the sole curate of St Bees. . . . And the cure being so greate and you soe very ignorant and unlearned, are not able or fitt to performe that office of curate your selfe.

Arising from this came the charge that he was unable to read either fluently or distinctly:

> You are so ignorant and unlearned that you can nott reade divine service truly and distinctly but you miscall many words in reading and . . . do become so very ridiculous to the Congregation and have caused them by your foolish gestures and ignorance in reading to laugh at time of Divine Service and . . . have given great offence & scandale.

The inability to conduct divine service decently and in order was not his only failing. He was incapable of administering baptism and had also administered Holy Communion to 9-year-old children in Gosforth chapel, as well as to persons who were standing excommunicate and to persons convicted of adultery. In addition he had refused to visit the sick and comfort the dying. In common with many others who were accepted from secular occupations of a similar nature and ordained, Coats was accused of turning his house into a 'common, drunken, disorderly alehouse', which was open to parishioners who came to drink, and afterwards ended fighting as well as being drunk. On sacrament Sundays he would invite the communicants to his house after the service:

> and have suffered divers and sundry disorderly people to

frequent your house and sitt drinking there till they were drunk, and to fight or quarrel in your house which was a great disturbance to your neighbours and a scandal to the ministry.

Indeed, Coates himself was often too drunk to read divine service, so that 'often tymes you have been carried home and in your drunkenness you have been like a dead man voyde of sense by reason thereof'. Coats was deprived and forbidden to hold another living.[38]

Another northern curate a century later who was charged with similar offences was Henry Nicholson, curate of Easby, Richmond. Following a marriage in Easby church, Nicholson had gone with the bridal party to Samuel Waller's alehouse where they sat drinking until long after the 'usuall time of going to Church'; and he had been 'so concerned in drink that he could not read the prayers'. He had arranged to baptise Samuel Waller's child on Easter Tuesday. The family waited all morning for Nicholson to appear but he did not arrive until mid-afternoon from Brompton, when 'he was so much Concerned in Drink, he could not perform the Divine offices . . . & read the Morning Service instead of the Afternoon Service'. In addition to his drunken habits he was also accused of indecent acts in an inn in Bargate, Richmond. On this occasion, during a drinking session, he asked the landlady to bring him a chamber pot in order to relieve himself. When she brought one into the room he said to her, 'help me out with it Bonny Face for it is grown rather short'. The landlady being a woman of more than 70 years of age turned to him and replied, 'so has my arm', to which he responded: 'Don't be afraid, it used to be a good one once but has been no use since Edward Robinson hit it on the end'.[39]

Causes of this nature are by no means rare in the remoter parts of the diocese but appear to have been less frequent in the archdeaconry of Chester. In 1640, Robert Holden and Charles Gregory brought a suit against John Holden, curate of Haslingden, for drinking and smoking as well as preaching a sermon in George Jackson's alehouse. He was also said to have been drunk at Blackburn on St Bartholomew's day, when he 'offered a book to Robert Gregory for five shillings as a pledge to bring in more ale'.[40]

It was a common custom in alehouses to undertake ale drinking for a wager. In 1676 at Over in a dispute between Littler Sheene the incumbent and Abraham Smith, his curate, it was alleged that Joseph Darlington, a witness in the cause, had gone to widow Cooke's alehouse, near Over church, at eight in the evening where he found Abraham Smith sitting there, 'full of ale'. Darlington and his friend had gone past Smith and his group into an upper room when they heard the noise of quarrelling.

> about twelve a clocke at night they heard the company quarrelling belowe and goinge downe found James Kettle on behalf of Mr Smith and Jonathon Robinson fighting together. Mr Smith having putt of his Coate was . . . kept by force in an inner room where they had been drinking to hinder him from coming to engage in that quarrell.

It took some little time to pacify the parties. Smith then took Robinson's hat by the brim and 'turned it round his head and with his fist gave him a blow on the ears', after which Smith offered to fight Robinson. It appeared that the quarrel had arisen over a challenge by Robinson to Smith whether he would 'pledge him a whole quart or flaggon' of ale which he had then agreed to do. Smith drank part of it but 'could not drink the rest' whereupon James Kettle, who was part of the company, offered to, 'and would have drunke it for him'. Smith refused, and Robinson and Kettle began to quarrel. Robinson admitted that Smith was regarded as a man of civil and sober life, diligent in visiting the sick and other pastoral duties, but he was penanced all the same.

Behind it all lay the fact that the vicar, Littler Sheene, and Abraham Smith were already at loggerheads. Sheene had criticized Smith for saying that the bishop of Chester 'was condescending to the Presbiterian faction and an uncharitable person in so much that the poore of Wigan were ready to fly in his face', and that Smith had 'combined with some persons disaffected to Mr. Littler Sheene and have disturbed & hindered him from performing his duty'. Smith, encouraged by his supporters, locked the church doors so that Sheene could not get into church and further had placed a lock on the pulpit door, so the vicar could not preach, and kept the key in his pocket. The matter did not end there, for John Tramlowe, one of Sheene's witnesses, stated that 'Mr. Smith in the house of Alice Baker widow, an alehouse in Whitegate parish did marry Thomas Burroughs and Mary Dod together'. Robinson countered for Smith by stating that Sheene had fathered two bastards, one on Marjory Maddock and the other on Mary Maddock. The climax came when Darlington served a citation upon Smith to appear in court, whereupon 'you snatched the Citation from Thomas Darlington and threw away the seal of it, defaced the citation saying, "you cared not a fart for it"'.[41]

This is by no means an isolated case, for at Thurstaston the incumbent, John Groome, was charged with taking secular work and joining in indecorous acts, including violence to women. The suit is a lengthy and involved one but it was his parishioners who brought the charges against him and these throw light on life in Thurstaston at this date. He was accused of negligence in attending church on Sundays and holy days, of rendering divine service in a slovenly and irreverent manner, and altering, corrupting, and depraving the Lord's Prayer, accompanied by 'unseemly gestures of his body, and often pulling of his periwigg and ordering of it, and in saying the Lord's Prayer it is soe that the Congregacion seldome can heare him or know whereabouts he is'. Arthur Pemberton, one of the witnesses, alleged that the sacrament had not been administered more than once in the year since Groome came to the benefice. It appears that the number attending church had declined to some fifteen souls and on Easter Day 1677 there were only two old men in the congregation. Groome was said to be a frequenter of alehouses and tippling houses, a man who drank to excess so that he 'fomented strife and contentions' against the poor and helpless. Indeed Groome had spent Holy Week in fights and brawls with his parishioners. He was also in the habit of sending children to the alehouse to obtain ale for him but never paid for it. Pemberton continued, 'he hath for all the time articulate much frequented Alehouses both night and day, and one night he was danceing in the Alehouse with some young Women and people of the towne'.

Now Alice Pemberton's daughter, then aged 10, had seen this incident and childlike reported the story to the maid at the house where Groome lodged; naturally the maid reported it to Groome. Shortly afterwards, Groome met Alice's daughter 'in the towne lane and there fell upon her & threw her down, and sett his feet upon her neck and did beat and hurt her very sore'. Some time

later when Alice Pemberton met Groome and asked him the
reasons why he had so brutally attacked her daughter, he

> fell upon his deponent in a very fierce and violent manner
> and took her by the throat and putt his hands about her
> necke and squeezed her very hard and almost stopped her
> Wind . . . and thrust her head and arme to a stone
> Chimney . . . and swore by the liveing, eternall God that he
> would send her to the house of Correction.

Five other witnesses testified to this, and also to the facts that he
had been seen 'spreading Mucke in the field with a spade or
pickoll' and that they had seen him working on holy days by
foddering horses and cattle, driving them to water, ploughing,
harrowing, and carrying corn, such secular work as clergy were
not supposed to perform since it lowered their professional status.
Groome was sentenced to suspension from his living for three
years, the profits to be sequestrated and public notice of his
sentence to be announced in the churches of West Kirby, Shotwick, Backford, Heswall, Neston, Eastham, Stoak, Bebbington,
Bidston, and Wallessy, together with his sentence of excommunication, so that the entire community would know what had
taken place.

The intruding of a clerk in holy orders into a parish could lead
to disputes between the patron and the congregation. In 1604,
Thomas Short, who had been curate at Macclesfield for some
thirty years, 'to the likeing of the chapelrie', was removed from
office by the mayor, William Rowe, who gave no reason for his
action. Although the stipend was only £5.6s.8d. per annum Short
was content with his income, but a request from the inhabitants
that Short should be allowed to retain his curacy was rejected. The
intruder, Francis Jackson, read divine service, buried the dead, yet
he made 'exposition of the scriptures according to his own mind
and reading books in public not allowed', which were indications
that Jackson had puritan attitudes and the town was one of those
where puritan exercises were conducted.

Contrary to canon law, Jackson had undertaken a secular
occupation, as John Groome had done at Thurstaston. The petition of the townsfolk of Macclesfield stated that

> he was a man of lewd conversation, scandalous life, being a

man of many trades, contemptuous to his neighbours, he has been a Butcher, a Drover, a Wyneman, a Button man, a tradesman of Manchester Ware viz. Inkle, sacking, and baggs and many other courses which seem God hath not blessed his labour and is odious in the face of the Congregation.[43]

Unfortunately, the result of the petition is missing but it does not appear that Short was restored to his curacy.

A parallel case comes from Bunbury where the curate John Swann was accused of disgracing his calling by keeping 'a Merchants or Tradesmans Shoppe and you . . . doe sell Wares in the same. And you have travelled as Tradesmen usually doe from Markett to Markett to buy and sell wares and such traffike'. Additional charges were brought against him for refusing to administer Holy Communion out of 'Mallice and Envye' so that he sent people away 'without anye at all'. His conduct at funerals was most unseemly for he did not meet the corpse at the 'lichyate' but 'goe sometymes before them a smilinge and laughinge in an unfittinge manner'. On another occasion, instead of conducting the funeral of Anne Marsh, he slipped out of town and left her unburied.[44]

Men who intruded themselves into the northern chapelries could be a nuisance. In 1638, Charles Knott, vicar of Bolton-le-Sands, had to take action against William Curwen, the pretended curate of Over Kellet chapel in Knott's parish. Curwen had abused a cleric, Mr Bashall, while conducting a funeral. He had also tried to pull the vicar from his seat in church and had stoned the parish clerk's cow, 'so that she pist blood', a cruel thing to do. He had committed adultery with a travelling beggar woman, Jane Maire, in Warton schoolhouse after which she bore a child. He had permitted Agnes Stockdale to perform her penance in an alehouse, and received 8s. from Agnes Stead to free her from a presentment. Curwen had also referred to the churchwardens as bastards. The outcome of this was an excommunication and eviction from his pretended curacy, for he was regarded as unfit to be either curate or parish clerk.[45]

One of the more detailed cases arose at Maghull in 1704 where George Burches was curate. Liverpool was becoming an attraction for both clergy and laity who wished to live a loose life. It was said that Burches daily frequented an alehouse in Maghull, The Ship, which was kept by a Quaker, Elizabeth Molyneux, and was accounted 'an alehouse of bad reputacion, entertaining bad persons'. Burches had been found there with three persons whom he said were strangers, one a cider merchant, the other a fencing master, and the third a sailor. All four stayed at The Ship for three days and nights during which they arranged two horse races and a foot race. It was clear they were not strangers but knew each other well. Indeed, Burches often spent the greater part of the week in Liverpool at Margaret Pye's alehouse, not returning home until Saturday night after the Saturday market. Francis Ireland, a witness, stated that he had offered to pay boys to write his sermons for him but when he had then refused to pay them they spoke out. Burches was very friendly with two women, Margaret Pye and Betty Gregson, to whom he sang 'unseemly songs'.

On another occasion he was in an alehouse at Upholland when Francis Ireland and Richard Hesketh criticized his excessive drinking habits. But Burches, 'taking it ill to be admonisht by this deponent, fell into a passion and with his whip (and he believes the heavy end of it) strikeing this deponent (Ireland) broke his head'.

When William Tyrer was at Pye's alehouse he found Burches and two women 'And a fidler being sent for, came and played to them and . . . Burches danced withe the bigg belly'd woman'. While this diversion was in progress, some carpenters came and called Tyrer outside where, 'in a derideing manner, threw snow balls at him and at the doors and call'd him the parsons pimp'. In addition, Burches had married Thomas Hesketh and Elizabeth Birch in James Taylor's alehouse in Rochdale and Richard Molyneux to his wife in an alehouse in Ormskirk. The real crunch came when Francis Ireland reported that

> Alexander Hesketh, Mr Burches and Thomas Tyrer kept a whore among them . . . and that there was indeed twelve shillings a month for a young woman who was said to bee sold to go to Virginia at one Pye's in Liverpool. . . . And that Thomas Tyrer had brought her to the Staggs head in Aintree where they could have her kept for 8s. a month.

Tyrer admitted that both Margaret and Betty Gregson were very lewd women and were 'reckond as common whores'.[46]

The case came before Bishop Stratford at Chester when Burches attempted to clear himself with a variety of excuses, but the bishop deprived him of his benefice and degraded him from his orders.[47] For clergy with weak characters and low moral standards the attraction of growing towns like Liverpool was difficult to resist. The same type of cause can be found at Cockermouth and Ulverstone.[48]

The case against Thomas Proddy, vicar of Cartmell, was, as he stated in his reply to questions, the result of illness and drink. He openly admitted that he drank too much which resulted in oaths and curses. The reason for his neglect of his parochial duties was his affliction with dropsy and the gravel which forced him to spend considerable time in bed. This complaint also caused him to fall into a violent temper; he admitted that, in October,

> with a stick, rashly and suddenly, [he did] strike Her [his
> wife], of which he repents him: but doth deny that hee then
> knockt her down or that she was . . . put into a Cart
> carry'd to the Town or was in danger of her Life from that
> stroke.[49]

He duly appeared before Bishop Stratford and made his humble submission and promised to amend his ways. Two years later, in 1706, he was again before the bishop for 'being disordered in his mind and cutting up his wife's bed'. On this occasion the bishop had no alternative but to deprive him of his benefice.[50]

The case of William Dennis of Doddleston in 1698 is of interest since it gives medical information that is rare to find in a case of disordered mind. The dean and chapter of Chester had presented the rector on charges of excessive drinking, being drunk, playing 'illegal games', incontincency, and adultery. The details of the charges are not recorded in full but it appears that in 1695 Dennis had been afflicted with a fever which lasted some three weeks, during most of which he was delirious. He was eventually cured but his brain continued to be disordered, 'being affected with a deep Melancholy which being increased & heightened by . . . having a Sonn of his run away from him to bee a soldier in Flanders'. Later he had a fall from his horse which so damaged his head that

> sometimes hee has been Frantick, att other times so melan-
> choly that hee has sitten whole days together & would not

speak a word . . . sometimes he would . . . sing strange
Rhymes part Latin part English of his own composition
extempore.

He also took up the habit of smoking 'most immoderately'. Henry
Williamson, the doctor, said that he suffered from 'Synochus
putrida', a fever he contracted by getting wet travelling from
Lancaster. The doctor gave a detailed account of the symptoms,
including a peculiar hiccough which continued for some time.
This, he said, 'was accompanied by perpetual deleriums or Rave-
ings and a clammy coldness of the lower parts. I gave him a very
sharp Glister by which . . . he ejected many yellow greenish and
fetid humours which caused him to faint'. The witness who had
come to give evidence for his adultery were objected to as being
'poore, indigent & scandalous people'. Anne Larke, one witness,
was 'an evil woman' suspected of having two husbands; 'she
forced her former husband to go into the Army . . . and hath
threatened her present husband to cutt his throat if he would not
do as she bade him'.[51] Dennis's sentence was one of suspension
for three years with sequestration of the revenues.

Alongside the drunken, dissolute clergy were those who held
puritan attitudes to worship by refusing to use the sign of the cross
at baptism, to church woman after childbirth, to observe the
Rogationtide procession, or to wear a surplice when taking
services. Undoubtedly the latter could be a mark of puritan
sympathy but one has to remember that the surplice was an
expensive garment so it is essential to differentiate between those
cases where the clergy openly refused to wear it and those where
the parish neglected to provide one. The visitation of 1578
revealed some seven parishes in the deanery of Catterick where the
excuse was given 'that there hath been none to wear and when one
shalbe provided he will wear it'.[52] From time to time the Richmond Consistory ordered the offending churchwardens to buy the
cloth and bring it back to show the court the order had been
executed.[53] By 1609 the presentments against the puritan clergy
increased. By then they were not only about the lack of a surplice
but, in the case of Henry Stubbs, rector of Wath, for

> not reading homilies for not catechising the youth, for admit-
> ting persons not being of the parish to receive the commu-
> nion and for expounding homilies not being a preacher, not

wearing the surplus and for milking Ewes in the church-yard.[54]

Edward Fleetwood, vicar of Kirkham, neglected to wear the surplice when celebrating Holy Communion, and at baptisms, when burying the dead, and reading divine service. Not only had he refused to bury the body of James Dixon for some time and then refused to have the corpse brought into church, although the boy's parents requested this, but he had quarrelled with his churchwardens and refused them entry to church. On All Souls' Day 1638 he abused his son in a violent manner; he was told: 'you did beate and violently strike and buffet your Sonne in the Church of Kirkham for that he opened the Chancel dore and suffered the churchwardens to enter the church'.[55]

Puritan ministers failed to conform to ceremonial prescribed by the Prayer Book, particularly in refusing to stand when the gospel was read or bow at the Holy Name. A great deal of this kind of defiance is found in the strongly catholic areas where puritan clergy had to struggle to gain acceptance. Edward Fleetwood was said to have deliberately 'overslipped the name of Jesus so that people were unable to bow and bend the knee'.[56] Hugh Burrows, vicar of Shotwick, was another who had stated that 'it was not lawfull . . . to bow the knee or body at the repeating or nominating of the name of Jesus and that whoever did so did bow his body or knee to the devil or words to that effect'.[57] Another who did not conform was John Lumley, curate of Pilling, who not only refused to wear the surplice but also kept a disorderly house in which he drank with recusants, (it was a strong catholic area) and referred to the clergy as 'fooles, asses, ninny hamers, divels, rascalls and rogues'. In addition, with the connivance of the churchwardens he solemnized clandestine marriages.[58]

Manchester, with a huge parish and growing population, which was difficult to supervise, was attractive to puritan ministers. Ralph Kirke, a curate there, was opposed to the use of the sign of the cross in baptism since it had no biblical foundation. When parents came for baptism and asked for the sign of the cross to be used, he asked 'them whether they will have a blacke, a Redd or blewe, or a headless cross and such other contemptuous words'. He objected to the surplice as a rag of popery and a heresy. Kirke was also charged with marrying persons in alehouses late at night when they were drunk. Although he was excommunicated, he continued to minister in Manchester.[59] Certainly, Manchester was a conveniently large parish for puritan refugees from elsewhere, for Thomas Smith, a former bookseller from Barnstaple, a 'hot zealot and strict nonconformist' who had been punished by Star Chamber and sentenced by the High Commission, was found preaching openly and illegally in the town.[60]

John Broxopp, vicar of Ormskirk, was cited into court in 1637 on the grounds, amongst others, that he did not wear a surplice. When he was questioned upon this matter, Broxopp explained:

some few times within the years [mentioned in the articles against him] when he did officiate and minister the holy communion he did not wear the surplice because sometimes it was at washing, sometimes at mending so as he could not always have the same to put on.[61]

On the face of it this is an innocent reply probably designed as a cover for his Puritanism. When it came to the charge that he held conventicles at his house during the night, it was clear that he was a strong nonconformist.

As late as 1683, Joshua Ambrose, vicar of Childwell, was cited for negligence in not reading the daily offices, neglecting to wear a surplice and solemnizing clandestine marriages in the house of John Bolton.[62] Another who changed the rubrics of the Prayer Book was Brian Wilson, curate of Colton in 1639, when he was said not to observe the 'rubrics of the prayer book', and held no prayers on Wednesdays, Fridays, and holy days. He had also amended the absolution at morning and evening prayer and the absolution in the communion service.[63] Another supporter of those clergy who refused to observe the rubrics of the Prayer Book was Thomas Holford of Plemondstall, who preached a sermon in 1637 in St Peter's church, Chester, in support of those who refused to conform to the Church of England.[64]

By the 1630s some ministers were becoming bolder in their attacks on the Church. In 1631 action was taken against Ralph Hulme, who came from Batley in the diocese of Lichfield to preach at Harthill. In his sermon he attacked cathedral chapters and choirs as unnecessary institutions. It was alleged that he had said the sums of money spent on unnecessary ministers and members of cathedral churches would be better spent on preachers of the word of God. In his answers to the questions put to him about his remarks he denied having said that 'soe much is bestowed upon Idle persons to singe Morninge & Eveninge prayer in Cathedrall Churches which would Maynteyne a sufficient minister for every parish or words to this purpose'. He tried to remedy his error by stating that Chester was well supplied with preachers, 'for which hee doth bless god . . . and denie that hee spoke otherwise'. However, he was unable to deny his comments on the Lord's Prayer, that 'the Lords Prayer was no more holy than others and any Minister might make as good a prayer as the Lords Prayer was', thus encouraging extempore prayers, a practice which the Prayer Book was designed to replace.[65]

By 1637 it was evident that trouble lay ahead for the Church. Laud had introduced his Prayer Book in Scotland and roused strong antagonism which added to the feeling which led to war in 1640. Preaching in Manchester on Christmas Day 1638, Thomas Case referred to the persecution of protestants in Europe as the Thirty Years' war dragged on: 'there were many others which were in persecution which you would not name. Under which, "many others" divers of your auditors conceived that you meant the kingdom of Scotland as indeed you did'. Again when Case went to preach in Didsbury Chapel it was said that

he desired people to pray for a sick member of the Church and when people gazed and expected to hear the name, you said it was sick and dying England, the Church of England was sick and ready to die.[66]

Even bolder was William Ellison, curate of Archolme in the parish of Melling. He ministered in a community that was hostile to Puritans and, like Broxopp, he had to hold conventicles at night. The principal charge brought against him was not holding conventicles but one of supporting Mrs Henry Burton. Henry Burton, together with Bastwick and Pyrnne, had been sentenced by Star Chamber to stand in the pillory and have their ears cut off for having written pamphlets attacking the bishops, the Church, and the masques held at Court. Ellison admitted that he had supported Mrs Burton in her time of trouble and while he thought Burton was wrong he had tried to encourage her to conform. It is evident that some support was forthcoming for Mrs Burton,[67] for Hugh Wyldbore, vicar of Eriholme in Richmond deanery, was also said to favour Burton's opinions and to visit his wife but he too hastily tried to deny it.[68]

A layman might accuse a minister of preaching false doctrine only to find himself in court for defamation, as at Stockport: 'Samuel Pickforth saying to Mr. Hornasall . . . Thou dost preach false doctrine in that a man should restore things unjustly gotten for a man could not restore Twelve Maidenheads he had taken from wenches.' Pickforth, by his remarks, revealed an attitude common in many northern areas that the preaching of the clergy should not be taken literally.[69]

By 1640 some began to be bolder in their attitude as is seen in the suit for blasphemy brought by John Edwards against Richard Broster of Chester in Hugh Anderson's alehouse in Foregate Street. When threatened with a citation to appear before Star Chamber, he replied with some glee that 'Starr Chamber be suspended, avoyded and put down by Act of Parliament as he hath heard'.[70] There was no doubt some anticipation aroused that relief from the control of the prerogative courts was at hand. In fact it was not until July 1641 that both Star Chamber and High Commission were abolished.

Those who lived in the archdeaconry of Richmond were little better in their behaviour. In 1633, during Richard Neile's primary visitation, a suit was brought from Nun Monkton that the vicar there had been subjected to 'abusive and irreverent speeches in the street'. At Kirby Fleetham, Anna Thompson urged her husband to give the vicar 'manie bloddie woundes', and John Bell of Barton Cuthbert 'cursed the church and prayed the devil to pull it down'.

A case from Aysgarth, during the same visitation, appears at first reading to be one showing puritan tendencies but careful reading gives an alternative interpretation. James Nicholson had said that 'the preaching of the Gospell is but bibble babble and I care not a fart for anie black coate in Wensley Daile. I had rather hear a cuckoo sing.'[71] This could well be an example of what must have been familiar in these moorland parishes, that the incumbent was not a local man and could not speak the dialect, so his words were not understood by his parishioners who doubtless felt the whole thing was a waste of time. This is borne out by a comment made by John Wesley when preaching at Clifton in Cumbria. In his diary he recorded: 'I preached at Clifton to a civil people who looked just as if I had been talking Greek';[72] this was a full century later.

Attitudes towards the clergy and offering them abuse were evident after the restoration of the Church in 1662. At Eccles, John Smith accused the incumbent Mr Marsden of preaching against the Solemn League and Covenant, an ordinance suppressed at the Restoration, which he said was 'mere prating'. He uttered this statement while standing in the church, wearing his hat and with his hands on his hips.[73] John Broughton of Walton was another who had a low opinion of the rector, John Meanwood, when he said that 'he could preach no more than a tub and was fitter to drive the plough than preach for he was a dumb dog'.[74]

The underlying problems that gave rise to such attitudes were the result of the religious changes in the north. True, the Elizabethan Acts of Uniformity and Supremacy, with the Book of Common Prayer, visualized an organized and disciplined national Church that would bind all Englishmen together, with the Thirty-Nine Articles as the foundation of its doctrine. This may have been the view of the Church from York or Canterbury, or even at diocesan level, but viewed at the parochial level it meant something very different. Here it meant supervision from cradle to grave, discipline from above and the introduction of religious practices and beliefs that cut across centuries of old custom, folklore, and habit.

Anti-clericalism was evident especially at Burton-in-Kendal in 1633, when John Crossfield gave the vicar 'base words', and at Pennington the curate suffered at the hands of Edmund Tell, who 'burst his face causeing it to bleed upon the 16th day of December last 1632'. Much more serious was the attack made on the curate of Torver when Edmund Atkinson abused him by calling him 'rascally priest' and broke his head with a pair of tongs, while his companion, James Brocklebank, 'broke his head with a crabtree cudgel'.[75]

Attempts by the clergy to suppress the old social customs of rural communities were met with opposition. In July 1588, Joseph Rhodes of Aldborough was one of a number of persons who had been rebuked by the vicar for holding a rushbearing and coming into church during divine service in their disguises. According to the vicar this event had been accompanied by 'a noyse of pyping, blowing of the horne, ringing or striking of basons and shouting . . . that the minister was constrayned to leave of redinge of the prayers'. Angered by the rebuke, Rhodes went into the alehouse, where he found Richard Scruton and gave him twopence to have the loan of his gun; he asked

> to have a shott in his gonne and having charged the same gonne with paper came into the church . . . and discharging the gonne, aiming directly over the minister eyther to hit him or as was reported to affray him and the paper blew about the minister his ears.[75]

Abuse of the clergy continued after the Restoration, but ecclesiastical control was weaker, since the prerogative courts were not restored and the only punishments available were penance and, if necessary, excommunication.

In 1666 two parishioners at Urswick church refused to stand for the gospel or kneel for the prayers; all the time they were 'laughing and Gearing at their minister when he did wear a surplice', and Ellen Garner called him 'a Babbling ass & foole'. The church at Eldroth was so little respected that John Taylor was able to use it as an ale store in 1668 and defy the vicar when he raised an objection.[76]

In 1778, Thomas Hest, the 70-year-old vicar of Warton, summed up his own opinions on the attitude of the northern parishioners towards religion and the church.

> We have alas many who have no Regard for Religion, who commonly absent themselves from the public worship of God, some I believe, thro Indolence, others thinking themselves witty, employ their Talents in ridiculing the Scriptures, and laughing at those who are disposed to be serious . . . for what Reformation can be expected from the rising Generation, when they have daily before their Eyes such very bad Examples of their own wicked and profane parents.[77]

It was clear by the mid-eighteenth century that those who offered themselves for ordination were often ill-prepared. Those who had been university-educated were often no better than those who were ordained directly from local grammar schools. Although many ordinands, both graduate and non-graduate, were men of some calibre, some had not the slightest idea how to undertake the pastoral care of the smallest country living. The seventeenth-century clergy were, like all men, sinners in a variety of ways:

> Servant of God has chance of greater sin
> And sorrow than the man who serves a king.
> For those who serve the greater cause may
> Make that cause serve them.[78]

The impression gleaned from the consistory files indicate that many members of the clergy could not resist the attractions of the world, the flesh, and the devil.

Economic conditions and changes affected the clergy. The increase in enclosure for pasture reduced clerical income. Tithes, which from the early Middle Ages had been the main support of an incumbent's stipend, were diverted at the Reformation into the hands of laymen, who often came to an agreement with the incumbent that meant virtually a reduced stipend. In the chapelries it was the inhabitants who often had to contribute towards the curate's stipend and often with some reluctance. Little surprise need be expressed that many curates were unwilling to accept such a chapelry, so many curates who served in them, such as William Coats of St Bees, were poorly educated. The problem of finding a supply of suitable candidates for ordination was serious in the northern province, so that often the moral and educational standards of many clergy fell far below the desired levels and led to quarrels, sometimes violent, between incumbent and parishioners.

Chapter Five

SIN AND THE CHURCHWARDENS

The office of churchwarden is one of the oldest positions open to laymen in the Church of England. Today it is regarded as an honoured office and is much coveted, but originally it was one to be avoided, if possible, for the responsibilities attached to it were onerous. There is little evidence available as to the precise date when the office of churchwarden was first adopted in England, but the earliest reference is in 1270, from the Oxford church of St Peter-le-Bailey, and five years later at St Mary the Virgin.[1]

By the close of the fourteenth century, churchwardens were attending to repairs to the nave, steeple, and bells of their parish church (the chancel was the responsibility of the rector be he incumbent or lay impropriator). Alongside these duties went the costly task of fencing the churchyard to keep out animals, especially pigs which 'root up the bones of the dead'. In addition they had to provide all things requisite for divine worship according to the canons and rubrics of the Prayer Book. Deficiencies in furnishings were often concealed until brought to light at an archdeacon's or episcopal visitation.[2]

In 1571, Archbishop Grindal drew up a set of regulations for the churchwardens in the northern province. They were to hold office for one year only unless re-elected to office at Easter. They were not to sell the bells nor dispose of church furnishings without the consent of the bishop. At Easter they were to present their annual accounts, showing the financial state of the parish, to the vestry meeting.[3] The cost of repairs could be a burden, for raising money was difficult even with the levy of a church rate, especially in a parish where the number of parishioners was small and there were no persons of substance to bear the greater proportion of the assessment the churchwardens made. As time passed, other duties were added such as responsibility for maintaining law and order in the church and churchyard, and for ensuring that there were no feasts or drinking in church and no markets, fairs, or dances in the churchyard. Churchwardens were charged with levying fines on all who failed to attend church on Sundays and holy days and reporting them at the visitation. The Elizabethan poor law legislation of 1597 and 1601 required them to co-operate with the overseers of the poor for the relief of the needy within their respective parishes. Finally they were to present at the visitation all who were 'common swearers', drunkards, scolds, unmarried couples who cohabited together as man and wife, all unlicensed schoolmasters, midwives, and surgeons, all recusants and Dissenters, and finally to search alehouses during divine service to discover those who were absent from the Sunday roll call in church.[4]

Faced with this formidable list, the consciences of many churchwardens were severely strained as the time for the annual visitation approached, for they could easily find themselves in the consistory court on charges of negligence. It was no soft option to be guardian of the morals of the parishioners, and it is not surprising to discover that many men attempted to avoid, if possible, the duty of serving as churchwarden for one year.

The method of electing churchwardens was laid down by canon 89, which also provided for emergencies:

> All Churchwardens or Questmen in every parish shall be chosen by the joint consent of the Minister and the Parishioners . . . but if they cannot agree then the Minister shall choose one and the Parishioners another.[5]

Since the number of churchwardens to be elected to serve the office was not specified, the number varied according to custom. Normally there were two, but large parishes such as Manchester chose more, and at Kendal, for instance, the number was twelve, since that parish contained fourteen chapels of ease. As the numbers of churchwardens chosen varied, so did the method of election. In some parishes the office was held by householders in rotation, in others by house row or by the occupiers of specified premises. In a number of parishes the open vestry had become closed since the plutocracy and oligarchy of the parish replaced it by a select vestry. Such vestries acted independently of the parishioners at large. They chose the churchwardens from amongst their number but administered church property in the same manner as the open vestry.[6]

At the first visitation after Easter, the old churchwardens appeared to hand in their presentments and accounts, while the new wardens swore their oaths of office. Until they had taken the oath the new wardens had no power to act.[7] Once they were legally appointed the new churchwardens had to levy a church rate for repairs to the fabric and could be called to account for their expenditure. The office was unpaid, though some parishes made a small allowance to them for their services. On the whole the office afforded few perquisites and every suspected malversation of funds could lead to a long and costly suit in the consistory court. Certain civil duties were also attached to the office, namely assisting the surveyor of the highways to make an assessment for road repairs, meeting the expenses of the parish constable, and assisting with the collection of money towards a brief. From time to time, Parliament legislated to prohibit certain classes from serving as churchwardens.[8] Naturally, several men attempted to avoid the office, but this was difficult: in 1664 Christopher Ayscough refused to serve at Middleton Tyas, saying that 'he would not take upon him the Execution of the office of churchwarden', and upon his non-appearance to take the oath he was excommunicated for contumacy.[9]

In 1671, the chapelwarden chosen to serve at Hudswell refused, in open court, to take the oath of office. Eight parishes in the archdeaconry of Richmond had trouble with elected churchwardens refusing to serve and three parishes had to obtain orders from the civil court to compel them to serve.[10] The same problem arose in the archdeaconry of Chester. In 1682 Sir Edward Osbaldeston challenged William Duckworth for having connived in the public election of a chapelwarden for the chapel of Great Harwood in Blackburn parish. He contended that he had the sole right to appoint chapelwardens for the townships of Blackburn parish to serve on Blackburn vestry. The suit continued until 1686 when sentence was decreed in favour of Sir Edward.[11]

It was not admissible to send a deputy to take the oath, as the new churchwardens of Over discovered to their cost in 1702. The old wardens brought a suit in the consistory court against Richard Evans and Edward Moreton for sending a deputy to take the oath and then proceeding to levy an assessment without 'lawful authority'.[12]

In certain cases where reluctance was shown on the part of those chosen to serve, the coveted position could lead to some intrusion by rival contenders for office. John Appleby, the rejected rival candidate for Smeaton, attempted to intrude himself into office by collecting money towards the repair of the church and not submitting an account of the amount he had collected.[13]

There was a complaint from Pennington, by the new churchwarden, against David Myers, surrogate, and James Trotter, notary public of the Richmond court, for 'continuing James Steel and John Coulton our predecessors as churchwardens for two years successively contrary to the 89th and 90th canons'.[14] In 1635 the rector of Lawton cited Thomas Booth, tailor, for intruding himself into the office of churchwarden, 'not being lawfully chosen'.[15] In 1635 action was taken against the elected wardens for Manchester, on the grounds that the churchwardens had been negligent: 'Samuel Tipping [and others] contra John Hartley and Richard Lomax for refusing the oath of Churchwardens and not serving their office and neglecting their duties'.[16]

Following the primary visitation of his province, Archbishop Richard Neile resolved to have decency and order in his churches, and to that end introduced Arminian policy. He issued orders for the unifying of pews in churches, ordering that all persons should sit facing the east; the communion table was to be placed at the east and and railed in to prevent abuse by dogs and parishioners; church interiors were to be made clean and decent and all broken doors and windows repaired. This was an expensive exercise in that it meant levying more than one rate, so opposition was to be expected. A good illustration comes from Prescot where Henry Ogle and James Pemberton, with others, objected to the payment of lays (rates) to implement Arminian policies, as between May 1634 and October 1636 the churchwardens had levied eight-two lays.[17]

Some unscrupulous churchwardens attempted to make a little money for themselves by undertaking improvements. In 1636 John Upton accused the churchwardens of Chorley of falsification of the accounts in order to make profit for themselves. Similar suits were brought in the consistory against the churchwardens of Bolton, Colne, and Astbury, based on similar charges.[18]

Some parishes like Broughton refused to obey the orders. In this case the churchwardens and the parishioners refused to pay lays or raise money towards paving the church floor or railing the communion table with 'handsome rails, and unifying the seats, in height, length and width, as the order issued to all churches in the diocese by Bishop Bridgeman in 1635'.[19]

The Prescot churchwardens were more resourceful in raising money for improvements to the church. Unfortunately for them, Sir Henry Ogle found what they were doing and cited them into the consistory, on the grounds that 'they have taken up the gravestones and tombstones and sold them for building materials . . . and appropriated the timber from the amended pews for their own use'.[20]

St Bees was a parish that contained two most difficult, to say the least, parochial chapels, Ennerdale and Kinniside. Both refused to pay any of the lays levied by the churchwardens of St Bees towards the repair and improvement of the parish church, estimated at about £100, for both chapels tried to make a case for independence on the grounds that Ennerdale was a parish in its own right and Kinniside was a chapel within it. The suit dragged on interminably until the Civil War brought it, albeit temporarily, to an end.[21]

The occupation and title to a pew in church could become a source of contention because it was regarded as personal property, and as such often led to brawling during divine service. By law, every parishioner had a right to a seat in his or her own parish church in which to sit, kneel, or stand during the time of the service. Obviously a parishioner could not have the sole right to select the position of his pew, and in the interests of general order, seats or pews had to be allocated by some impartial authority having the requisite knowledge of the circumstances concerning each parishioner. In practice, the most suitable and natural arbitrators were the churchwardens, but to avoid disputes the allocation of seats in the diocese was undertaken by a commission appointed by the bishop or his commissary at Richmond.[22] Indeed, detailed information was readily available for church-wardens when faced with the problem of allotting pews and seats to parishioners.[23]

By canon and common law, the seats in the nave of a church were the common property of the parish and all the parishioners were to be seated in an ordered fashion, without the wealthy being accommodated to the detriment of the poor. The allocation of a seat or pew did not convey the exclusive right to occupy this permanently, as changes could be made as circumstances required. It is clear that the law did not anticipate the disturbance of one parishioner by another in his right to occupy a seat. In the nave, the right to a pew could be claimed by the holding of a tenement, or burgage house, but not by the heirs or successors of a tenant who had occupied the pew by right of his tenancy. Pews in the chancel or side chapel were frequently held by right of inheritance, or of social standing, together with the obligation to repair not only the pew but a portion of the chancel or chapel itself.

Towards the close of the sixteenth century, church naves had become filled with a mixture of square and straight form-like pews. Since they faced the pulpit, pews ran in all directions creating many odd corners and alleys in the nave. Occasionally, a vacant portion of the church floor would be let off for people to erect their own pews, a practice that often led to serious disputes involving violence.

The most interesting case of an allocation of pews in Chester diocese took place in Kendal in 1578. For some time, the parishioners had been engaged in controversy about their pew rights, so during his visitation in 1578 Archbishop Sandys settled the matter on the spot by allocating the seats to the various parties engaged in the dispute; so well was this task accomplished by Sir Thomas Boynton, an official of Archbishop Sandys, that the seating remained undisturbed until the nineteenth century.[24]

The growth of the textile trade and industry in general during the earlier part of the seventeenth century enabled many clothiers and others to make money. Unfortunately, they had little idea of how to use it and on average had as much knowledge of civilization as a nineteenth-century Californian gold miner. In order to exhibit this new-found wealth, it became the fashion to erect private pews of all shapes and sizes in churches; hence the continual flow of orders from the registrars at York and Chester during the 1630s to 'unify the seats'. A good illustration of this comes from Ashton-under-Lyne in 1638 when the churchwardens brought a suit against John Sandeford concerning his new pew.

[it] is not uniform, for it is built too high like a pulpit and

is of contrary fashion to the rest and is too large for it is couched and doth hinder them that sit below from beholding the communion table and further it encroaches on the Alley.[25]

They demanded that all such exhibitions of private enterprise be cut down to a uniform size.

Churchwardens were not always honest and reliable. In 1631 the Warrington churchwardens were cited to appear in the consistory for making a false presentment of faults to the visitor in as much as Warrington church was not uniformly pewed and Thomas Ireland, the impropriator of the tithes, had constructed a pew 'in the manner of a scaffold twelve feet above the floor standing on pillars of wood and it over looks the congregation and the parson in the pulpit'.[26]

The churchwardens of St Michael's, Chester, became the centre of an investigation into the interior condition of their church. It appeared that in 1640 the churchwardens had demolished and defaced the chancel screen, and the chancel seats were not 'choir wise', nor were the seats in the nave uniform. They were ordered to erect a new screen, with long pilasters, to divide the chancel from the nave, as well as the north and south aisles. The order went on to deal with the nave: 'the seats in the nave are to be uniform so that none sit with their backs to the communion table, they are to be uniform in height, length and breadth so that people may face the communion table'. The puritan practice of administering the communion to people seated in their pews was to cease in St Michael's, and all were 'to go in rank according to their quality & condition to receive and then return to their seats'.[27]

In the second half of the century the population was beginning to increase, and this brought with it a demand for more private seats in the church, especially among the professional people in the parish. Ormskirk provides an excellent example of opposition to private pews. In 1672, Sir John Hurleston petitioned for a faculty to convert certain 'open and common seats' into private pews. The churchwardens pointed out that the parish had re-pewed and unified the seats at public expense in 1634. A petition was presented, signed by forty-seven parishioners, opposing the appropriation of common seats for private pews on the grounds that 'there are insufficient seats for the parishioners and private pews are not wanted'.[28] Six years later, Sir John Hurleston contested the right of Peter Rigbie to a pew which he said belonged to Hurleston House and, as in 1672, references were made to the unifying of the pews in Ormskirk church in 1635. The churchwardens stated that 'there are so many people in the parish that they sit where they can',[29] so highlighting a problem that was to become apparent in the next century with an increase in population. A year earlier, Sir John Entwistle opposed the claim of Jane Laithwaite to a private seat in Ormskirk church. Her claim was based on the fact that she owned a house, 'in Aughton Street at the corner of More Street', with a second house in Burscough known as the Little Mass House. She gave details of the Laithwaite family and an interesting account of the arrangement of the pews before the reordering of 1635.[30] She lost her claim on the grounds there were insufficient seats for the parishioners.

When Peter Weston of Christleton, who had married Elizabeth Golbourne, a descendant of Ralph Golbourne, laid claim to a seat in right of his wife's title, he traced the ownership of this pew from 1605 and confirmed that Ralph Golbourne had 'tiled' and 'flagged' the church at his own expense. In such a case it was virtually impossible to reject the petition.[31]

Today we should be shocked by the lack of reverence shown by our ancestors to a church interior. In the Middle Ages the naves of churches were used not only during worship but also for meetings and for conducting a variety of parish business. Abuse of the church as a consecrated building had so greatly increased by 1550 that in 1552 the government of Edward VI had to pass legislation to prevent sacrilege both in church and churchyard by brawls, fights, and disputes concerning ownership of pews, which often arose from social ambitions in the community; to these can be added the disturbances that arose from objections to the statutory services of the Church and to episcopal government.[32]

Occasionally the churchwardens had some difficulty in settling a pew dispute, and the easy way out was to refer the case to the bishop. In 1624, the churchwardens of Askrigg took such a course of action against Peter Thornton and George Macryas, who 'disturbed and trubled the parishioners of Askrigg by theire Struggleinge and Shuffleing in the Church about a contencion betweene them tochinge their several ryghts to a staule in the said Church'.[33] The case was heard before the bishop who settled the case in favour of Thornton.

Often the churchwardens were able to settle a pew dispute without recourse to a consistory hearing by requesting the commissary to arbitrate. At East Cowton, on Easter Day 1609, Elizabeth Barker was seated quietly in her seat when Catherine Masterman entered the church and came up to her seat so noisily that Elizabeth 'was disturbed & molested that she was urged to bidd her be quiett with some other reasonable woords to keep & maintaine her right as . . . by Marjorie Faile who did likewise disturbe her in cominge to hir seat or stall'. The matter was settled after apologies made by all parties before the commissary.[33]

The solemn occasion of a funeral could provide an opportunity for a violent dispute about a seat. Frances Akers had had the use of 'the fifth pew from the chancel on the south side of the middle alley over against the pulpit' in Bolton church for several years. On 5 October 1671 she attended the funeral of Thomas Heward's wife, and was sitting quietly in her seat when George Sutton entered the church. He violently objected to Frances occupying that particular seat:

> he did chide and brawle with Frances Akers and did smite
> and lay violent hands upon the said Frances and in a furious
> manner tooke her by the Arme, Shoulder and violently thrust
> her out of the said pew to the disturbance of divine service.[34]

Violence could lead to excommunication of the offender, as happened at Middleham in 1638. Thomas Spence became contemptuous towards the dean of Middleham when he admonished him in church. Spence retaliated by breaking a pew in pieces and cursing the dean.[35]

Cruelty to a servant while seated quietly in church was not unusual. In 1687 at Marbury, while the minister and congregation were assembled ready to begin prayers, John Sadler of Holyhyrst instructed his servant Thomas Evanson to sit in a certain seat. This displeased Thomas Heath, and 'maliciously & violently coming from his seat' to the one in which Evanson was sitting, he managed, with the assistance of John Barnet and Thomas Colefax, who were in the same seat, to 'pull Thomas Evanson out of the seat by the Hair of his Head into the Isle of the said Chappel and

. . . Thomas Heath called him a Rogue . . . and said the Stocks were fitter for him than to sit there'.[36]

Jealousy was often the root cause for disputes between couples, and often demonstrated itself in a brawl in church. In 1620 the pews in Stockport church had been reordered following instructions from the bishop. Elizabeth Chetham disliked the new arrangement as it meant Elizabeth Brookshaw was now placed one pew in front of her; she reacted by attacking Elizabeth Brookshaw during divine service: 'she did hale and pull her violently that her clothes did crack and pulled her from her seat and thrust her out of the Church door', which led to uproar in the church and an interruption of the divine service.[37]

A similar situation in Holt chapel in 1631 led to the churchwardens presenting John Yardley at a consistory for 'pushing back John Roden, when he attempted to enter the same seat'. Roden fell backwards and in his fall broke the partition between the pew of Mr Bostwick and Edward Broughton, causing 'great uproar' and a halt to the service.[38] A particularly violent incident took place at Saddleworth in 1684 when Isaac Lees and John Wylde openly created a brawl concerning the occupation of a certain pew during divine service. In this case, Wylde picked up Lees and threw him bodily to the opposite side of the aisle by which action Lees hit his head against the wall and was seriously injured. Two weeks later, to prevent any repetition of the incident, Wylde cut the seat 'half a yard shorter' so that only he and his wife could occupy it.[39]

Robert Jones and Anna Hewitt of Doddleston tried to occupy the same seat in 1680 whereupon she moved via the seat in front and would have entered the seat by the other end but was prevented by Jones. Her next action was to seat herself on the top of the seat, but Jones pushed her down with his elbow. She then 'went and took a boss out of another seat and sate down upon it at the entrance into that seat, but he forc'd her from that place also, pushed it away with his foote'. At this both the congregation and the incumbent reading prayers were disturbed and John Harrison, the churchwarden, 'desir'd them to forbear and be quiet'. Anna Hewitt claimed the seat because her mother had sat in it but Jones objected. When prayers began, Jones took her by the hand and when she cried out 'murder' he pulled her out. However Thomas Hewitt came and sat in the far end of the pew and Jones, unable to get him to move, sat upon him for a great part of divine service to the annoyance of all present.[40]

A churchwarden's wife was not above being attacked in church by an opponent. In 1632, John Meacocke intruded himself into the seat normally occupied by the wife of John Martin, churchwarden at Guilden Sutton, an action that was offensive to the congregation. At this, John Martin acted

> to prevent trouble, disorder & misdemeanour in the saide
> Seat, did goe into the seate . . . and sitt therein quietly for a
> tyme. . . . John Meacocke came into the seat next behind
> him and laid or took hould of both the shoulders of the said
> John Martin . . . and did violently hale and pull him
> backwards so that his body, falling backwards, his foote
> caught hauld of the next bence before him, otherwise he had
> fallen back upon his head into the seate behind him.[41]

In many parishes the jealousy and envy concerning who should sit in certain pews led to these violent brawls because the seating order of the parishioners indicated the pecking order in parochial society. Brute force was often used to remove someone from a seat. In 1639, John Dennis of Hatton annoyed Anna Taylor in Daresbury church by attempting to elbow her out of her seat, and because she refused to move sat on her so that she cried out 'Oh, how he hurteth me'. Her hat was almost removed, and her neck band crushed and 'turned about her neck', all of which caused offence to the congregation.[42]

To attend church wearing spurs was contrary to law for these were classed as armour, yet at Wrenbury William Cudworth accused George Taylor of Audlem, saying that he 'kicked him with his spurs and tore his stockings abusing him in his seat'. As a result, Taylor had to perform a public penance in the churches of Audlem and Wrenbury.[43]

Fights and beatings were commonplace. At Liverpool, Sarah Melling accused Margaret Griffiths and Elizabeth Lorting of 'Striking her servant, also Sarah Melling and her child in church'. (Child abuse was, as will be seen later, by no means a rare event.)[44] At Wybunbury, William Gamvell of Audlem charged William Reeve with 'striking him on the cheek and boxing his ears during Service and Sermon'.[45]

Re-pewing of churches gave rise to a great deal of trouble. At

Liverpool, on Sunday, 28 August 1631 Katherine Hedley 'did strike Margaret Moore on the face and abuse her with evil words' during the sermon.[46] In a similar manner Elizabeth Witters of Christleton accused John Bevan of brawling with her and her children about their right to occupy a certain seat, all the while 'grinning and gripeing his fist at her'.[47]

Pews were not the only cause of disturbance in church, and there were other sorts of incidents, such as the one at Crosthwaite chapel when John Cartmell 'did cutt or make holes in the cloaths of James Docker . . . and did stick Burrs upon his coate which he did weare in the Chapel', an incident that disturbed the service and was said to be 'an evil example to others'.[48]

As the population increased so did demands for seats, with the result that many disputes were concerned with several sitting in a single pew. Such a case at the Richmond consistory court was heard on appeal at York. It concerned Mrs Bulmer's title to a seat in Coverham church. Anthony Topham, who lived at the Manor House, had obtained a faculty to erect a pew at the east end of the Lady Quire; the Topham family had previously sat at the west end. The curate confirmed he had seen a faculty granted by Bishop Lloyd to Sir Adam Loftus, and Christopher Loftus and Mrs Bulmer, who was a Loftus, had erected a pew. It appeared that Mrs Bulmer and two of the defendants in the cause had hurled lively insults at each other about the pulling down of the pew. Mrs Bulmer remarked that should would like to know any who dared to pull down the pew without her authority.[49]

In some parishes allocations of seats were made jointly by the churchwardens and the majority of the parishioners. This was the custom at Whixley, and when an allocation was made without the consent of the third party trouble could arise as it did in 1603 when William and Dorothy Atkinson had been given a site for a pew in the church. The complaint was that

> the said piece of ground so sett furth and appointed by
> Thomas Dawson and George Kidd with the consent of
> Walter Ellis Vicar of Whixley, was not sett furth and
> appointed by the consent of the more part of the parishioners
> . . . but was a place wherein the servants and children of
> William Stockdail of Greenhammerton . . . had used to sitt
> or kneele for the space of twenty yeres before.

This was the prelude to a case which finally came to a conclusion in the chancery court at York some five years later. The dispute surfaced again in 1605 when the two families of Atkinson and Stockdail openly quarrelled in the church during the service on St James's day and created a disturbance. It appeared that William Atkinson had sent one of his servants to church to occupy his master's seat and prevent access to the seats in the pew by others. One witness, Nicholas Hopperton, said that he 'did see James Pawson stand in the upper end of the closett called Hammerton Closett . . . and did see him stop and stay the servants of William Stockdail . . . from going into the upper end of the closett called Hammerton closett'. Pawson successfully prevented any from entering the pew except Brian Sharpe, who dodged round and crept underneath, so taking possession. A violent dispute arose, so that 'the vicar Stayed Service for a time and one Henry Atkinson then churchwarden went unto them requesting they were quyet'.[50]

Three years later the cause went to appeal in York as the parties were unable to come to an agreement. In his evidence William Atkinson confirmed that there were two chapels in Whixley church:

a closett on the south side of the church called Hammerton Closett and another on the north side called Whixley Closett. His wife Dorothy did sitt in the seate appointed for her nere the font which belongs to her house, while he did sit in a stall adjoining the High Quier dore but his wife before the said time did sit first in one stall and them in another.

William Stockdail said he had lived at Greenhammerton Hall for twenty-three years, and before him William Charlesworth and others had always sat in Hammerton Closet. Gregory Man, aged 80, confirmed that he

was born in the house where William Atkinson now dwels and he lived there for sixty years. He has seen divers and sundrie sitt in Hammerton Closett as well as the occupiers of the manor house. One was Butler, another Syninge, tenants of Greenhammerton as well as Mistress Bancke of Whixley. He had never seen any placinge or displacinge of parishioners in different stalls but of late Adam Hopperton, the churchwarden, had moved some parishioners to place the vicar and parish clerk there.

A key witness was Thomas Banckes who provided details of the background to the two chapels and the seating arrangements. He stated that there

is a manor house in Greenhammerton nowe in the possession of Mr. Francis Swale in which manor house the Lords Courts are kept and hath lands belonging. . . . He had once dwelt in the house where nowe the said William Atkinson dwelleth. By reason whereof he knoweth well the stall at the Quier dore on Whixley church where nowe William Atkinson sitteth is belonging to the said house where noe women did sitt but men.[51]

It appeared that when Atkinson realized that they occupied the bailiff's house they thought they were entitled to a seat in Hammerton chapel alongside the tenant of the manor house. There is little doubt that Dorothy Atkinson was responsible for the dispute, by seeking to advance herself socially in the parochial hierarchy.

The chapelries in the Pennine moorland areas, inhabited by clothiers, peasant farmers, and artisans, had been attracted to Puritanism, an attraction that led to Dissent after the Restoration in 1660. One feature of those who were addicted to Puritanism was to try to intrude an unlicensed minister to provide divine service, as occurred at Saddleworth in 1618. Edward Percival, curate, cited Richard Wrigley, Robert Whitwell, and John Harrop to court for disturbing divine service on 14 June 1618. On that Sunday, Wrigley entered the churchyard, bringing with him an unlicensed and 'unconformable' minister, whom he led into the church while Edward Percival was reading evening prayer at the entrance to the chancel. Wrigley then 'did cry out with a loud voyce & say, "Shrd, Shrd, come this way for we will have a sermon of our owne" or words to that effect'. He then led the intruder to the upper end of the churchyard to preach to those who, by Wrigley's efforts, had been drawn away 'from hearing the divine service of the church . . . to the grief of well affected people'. The second member of the trio, Robert Whitwell, was anxious to get Percival removed from the parish, so he spread abroad the rumour that he had never been called to be a minister. To give some weight to the rumour, Whitwell had drawn up a petition implying Percival had sinned grievously. Armed with this, he went round the parish saying that those who signed the petition were showing their repentance, and pressure was put on many to sign. The third member, John Harrop, had entered the church in April during divine service to create a disturbance: '[he did] Continually exclayme & not cease to call upon him . . . not to reade any longer: so that Edward Percivall being reading the second lesson . . . was constrained before he had ended to cease & leave off'.[52] The service had to be abandoned as the result of this disturbance, but the officers were cited to court, penanced, and in some cases, excommunicated.

When the High Commission undertook an investigation into the conditions in the hundred of West Derby in 1633, they found a scandalous case of sacrilege in West Derby church on 14 and 21 August 1631. Two brothers, John and Richard Nichol, and George Massie had locked the church door to prevent any Prayer Book service being held. On these occasions, the sermon was preached by the incumbent who had to stand upon a gravestone 'or on a chair in the churchyard'. The three men had also placed a horse lock on the pulpit door to prevent anyone entering without their permission. Worse was to follow, for on Palm Sunday the following year Thomas Glover, the rector, had placed a bottle of wine upon the altar for the communion. The three accused were said to have removed the bottle and, 'by their enormous carriage', had spilled the wine and thrown the bottle on the floor. Richard Nichol then kicked the bottle with his foot, and George Massie and he then sat in the chancel to gaze on the communicants in an irreverent manner. Meanwhile, John Nichol, 'in a prophane manner took tobacco leaning on the font stone'. Nicholas Sachell, the curate, was suspected to be an aider and abetter with the others, because 'he doth keep an alehouse in the parsonage and sells ale therein & has been divers times in a beastly manner drunk so giving offence to his calling'.

The punishment was severe. The three principal offenders were to perform a public penance and pay £20 each to 'the use of the poor', while Sachell had to exhibit his Letters of Orders and was then to be unfrocked for his incorrigible drinking and irreverence and enter bond to perform his penance and amend his ways.[53]

On 1 August 1634 Sachell appeared in court and was then suspended from holding any clerical office in the province of York.[54] The court was able by its powers to impose a heavy fine accompanied by a term of imprisonment if necessary.

Doubtless many churchwardens, faced with the possibility of disorder, issued orders for the conduct of the parishioners in church. One set has survived for Kendal, drawn up in 1601. It is clear from these orders that weddings and funerals took place on Sunday, as 'Those who come to be married while the sermon is being preached shall not go up the centre aisle but sit quietly in some convenient place until the sermon and psalm are concluded'. Only at that point could they proceed forwards to be married. In the same way, those who brought the dead for burial were not to go into the chancel but quietly up one of the side aisles. None were to sit in the chancel except those who could sing and 'help to furnish the choir or are invited by the vicar and churchwardens for the time being'. Then follow detailed instructions concerning the conduct of the youth of the parish who, judging from the orders, appear to have been as disorderly, irreverent, and ill-mannered as any in the present century:

> Whereas many young persons and others, voyd of all reverence and Civil behaviour, have been and are accustomed to stand upon the stalls and seats to gaze about them at the time of any wedding or marriage. . . . It is enjoined that none shall use any unreverent gestures or behaviour but quietly keep their places . . . at the time of any wedding or other wise.

There follow details of the order in which the parishioners are to be seated whether aged, single, married, apprentices, servants, or young women. The list concludes with a general warning:

> concerning walking, talking in the church and loitering in the churchyard, frequenting of alehouses, departing out of church in time of service and sermon, the law has provided remedies regarding abuses . . . as they will answer to the contrary at their perill before the ecclesiastical authorities.[55]

The Civil War and Commonwealth abolished the church courts and, according to Christopher Hill, who compares the religious state of England at this period with the 'Island of Great Bedlam', there had been not only a political revolution but a religious and sexual one also.[56] The revision of the Prayer Book at the Restoration by that ecclesiastical quango the Savoy Conference alienated the Dissenters. This alienation was marked by the wording of the prayers for the established holy days of 5 November, 30 January (the martyrdom of Charles I), and 29 May (the restoration of Charles II).

In April 1662 Parliament approved the revised Prayer Book and attached to it an Act of Uniformity which made it not only compulsory to use the book but also to attend the Anglican church services each Sunday and holy day, and compulsory for the clergy and schoolmasters to subscribe to the Thirty-Nine Articles *ex animo*.[57] They were to renounce the Solemn League and Covenant, and to swear to the oath of non-resistance and supremacy.[58] Those clergy and schoolmasters who failed to subscribe were to be presented by the churchwardens as well as those who retained their livings by avoiding subscription to the Act of Uniformity.[59] This legislation raised the question of a possible fear that a return to another Cromwellian type of government was a possibility and moreover whether it was possible for a subject to differ from his monarch, who ruled by divine right, in the matter of religion. If so, a subject could possibly be regarded as subversive and an ever-present danger to the State. In many northern parishes and chapelries, especially in those areas that in the next century were to be influenced by the Industrial Revolution,[60] the restoration of Anglican worship, with all that it implied, was unacceptable. Dissent obtained a strong position in these parishes, which it continued to hold.

The Laudian Church was restored in framework but not in power. The prerogative courts of Star Chamber and High Commission were not restored so there was no coercive authority to discipline obstinate opponents by imposing prison sentences and crippling fines on them, for opposing the Church Settlement of 1662. In the absence of any official instructions concerning church administration, the old courts and vested interests came to life as though they had never ceased to exist. The Chester diocese was back in operation by 1661 to be followed in a piecemeal fashion by other dioceses.[61]

When Archbishop Accepted Frewen held his primary visitation of the dioceses of York and Chester in 1662/3, he discovered that many churches were in a poor state of repair and lacked furnishings. Scarcely one church possessed a surplice, many had lost their bibles, chalices, patens, and communion tables had disappeared, while the prayer books, where they survived, were dilapidated. Some eight years passed before all the churches in Chester diocese were furnished with the items requisite for the celebration of divine service.[62] It must also be remembered that many northern parishes were areas of extreme poverty where, in the 1660s, as many as 25 per cent of the parishioners were receiving parish poor relief. This meant that the churchwardens could never collect a full church rate.

Churchwardens had problems to face concerning the refusal of incumbents to use the Prayer Book. In June 1662, John Bennett, churchwarden of Walton, gave in evidence in a case against Henry Finch, vicar of Walton, that he had asked Finch to execute an order sent to him in 1661 for providing a new Book of Common Prayer for the use of the parish. Bennett purchased a copy and asked Finch to use it, but 'this deponent [Bennett] . . . tendered it to Mr. Finch who told this deponent he would need three weeks to consider of it but he never read or used the same . . . and he as churchwarden did present Mr. Finch to the Rurall Deane'. He affirmed that he had never seen Finch administer the communion and when he baptised children he never used the rite in the Prayer Book.[63] Another incumbent who acted in a similar manner was Robert Constantine, vicar of Oldham, who did not use the Prayer Book but 'despised the same and the sacraments' by preaching sermons against the book.[64]

The laity were more forceful in registering their opposition. In 1662, Lydia Turner of Manchester was cited to appear in court for attacking the Prayer Book in public. One witness, William Marshall of Manchester, stated

that on or about the 23rd April 1662, he did hear Lydia
Kay alias Turner in a very bitter and angry manner say that
she hoped to see the Book of Common Prayer trampled
underfoot and brought as low as . . . the Solemn League
and Covenant and did . . . stamp her foot upon the ground
. . . he wished her to take heed of what she said for these
were dangerous words.

Her response was to reply in a stronger manner than before.[65]

Reaction of this nature was to be expected in Manchester which had been a strong Presbyterian centre during the Commonwealth and a supporter of the parliamentary forces in the Civil War.

One case of interest arose in Marple in 1662. The documents in the case throw light on the tensions that beset the parish immediately after the Restoration. The libel names two men, Ottiwell and Oliver Higginbotham, who were notorious Dissenters and refused to attend divine service at Marple. It was alleged that on Trinity Sunday, 1662, which that year fell on 25 May, they had fastened the chapel doors with staples and hasps to prevent the curate, Francis Lowe, and his congregation from undertaking divine service, since at that service notice was to be given of the 'anniversary of the observance of the 29th May' (the date of the King's Restoration). As a result the curate and his congregation were forced to break down the door. Three days later, they once more fastened the door to prevent the reading of the new service honouring the Restoration, and Lowe and his congregation again had to break down the door and make a forcible entry.

The following Saturday, the Higginbothams again broke into the chapel and removed the lock, replacing it with another. Finally on Sunday, 8 June, they surpassed themselves, as

> the minister and the people meeting according to their accustomed manner to perform . . . the duties of the day, found the old chapel doore taken away and a New strong doore full of Great Nayles and a new lock . . . that neither the minister, sworne men or their assistants could enter the said chappel . . . the Minister was Constrayned to reade prayers in the Chappel yard.[66]

The case first appears in the court books on 19 June 1662 as a case promoted by Francis Lowe, from which we learn that seven men were involved in it. The depositions of the four senior inhabitants of the chapelry are dated 17 July 1662. The former witness accused Lowe of a scandalous life and of retaining his office against the wishes of the parishioners. The other witness, Robert Higginbotham, stated that Lowe had been their minister for fourteen years, and

> at first came among them with a general consent except of some fewe of the meaner sort . . . he is nowe very well liked

of all except the partyes nowe in question and some fewe
more whoe are factious and not Conformable to the Church
of England as nowe established by some . . . Inhabitants of
Marple.[67]

The case dragged on for some months, and as there is no record
of any sentence the proceedings may have been abandoned when
Francis Lowe moved from Marple in 1663 to the much richer
benefice of Taxal.[68] Despite this the case is interesting and
demonstrates the difficulties that could arise in a small country
chapel remote from the centre of ecclesiastical authority. It would
appear that the chapel had a history of favouring Dissent for in the
1630s it had a curate, John Jones, who had been prohibited from
preaching before the Restoration. Perhaps his ministry was more
acceptable to the Higginbothams than that of Francis Lowe. There
could also have been some political tensions at work as there were
in many rural areas.

Another case that involved the removal of locks and keys to
prevent the statutory services being held took place at Altham
chapel in Whalley parish. Thomas Jolly, a Presbyterian minister
ordained during the Commonwealth and a friend of Oliver
Heywood; who was leader of a group of Dissenting ministers based
on Coley chapel, Halifax, was brought before the consistory by
William More, vicar of Whalley, for his Dissent. James Whittaker,
one of the witnesses in the cause, stated that Thomas Jolly had
been at Altham chapel for twelve years and that he was 'ordained
by the presbytery that were in those parts upon his promise to
defend the presbyterian government to the last drop of his blood,
for at that time they suspected him to be inclining to
Independency'. According to the witnesses, Jolly had formed his
own society and would baptise and bury only those who belonged
to that society. When the Prayer Book was handed to him he
refused to use it, and 'tore a great part of it out'. Furthermore he
had refused to read the thanksgiving for the Restoration of Charles
II, 'though desired thereto and refused to observe the day'.

According to Henry Whittaker, Jolly had expounded scripture
and had prayed and preached in the chapel but it was 'contrary
to the liking of all the inhabitants of the said Chapellry except two
or three families of the poorer sort'. Also he had heard Jolly
'openly in his sermons preach and invey against Common Prayer

as an invencion of man and made by the papists and there was not a true word in it'. He had also preached against the Lord's Prayer.

He was then barred from the chapel by a Mr Bannester, an inhabitant of Altham who

> got the Key of the Chappell dore would not permit the said Jolly to goe in and preach because of his nonconformity . . . whereupon the said Jolly broke open the Chappel dore & got a new locke and key made for the same which his Clarke hath kept ever since and preaches there at his pleasure.[69]

Jolly managed to avoid a presentation at the Lancashire quarter-sessions by slipping across the Pennines to the safety of Coley, in the ungovernable parish of Halifax and outside the jurisdiction of the Lancashire justices.[70]

The extent to which some persons would go to demonstrate their opposition to the Prayer Book is well illustrated by a case from Ratcliffe which was heard in the consistory court in January 1663. It had been reported by some parishioners to John Angier, curate of Ringley chapel, that two parishioners had brought a horse into the church in order to parody the rites of baptism and Holy Communion as set forth in the Prayer Book. In an attempt to ascertain that the report was correct, Angier went to see the sexton, John Lowe, whom he 'found something unwilling to give him a full and true relacion of the whole matter though he was present'.[71] Accordingly Angier reported the whole affair to Thomas Tong, the vicar of Ratcliffe, who brought the charge.

From the evidence it appears that Otto Holland and Peter Walker had brought a horse into the church on 5 November, the church being open 'to ring the bells for the solemnitie of that Day', but the sexton seemed unwilling to speak the truth; he said 'hee did not much mind it for he turn'd from them & went into the belfrey'. However, it seemed that Holland and Walker led the horse up the church, made it kneel near the communion table, and there 'gave him a piece of bread with some blasphemous expressions that this deponent doth not well remember to depose. And that he was as good an Episcopalian as any of them for he had bowed to the Altar'. After this the two led the horse down to the font, one of them removed its cover, and 'either he or thother sprinkled water upon him and called him Surly Boy'.

The affair evidently gained some notoriety in Ratcliffe and its neighbourhood, but in such a parish, where there were many Presbyterians, attacks on the liturgy of the Church of England were to be expected. Later Holland claimed that he had compounded with the officers of the consistory to 'take off his punishment for his delinquency', and the case disappears from the court books.[71]

Attacks by Dissenters continued for several years after 1662. One case of some interest arose in the chapel of Hutton Roof, in the parish of Kirby Lonsdale, in 1668 when a group of Dissenters broke into the church and one of them preached a sermon with the knowledge and connivance of the chapelwardens.

> On Trinity even . . . the Window thereof was broken open
> . . . the locks was pulled off the doors . . . the booke of
> Common Prayer and a Psalm book was likewise stolen away
> . . . the book of Homilies was rent assunder . . . And the
> next day . . . James Greenwood a nonconformist did preach
> at the request of Edward Mann. . . . Greenwood did take
> away the Booke of Common Prayer and the psalm book . . .
> and since could never be heard of nor found.[72]

Dissenting opposition to the Church, especially of this type, surfaced from time to time in the western deaneries of the diocese.

Attempts were occasionally made to discredit churchwardens by accusing them of theft and fraudulent conversion of church property. One good example comes from Lancaster, where George Harrison, who succeeded James Thompson as churchwarden, was determined to bring his predecessor in office before the court on a charge of embezzlement. It appears that Thompson had erected two new pews for the bellringers but Bishop Gastrell refused to issue a faculty, so they had to be removed. To install the pews it had been necessary to remove the flagstones from beneath them. Thompson was building himself a new house in China Lane, and according to Harrison he had removed all the

> valuable flags he could meet with in the Church as well as
> those placed under the stairs leading to Dr. Fenton's and
> Mr. Fisher's seats as others, as well as those taken from
> over Graves when Grave stones were laid down as from the
> Chancel and other parts of the Church.

At the same time new stairs and rails were provided for the pulpit, though 'the old ones were sound and would have lasted many years'. Like the flagstones, the stairs and rails went to China Lane.

Harrison then commented upon the church clock which would not go because it required cleaning. Thompson had removed the clock weights but when his term of office ended he brought some lead weights, 'which he had hung in a Chimney for some time to make them black', so that they would resemble the originals. Harrison stated that Thompson had obtained the services of Gavin Wingreen , a glazier, to melt the weights and cast them into sash weights for the new windows in his house. Young Gavin Wingreen, apprentice to his father, confirmed that he had helped his mother to melt down the clock weights and he had seen them in Thompson's new house.

The masons were then brought into the cause. James Fell had helped to load the flagstones into carts, after darkness had fallen, and they were then driven to China Lane. Fell and his assistant Robert Gibson laid the flags in the kitchen and the cellar. During the time that Fell was engaged in laying the flags, he observed the pulpit stairs lying in the kitchen. What John Wallis the blacksmith was questioned about the flags he replied that when he was walking up Castle Hill, 'at sun rise in May or June', he saw a horse and cart in the churchyard with three men loading the same. Observing that they were noticed they moved out of sight, but later the same morning Thomas Cornthwaite the carrier took the cart with the load of flags to China Lane.

In his defence, Thompson stated that the church floor was not entirely flagged but that 'the pews on the north side are not flagged but strewed with rushes for the convenience of kneeling as most of the seats in the church were & are now'. He had purchased the flags from Dr Fenton, vicar of Lancaster, and they had been removed when large gravestones had replaced them. He denied both that he had removed the flags by night and that he had told the carter, if questioned by the sexton, to say that 'he was removing bed stocks from the Marsh'. Had he desired to keep the matter secret he could have taken the cart between the castle and the churchyard wall where the sexton would have observed nothing untoward. In the matter of the clock weights, he had asked permission to remove them to convert into sash weights because there was no lead for sale in the town. When supplies arrived he immediately replaced the lead he had removed. Thompson also pointed out that Harrison had removed lime from the church in order to make mortar for his own new house, and he hoped that 'he had restored the same quantity as he had removed'.

The commissary of Richmond questioned the plaintiff as to the reason why he had not preferred this cause to court before. Harrison replied with three reasons: first, Dr Fenton said it was a dangerous step to take since if Thompson was convicted he would appeal to the Archbishop of York; secondly, if he failed to prove every single point of his allegations, through reliable witnesses, he would be condemned in costs; and thirdly, he had no reliable witnesses to present proof at that time and had but hearsay for the case. Since Harrison had completed his term of office as churchwarden he was free to bring a cause.

Analysing the evidence, it appears that George Harrison brought the suit not on grounds of fraudulent conversion of church property, which formed the basis of the suit, but because Thompson had 'opposed the said George Harrison's imperious demands and designs for enslaving the Corporation of Lancaster'. Harrison threatened to have his revenge so he made it his business to abuse Thompson 'in the public rooms of all the alehouses in Lancaster'. In order to achieve his ambition, he obtained the support of the Dissenters, who were opposed to the Church, to prosecute Thompson and they had signed a defamatory libel in which they promised to assist the prosecution. In fact, Thompson openly asserted that 'George Harrison has abused, defamed, aspersed and railed at, in public alehouses the persons concerned in advising James Thompson in his defence against the malicious designs and revengeful prosecution of George Harrison'.

Harrison lost his suit and was condemned in cost.[73] This is not an isolated cause for jealousy and envy played a not inconsiderable part in relationships between churchwardens.

One duty churchwardens found irksome was the obligation to collect the fine imposed by the 1559 Act of Uniformity from all persons who failed to attend their parish church each Sunday and holy day, so making themselves liable to pay 'twelve pence to be levied to the churchwardens . . . to the use of the Poore of the Parish'.[74] One of the few references to the collection of this fine comes from Brignall, where the churchwardens in 1619 pointed out to the visitor the difficulty involved:

> We answere yt hither toward they yt use to be absent from divine service upon Sundayes have not bin observed for xii pence for every absence, neither hath any such forfeiture bin collected, because we know no course as yet how to enforce them to pay such mulctas.[75]

When Richard Neile held his primary visitation in 1633 he gave orders to the churchwardens of Aysgarth, Buske Chapel, Clapham, Gosforth, Hale, and Lamplugh to make such collections, but the churchwardens of Millom, Warton, and Kirby Lonsdale said the fines had never been collected.[76]

The fines were omitted from the 1662 Act of Uniformity which envisaged that all persons would be members of the Church of England and to that end the various acts forming the Clarendon Code were passed. Although under severe penalties, Dissenters attempted to avoid the legislation by meeting secretly wherever possible. The 1672 Declaration of Indulgence had weakened the hold of the Anglican Church in so far as some toleration had been granted. The Exclusion Crisis led to the emergence of an elementary party system which led to increased tension. In 1681, following the dissolution of the Oxford Parliament, an attempt was made to enforce compulsory attendance at church by suppressing religious meetings held by Dissenters, arresting persistent offenders, and enforcing penal laws against papists. Many court suits of the 1680s show that non-attendance at church was the reason for the summons to appear in court.

As usual, the churchwardens had the task of presenting such absentees for action to be taken. The first suit appeared in 1681 from St Peter's, Chester, when Thomas and Sara Fernihough had to explain why they were absent from church services. The following year saw a spate of suits. Anthony Henthorne, sugarbaker, of Whitefriars had not attended church for several years, William and Anne Pickering for seven years, and Ralph and Anna Dicconson, Thomas and Anne Fernihough, and Nathaniel Basnett, apothecary, for varying lengths of time; all of these defaulters appeared at the citation to confess.[77] Two Liverpool sugarbakers, Richard Cleveland and Daniel Danvers, ignored the citation to appear and answer for their non-attendance at church. Since they did not make an appearance in court within forty days, they were declared contumacious and a Significavit was issued for their arrest. When they were brought to court they were sentenced to enter bond for £20 each to attend church, and surety was given by Nicholas Johnson, 'sopeboiler', and Thomas Buck, grocer, of Chester, who were obviously known to the Liverpool offenders.[78]

Three persons from Leigh, Mary Eaton, James Bannester, and Edward Hilton, had been before the assizes at Lancaster on the grounds that they were recusants and so were convicted under the penal legislation.[79] It was never easy to compel people to attend church, and the Quakers defied legislation on compulsory attendance. The rural deans, or their surrogates in the western deaneries, compiled lists of excommunicate persons who refused to appear in court, the majority being Dissenters of one kind or another. In Kirby Lonsdale deanery there were 262 persons standing excommunicate 1682 but by 1685 the number had risen to 452. In Furness deanery there were 175 excommunicate persons in 1682 but by 1685 this figure had increased to 241, with a total of 300 in Copeland deanery.[80] The Toleration Act of 1689 saw a dramatic fall in these numbers as Dissenters were no longer persecuted with such vigour.

Wherever there were large numbers of excommunicate parishioners the churchwardens faced a difficult task, that increased at time passed, in collecting church lays. The only method of financing church repairs and maintenance, apart from charitable bequests, was by means of a lay or rate. In fact it was the duty of the churchwardens, once they had been sworn into office, to make an estimate of the amount of money they would need to raise to meet expenses during the ensuing year. Frequently the churchwardens' popularity depended upon the skill by which they were able to keep church lays at a minimum level. If they were negligent in executing repairs to the church fabric, or churchyard walls, it could lead to excommunication without the possibility of obtaining a writ of prohibition from the civil court.[81] Occasionally alternative but less creditable means of raising money were resorted to by holding a church ale and similar jollifications.

The church rate had been established by a constitution of Archbishop Stratford in 1342 whereby all persons who possessed lands or houses in a parish (with the exception of tenants on the glebe), whether resident in the parish or not, had to pay together with the parishioners the charges levied by common right or custom.[82] Having decided upon the total amount of money to be raised, the churchwardens then presented the figure to the archdeacon or rural dean for his approval, followed by notification to the parishioners of their individual assessments. Although those who defaulted in paying their rates could be cited into the correction and consistory courts as yet no process could be entered against them in the civil courts. In 1692, the Commons had attempted to place church rates on the same basis as poor rates but the bill was thrown out by the Lords.[83]

Objections to their rate assessments usually came from the landowners, both large and small, and tenants who resided in another parish. The common excuse was that the lands assessed lay beyond the boundary of that particular parish. The annual perambulation of the parish boundary at Rogationtide was designed to minimize such disputes at a time when cartography was very elementary and ordnance surveys had not as yet been developed. The laity, especially in those areas where Dissent was strong or industry expanding, did not always realize the importance of this perambulation, so they tended to ignore or neglect the custom. Dissenters ignored the custom as a waste of time since it interfered with work and in some parishes some parishioners would make fun of those that went on perambulation. In 1638 at Mobberley, Robert Robins found himself before the court for 'jesting and geibing [sic] those who went on the perambulation upon Holy Thursday last calling them many fooles for soe going'.[84]

In 1631 the churchwardens of Woodchurch cited John Hockenhull to appear in court and explain why he had not paid his church lays for the past twelve years, and William Vaughan of Bangor on Dee for refusing to contribute towards the repair of the church fabric.[85] Refusals to pay lays were frequent from Farnworth, Chester, Ashton-under-Lyne, Frodsham, Backford, and Thurstaston, where Elena Keene said the churchwardens made an attempt to get her husband to pay his lays by making him drunk.[86] Manchester churchwardens had considerable trouble in collecting lays from Lady Cecilia Trafford for her manor of Trafford and the dues from her lordship of Stretford, as evident from the entries in the lay books for 1617–34 which were produced by the churchwardens. Also in trouble was Lady Anne Moseley for non-payment of her assessments and dues on her property at Hoosend in Withington.[87]

The large number of orders issued by the diocese to the churchwardens to make their seats in church uniform, to enclose and rail off their communion tables, to pave their church floors and fence the churchyard raised objections from many parishioners. When the churchwardens of Stockport levied a lay to carry out such an order, Lawrence Wright obtained a prohibition to have the case heard in the civil court, an action that the churchwardens were unable to undertake by law.[88]

Very few churchwardens escaped a suit in the consistory court when faced with the problem of executing episcopal orders to unify seats and 'beautify' the church. In 1635 the churchwardens of Christleton refused to reorder the interior of their church and in consequence found themselves in court for refusing to obey orders.[89] At Prescot and Chorley the churchwardens spent very large sums of money on reordering and beautifying their churches. At Prescot, although the lays between May 1634 and October 1637 raised £248, the churchwardens had spent £250.2s. There were also objections from four of the parishioners who lived at Euxton Brough who in consequence found themselves before the High Commission at York.[90]

Workmanship in the sixteenth century could be as shoddy as that in the present century. When the churchwardens of Colne had removed the pew of John Robinson lower down the church to make room for the new pulpit and reading desk, he cited them into court not only for moving his pew but also for bad workmanship: 'the soletrees are only two inches thick instead of five inches and are made of rotten timber and full of mortice holes'. He also opposed the conversion of the pews into double seats instead of single, for some persons would be seated 'looking down the church with their backs to the communion table'.[91] At Astbury Edward Drakeford refused to pay his lay of 28s. to the re-pewing of the church which, according to the churchwardens, was in utter confusion: 'the pews were some high, some low, some wider, some longer, and some of one manner and fashion and some of another'.[92]

Parochial chapels could be at the root of financial problems. The churchwardens of Bolton entered into a long and costly cause against the chapelwardens of Rivington concerning their obligations to contribute towards the repairs of Bolton church.[93] Broughton chapel was another that openly refused to contribute any money towards the re-pewing and reordering of the church of Kirby Ireleth, following 'the order issued to all the churches in the diocese'.[94]

Parochial boundaries in parts of Lancashire were difficult to define and occasioned a great deal of argument. In 1641 when John Ormerod and Richard Whittaker were cited for non-payment of their lays and dues towards the repair of Haslingden chapel and a proportion of the curate's stipend they raised an objection. According to the two defendants the hamlets of Low Clough Booth, Crawshay Booth, and Newhall Hey were in Haslingden but those of Goodshaw Booth and Higher Booth were in the castle parish of Clitheroe, so as residents in that chapelry they did not pay lays to Haslingden.[95]

After the Restoration church lays proved even more difficult to collect since the Quakers openly refused to pay and the Dissenters were equally reluctant. Occasionally one finds a case where the petitioner hoped to be released from paying lays because he was on the losing side in the Civil War. In 1664 John Sefton of Shotwick refused to pay 2s. lay on his 'coate built on Capenhurst Waste'. He claimed that he had been a soldier in Ireland and had lost everything fighting for Charles I.[96]

The city parishes of Chester had boundaries extending beyond the city and objections were numerous to the payment of lays. When the churchwardens of St Mary on the Hill cited Francis Massey of Moston Hall for non-payment of three lays in 1684, although he agreed that Moston lay within the parish of St Mary he claimed that 'people of Moston worship at Backford and the same parish relieved the poor of Moston'. This problem was common in places where the boundaries of the civil and ecclesiastical parish were not identical.[97]

At Sefton the road to Lord Molyneux's mill went through the churchyard and was used by carts and carriages. When the Archbishop of York held his visitation in 1685 he ordered the road to be closed and diverted round the exterior of the churchyard. The churchwardens estimated that five lays would be required to construct the diverted road and that the constables for Ince Blundell and Crosby should collect the lays. Sir William Blundell objected as he considered that it was not the responsibility of the churchwardens to construct the road. The cause went on appeal to York but no trace of the decree can be found.[98]

The cost of maintaining church bells is an ever-recurring theme; parishioners do not appear to have been over keen to add to the number of their bells as these could be costly to maintain. When in 1691 the churchwardens of Leigh proposed to add a fifth bell, several parishioners objected on the grounds that the steeple was too small and the fabric would be endangered by the additional weight.[99] At Manchester, where the churchwardens wanted to repair the tower and recast the bells, there were objections to the cost from the parishioners who lived in Manchester, Crumpsall, and Cheetham who insisted that only two bells required recasting and not the whole peal of six.[100] An attempt by the rector of Doddleston to install new bells, ropes, and a bell frame brought protests and a suit in court by the churchwardens who accused the rector of 'irregularly levying a church rate'.[101]

The cause papers in the consistory files concerning payment of church lays contain details that are sufficient to given the impression that some churchwardens were reluctant to collect the lays even if opposition was small. In 1595 the church of Middleton Tyas was in a bad state of repair, so the visitor told the churchwardens to make an assessment, and then to 'collect it sufficient for the repair of the Church with all convenient spede and if they refuse to contribute to certifie their names and to begin so sone as they can with the repair thereof and to certify'. The churchwardens duly appeared at the next visitation, and said 'they have made a Cessment [assessment] but have collected nothing'. They were duly warned that they must make a serious effort to collect the assessment, but 'if they collect not at all before the end of the year then to give up a rite account to the Churchwardens that shall succeed them and acquier them with the whole proceedings'.[102] An attempt was made to collect the lay but it was undertaken in a half-hearted manner and their successors had to complete the collection.

On the other hand, when churchwardens of Marrick, a neighbouring parish, were cited to appear for the same offence in 1702, they were able to plead successfully that the poverty of the parishioners rendered it impossible to collect any lays at all.[103] At Great Harwood, Ambrose Peacock and Richard Constable refused, as constables, to collect an assessment of one-sixteenth for the repair of the church in 1623, but their negligence was eventually disclosed and seven years later they found themselves in court.[104] Similarly, at Upholland William Lewis, the curate, cited Christopher Robie, churchwarden for the lower end of the town, for not collecting the pew rents of 8s.4d., 'being part of the salary of the curate'.[105] From evidence in court files, the collection of the curate's stipend in the parochial chapels was frequently a problem, often arising from economic conditions.

The inability and reluctance of some churchwardens to collect the church lays for the repair of the parish church led to some serious problems in the state of the fabric. One good example is provided by the church of St Mary, Chester, in 1697: 'the south aisle has fallen down and the paving of the churchyard is defective. Charles Fletcher the parish clerk has taken ten pounds towards the repair of Troutbeck chapel'.[106] When the churchwardens of Rostherne cited Peter Leigh for refusing to pay his lays towards the repair of the church, they described the appalling condition of the fabric:

> the seats are not uniform, we want repairs in the roof, walls and windows, the floor is not flagged, the belfrie farr out of order, the windows unglassed and the font very unhansome, foule and indecent. The walls of the church raine and wett dropping and running thereon are turned green and mouldie, The doors of the church are broken and the church porch decayed.[107]

This was undoubtedly a shocking state of affairs, but matters were not much different when Archbishop Sharp visited Cockermouth in 1707, as his report on the church presents a depressing picture: 'The Church is most deplorable in conditions both within and without. The walls rotten at the top and the Timber decayed. The Creed, the Lord's Prayer and the Ten Commandments are not legible.'[108]

Troutbeck chapel was in an even worse state of decay. The Reading Desk had been cut down and moved into the belfry, the chapel gates were so decayed that it was impossible to restore them, and the locks were missing from the chapel doors. Ten years later the windows were broken and shattered while the chapel yard walls had collapsed, leaving the yard open to the neighbouring fields. By 1727 the roof and steeple were so decayed that 'the bell dare not be tolled upon any occasion' and the congregation attended church at the risk of their lives; a complete rebuilding had to take place in 1735.[109]

There were many variations in the methods of assessing parishioners for their proportion of the church lays. At Kendal the vestry met on St Peter's day (29th June) to assess themselves and the lay was collected at three intervals in the year, 18 October, 27 December, and Easter Tuesday. The inhabitants of Broughton-in-Furness assessed themselves by quindam (fifteenth) whereby all estates in the parish paid the same amount irrespective of acreage or value. The residents of Cockermouth over 16 years of age, were assessed at $1\frac{1}{2}d.$ each, while in Millom the church lays were raised by fattening inferior cattle for sale on the open market.[110] In the archdeaconry of Chester the parish of Aughton assessed the parishioners at a flat rate of two-fifteenths and that of Halsall at three-fifteenths, but Culceth managed with one-fifteenth and 'one and a half lays'.[111] When the churchwardens of Prescott attempted to assess Cuthbert Ogle for his glebe land he was able to prove that this land, being church property, was exempt from lays.

The obligation placed upon churchwardens by canons 20 and 21 to provide the elements for the communion was one that some attempted to avoid. At Cheadle in 1633, the churchwardens had provided neither bread nor wine for the communion, no Book of Common Prayer, and had not collected the lays from Handford Quarter.[112] Evidence was given in the suit brought against the Warrington churchwardens in 1673 that they were supporters of Dissent for not only did they fail to provide the elements for the communion on Whit Sunday but also on St Peters day. Robert Curren, innkeeper, who preferred the charges said that

[they] doe very many Sundays and holidays absent
themselves from their parish Church . . . and upon these &
other days doe frequently repair to those places commonly
called Barn-Churches or unlawful Assemblies or where Nonconformist Ministers . . . doe preach and expound the Scriptures.

The effect of this was that those who required sacrament certificates to comply with the Test Act of 1673 were unable to obtain them, the churchwardens being absent.[113] One ruse adopted by the churchwardens of Warmingham when asked why they refused to provide the elements was to reply that 'it is the custom in the parish for forty years that the rector provide the elements'.[114]

There appears to be very little evidence in the Chester consistory court files of the excesses that occurred in the York diocese in connection with the provision of the elements. The parishes of Kirk Smeaton, Drax, and Hatfield provide examples of the use of beer, water, and unconsecrated bread at communion. The cost of providing wine could be heavy for large quantities of wine appear to have been purchased. At Cawthorne (York) in the Doncaster deanery some twenty-three gallons of wine were provided for 200 communicants for six celebrations annually.[115]

Undoubtedly, want of funds encouraged some churchwardens to adopt a policy of 'make do and mend', as at Kirkham in 1632. They were cited into court for having patched the pulpit with iron bands to hold it up, and had provided no cover to prevent defilement by owls and other birds. It was also too narrow to preach in and they openly refused to pay the joiner to make a new one as instructed by the vicar, Edward Fleetwood, but were content with a patched-up job.[116]

If control of the congregation in church could be somewhat of a problem at times, controlling behaviour in the churchyard was equally difficult. Churchyards were commonly used, in many places, for playing football, which was clearly against the law. The game was a dangerous one since there appear to have been no rules, so fights and other disorder, 'even beastly murder', took place. On Easter Monday, 1608, George Sumner and William Wilbraham played at football in Doddleston churchyard, where 'they did quarrell, brawle & chide one with the other in a most unChristianlike manner and afterwards the same daie did fight', for Sumner struck Wilbraham in the face with his fist. Two others, John Loram and John Howell, were also involved in the same game and fight.[117] Churchyard football was a common offence in York diocese especially in the growing towns of Wakefield, Halifax, and Beverley where the young people attempted to play on Sundays.[118]

Some churchwardens were reluctant to obey orders, as at Bury in 1631. When the vicar there, having read canon 118, ordered Charles Duckworth and Thomas Meadowcroft on the occasion of the fair on Sunday 23 April, to go 'and keep order in the church and town, they sat in their pew and would not move'.[119] Local custom continued to observe holy days abrogated at the Reformation, especially at Ripley where the fair in the churchyard continued to be held on the feast of the Assumption of Our Lady with the support of Sir William Ingelby, 'the lord of the town'.[120]

The civil authorities no less than the ecclesiastical ones experienced trouble with churchwardens in executing their civil duties. Quarter-sessions ordered the churchwardens of Ainderby Steeple to give more attention to the relief of the poor, so that 'they do not trouble this court'. Those of Askrigg were fined for continuing the market in the churchyard, those of Marske for not presenting absentees from church, and, most serious of all, those of Hornby for making false returns of recusants.[121]

Churchwardens could and did meet with their share of abuse. In Old Withington, a chapelry in Prestbury parish, Thomas Dale called them 'arrant knaves' who spent the parish money idly and did not attend church on holy days and 5 November.[122] When the chapelwarden of Selside was found in Kendal churchyard by the churchwardens, they asked, in the execution of their duty, why he was not in church and why he refused to go to prayers. He replied 'that the forms of prayer used in the Church were Odious and not worth hearing and made most scurilous reflections upon the devotion of the Church'.[123]

Occasionally they could present a comical side to their conduct by being very ostentatious and officious to the annoyance of the incumbent. In 1700, Thomas Richardson, the chapelwarden of Little Budworth, disturbed evening prayer by 'placing strangers with great ceremony in a pew', so disturbing the congregation, and then proceeded to 'thrust himself into the Reading Desk and ordered the clark to sing psalm 84 so disturbing the sermon and also the clark'.[124]

Churchwardens could be resentful of the pressure placed upon them by the commissaries. In 1609 William Harrison, churchwarden of Wath, was presented for uttering 'woords against Mr. Commissarie viz; that he perods [sic] the Churchwardens to set ther hands to thei known not what with other badd speaches'.[125] He duly appeared in court and was dismissed with a stern warning.

By 1712 some churchwardens regarded the preparation of a presentment as a waste of time. The Richmond registry was rejecting the ones the wardens had prepared and charging fees for one prepared in the office. The churchwardens of Eriholme entered a protest against this practice:

> We have to present . . . the Uncanonical practice of the Court in putting us on a hurrie on visitation dayes by oblidging us to call for a presentment from their office & rejecting those presentments made by ourselves deliberately at home & for rejecting the Minister's separate presentment as informal & Taking in none but from their office, & payed for. We know not whether their fees be extravagant or not, there being no Tables of Fees set up.[126]

The fees charged by the Richmond court were far higher than those charged by the Chester court.

An assessment of this survey shows that the position of the churchwardens in many parishes was an unenviable one for the raising of money was a problem not easily solved, and, as time passed, those who dissented from the worship of the parish church saw no reason why they should contribute to the support of a church with whose doctrines they did not agree. Furthermore, the delicate matter of presenting the laity for their offences could and did lead to acts of violence against the churchwardens. Much of the rural economy of the Richmond archdeaconry depended upon the prices of corn and wool with rye, oats, and barley a second, although corn-growing in this region was less than in the vale of York. Prices, then as now, fluctuated, and in times of depression little money would be available for church repairs, hence the long periods before the work was completed. On the other hand, there were always those who were indolent in office, content to carry on in the old ways and yield to temptation. Their main object appears to have been to keep assessments for church lays as low as possible.

The presentments and the court files reveal something about the backgrounds of those who were elected to office. In parishes such as Bedale, Tanfield, and Goosenargh, where the vestries were closed, the churchwardens exhibited a high standard in compiling their presentments and records. They were men with above average literacy and ability who were clearly the social leaders in their parishes. In those parishes which worked through an open vestry matters were very different. Here many men were illiterate, often unable to write their names; their spelling is often phonetic and here the evidence points to the office of churchwarden being regarded as a job to be avoided if possible. The parishes with closed vestries rarely appear in court and their presentments continue to be made in the old style long after their weaker brethren have resorted to an 'omnia bene'.

In general, the churchwardens can be regarded as a body of men who exercised responsibility in difficult circumstances and were the recipients of abuse from disgruntled parishioners. It was a hard task keeping order in church when pews were regarded as private property which could be transferred to others. Yet in their hands lay the destiny of their little kingdoms, for often local reputations were in their keeping. Undoubtedly, friendship, neighbourly feeling, pity, procrastination, social pressures, and downright corruption caused many churchwardens to ignore the numerous breaches in the law. Many were anxious to conceal their deficiencies, their sins of omission and commission revealed in the court files, and were encouraged to make a return *omnia bene* and hope that no searching enquiries would be made. This was the line of least resistance and doubtless many offenders escaped the elaborate net designed to catch them.

Chapter Six

SIN AND THE SCHOOLMASTERS AND READERS

The last ranks in the hierarchy of the parochial structure were the schoolmasters and the readers, many of whom were also acting as schoolmasters in addition to their duties as parochial readers. For many centuries English education has been closely allied to the Church. Virtually all early schools sprang from an ecclesiastical foundation and a large proportion of them were staffed by the clerks attached to the original foundation. For long periods in their history both the schools and the schoolmasters were supervised by the Church far more closely than they are now inspected by the State. During the greater part of its history, English education has been not only Christian in its teaching but for two centuries after the Reformation, with the exception of the Dissenting academies founded after the Bartholomew evictions of 1662, almost exclusively Anglican.

From time to time legislation concerning the conduct of grammar schools was enacted and some of the earliest legislation can be found in canon 55 of the Fourth Lateral Council of 1215.[1] In 1597, and again in 1601, provision was made for 'commissions of pious uses' to be set up to enquire into and amend all abuses in the conduct of schools, schoolmasters, and the management of their endowments.[2] From the sixteenth century onwards the grammar-school masters were subject to licensing by the bishop or his chancellor. Elizabeth I felt that bishops should keep an eye on all schoolmasters in their dioceses, 'forasmuch as a great deal of corruption in religion is grown throughout the realm . . . proceedeth of lewd schoolmasters'.[3] Canon 138 of 1604 ordered every bishop to summon all schoolmasters to attend his primary visitation in order that he might inspect their licenses. By canons

77 and 79 of 1604, the schoolmasters were required to subscribe to section 1 of canon 36:

> that the King's Majesty under God is the only supreme Governor of this Realm . . . as well in all spiritual or Ecclesiastical Causes as Temporal, and that no foreign prince, person or prelate . . . hath any jurisdiction or authority within His Majesty's said realm.

They had also to subscribe to section 2 of the same canon declaring that the Prayer Book and Ordinal contained, 'nothing contrary to the Word of God and that it may be lawfully so used'.[4] The intention behind this was to eliminate the recusant schoolmaster who could conscientiously feel unable to swear the oaths of Allegiance and Adjuration.[5] In addition the 1673 Test Act required all schoolmasters and officers to furnish a sacrament certificate, prior to being licensed, showing that they had received Holy Communion according to the Anglican rite and taken the oath against transubstantiation before the justices at quarter-sessions.[6]

This legislation militated against efficient teaching in the schools because a definite Anglican bias was implied, so from this date onwards an over-rigid control on the conduct of schools operated against good education.

Parishes could be reluctant to found a school even when funds had been bequeathed for this purpose. A classic example comes from Kirby Lonsdale where, in 1580, the High Commission at York asked for an account of the state of their grammar school.[7] In February 1581 the churchwardens appeared at York, and exhibited

> two scedules of paper th'one contyninge seven peas of paper wherein mention is made of the voluntary grant of severall somes of money as every particular person named in the same will give towards the same schole and th'other conteyninge in grosse what somes of money every Township such as are named in the same scedule will give towards the erection of a fre grammar schole at Kirby in Lonsdale aforesaid . . . two townships . . . viz. Killington and Firbank . . . have not full set down what they will bestowe towards the erection thereof.[8]

Some time later, an injunction was received by the churchwardens from the High Commission requesting a return of all benevolences made towards the erection of a school, and moreover to state

> what some they shalbe willing to bestow thereupon to the same in wryting with the names and surnames of everie the said persons and to exhibit the same this daye that order may be taken for the collectyon thereof and the erection of the schole not delayed.[9]

Those townships and parishioners who were unwilling to contribute were to have their names recorded and presented to the High Commission so that action could be taken against them.

Having built a school, there was no guarantee that the master elected by the feoffees, or trustees, would be efficient, or that the school would flourish. A school had been founded and endowed at Urswick by William Marshall who drew up the statutes of government.[10] In 1621 William Gardner, one of the feoffees, brought a suit against the then master, Nicholas Marshall, on the grounds that he had received a salary of £15 per annum for teaching but in return had neglected the school. Gardner said that Nicholas Marshall 'keepeth a youth or boy in the said schoole under you to execute your said place & being verye unfitt to execute the said place and teacheth but petties of very yonge Schollers'. In addition, the founder had left £10 per annum to place some boys in a university college, but Nicholas Marshall's teaching was so deficient that, 'you have not made nor sent any Scholler by you . . . taught, fitt for university or Colledge aforesaid'. The real problem, Gardner claimed, was Marshall's weakness for drink and gambling at dice and cards on a large scale: 'you have lost in one night the said Games played the Summe of tenn pounds . . . playing with Robert Kilner'.

His drinking bouts were not confined to Urswick but in other places such as Hawkshead, Dalton, and Harburroide. In fact he had sometimes been so drunk that he had no knowledge of what he had said or done, and had fought with others. He duly appeared in court and was given penance and dismissed with a warning.[11]

Seven years later, Marshall was once again in trouble for his neglect of the school for his drinking habits and committing adultery. Arthur Gardner, a witness, stated that he was in John

Fleming's alehouse in Urswick with other company where he also found Marshall drinking, when suddenly he 'fell on a sleepe and he . . . observed the water ran out at the knees of Mr. Marshall and ran down his stockings into his shoes but whether it was his owne he is unable to tell'. William Bowett of Dalton also confirmed that Marshall neglected his school and produced evidence that he had committed adultery with Agnes Lindoe, William Hodgkinson's wife, and others, in 'private places'. Such activity could not be permitted to continue so Marshall's licence was withdrawn and granted to John Shawe, the usher, who according to William Bowett was a scholar and 'a good grammar scholar and able to teach the Schollars the grammar and to make true Latten'.[12]

In 1689 Sir William Clegg brought a suit against Josiah Younge, schoolmaster at West Kirby grammar school, on the grounds that for the previous three years he had neglected the school to 'frequent alehouses', and was a drunken and idle master who rarely taught his pupils. Like Marshall at Urswick he had his licence withdrawn.[13]

The election of a schoolmaster was a somewhat haphazard affair. The man nominated usually appeared before the feoffees, was given a perfunctory interview, and then had to give a demonstration of his abilities, which included administering the cane efficiently. Usually a boy who was in need of correction was presented whereupon the master designate demonstrated his skill in administering the cane. The appointment of Richard Routh as master at Crosthwaite in Heversham parish involved a similar type of test.[14]

Once elected and licensed the master became the possessor of a freehold which gave him some security of tenure, 'quamdiu se bene gesserit', but made no provision for his removal when he became incapable of conducting the school efficiently or his mental powers began to fail. When a situation of this nature arose then the feoffees had to take action by petitioning the bishop for his licence to be withdrawn.

In 1634 Thomas Waryner, schoolmaster at Whalley for the previous ten years, was charged with neglect of his school in that 'the last years he has so fallen off from attending his Schole and Schollars that few have profited'. Naturally, parents took action and removed their sons to other schools, especially 'the gentry and those of abilitie' who were said to be placing their sons in other schools, 'remote in Yorkshire and elsewhere'. Those parents who were unable to afford the cost of 'education abroad' had removed their sons and placed them in occupations such as 'the plow, handy-crafts or as labourers' – actions which detracted from the reputation of the school in the area.[15] Twenty-four people signed a petition that Waryner's licence should be transferred to John Swinglehurst, to whom Sir Ralph Ashton, after he had removed Waryner, had given the post of schoolmaster. Waryner in an attempt to regain his office as master cited Swinglehurst to court on the grounds that the latter had been intruded or brought into the school to teach Latin which was Waryner's job. In their defence the feoffees stated that Sir Ralph Ashton and the 'neighbours' had hired Swinglehurst to replace Waryner, and he was duly licensed.[16]

Occasionally, a master would abandon his school without any warning or notice given to the feoffees. In such cases a temporary master had to be employed but he could cause difficulties when a permanent successor was elected. The mayor and corporation of Congleton were the feoffees of the grammar school when Royle, the schoolmaster, 'uppon a suddaine and unexpected occasion without any warning given of his departure to us', left the town. The feoffees approached Andrew Bowry, minister of Congleton, and asked him to take over the duties of the master of the free school until a replacement could be obtained. This he agreed to undertake.

By 1639 a new master, one William Overton, a man 'of good behaviour and ability', was engaged for a year and Bowry was dismissed on the grounds that it was 'too greate a task for him to execute the office of both Minister and Scholemaster they have become two difficult offices'. In effect Bowry could not meet the demands made on him by both situations. Bowry, annoyed by the action of the mayor and corporation, went to the Chester diocesan registry where he managed to obtain a licence to act as master of the school. On his return he was asked to surrender the key to the school, but to the consternation of everyone he 'peremtorilie refuseth to give upp the key and possession . . . assigninge no Reason for his obstinacy'. Doubtless, since Bowry had received both the stipend attached to the living of Congleton and that of the school, he was now unwilling to see his income reduced by a half.

His licence was withdrawn and granted to Mr Overton.[17] A similar case occurred at Thornton where the curate, John Soothill, who had also been acting as temporary master, challenged Richard Smith, the newly elected master, as an intruder because he resented the loss of the stipend of the schoolmaster.

Attacking the Prayer Book could be equally dangerous, as Richard Grange, schoolmaster at Ainderby Steeple, quickly discovered when he had his licence withdrawn and was forbidden to teach at any school in the diocese of Chester.[19]

Occasionally churchwardens would present a schoolmaster for being unlicensed, as they did from Kirklington, Pickall, Romaldkirk, and Marske. Some churchwardens could express sympathy for their master being unlicensed as at Stanwick St John, Ripon, on the grounds that he was 'a very pooreman and a Scott who acted lately as Usher under Mr. Phillip . . . we have nott put him to ye charge of taking a Licence'.[20]

During the rather tolerant episcopates of the earlier bishops of Chester, several parishes had allowed schools to be conducted in their churches. When Archbishop Neile held his primary visitation of his province, he discovered schools being taught in the churches of Hipswell, Scorton, Catterick, and Marske in the eastern deaneries of Richmond, while they proliferated in the western deaneries, especially in Muncaster, Broughton, Cockerham, Goosenargh, Kirkham, Lytham, Preston, and Ribchester, where the condition of the fabric was dirty, the walls were covered in graffiti, and the building was in general very untidy.[21] The curate and schoolmaster of Weaverham was cited to appear in court for having no licence for either office. Moreover, he taught the school in church, and it was said that 'the parishioners are annoyed by fleas and lice by schole keeping'; hence the flow of orders to remove pupils from church and to build a schoolroom.[22]

During the Commonwealth the 'unsatisfactory' schoolmasters were removed from office, especially those who were suspected Royalists. The other side of the coin was that the Commonwealth was anxious to encourage the growth of education and see the masters adequately remunerated. The salary of the master at King's School, Chester, was augmented from the tenths collected in Derbyshire during this period.[23]

At the Restoration, Commonwealth educational policy became suspect on the grounds that it was a possible breeding ground for potential enemies of the State. Hence the Act of Uniformity required all schoolmasters to subscribe, to swear the oath of non-resistance, and abjure the Solemn League and Covenant. The bishop was to license each master and usher at a charge of 12*d*.[24] Those whose consciences would not permit them to continue then resigned, but a number in the remote chapelries and parishes were discovered at visitations to be teaching illegally.

In 1663 the master at Northwich School, Thomas Swinton, was cited to appear at the consistory for being a non-graduate master intruded during the Commonwealth by 'persons disaffected to the government', and for not subscribing on 24 August 1662 as the statute required.[25] When Edward Chandler caused an investigation to be made into the status of Peter Hurdie, master at Walton School, the latter replied that he only went to church to hear the sermon for his 'conscience would not allow him to conform'.[26] Zachariah Taylor, who had been ejected from his benefice in 1662, was found to be teaching a school in Ringley chapel and was cited to appear and explain his conduct. However, Taylor was regarded by Archbishop Frewen as such an outstanding master that he licensed him to Kirkham school despite the bitter opposition of the incumbent.[27] Another was William Wales, curate of Farnworth in 1663, who was said to be a negligent attender at church and one who held conventicles in private houses. This is by no means surprising for Bolton at this time was regarded as the 'Geneva of the north'.[28]

The watershed in education was the 1673 Test Act which made it compulsory for all schoolmasters to produce a sacrament certificate and make a declaration against transubstantiation under the hands of the incumbent and churchwardens and the justices at quarter-sessions.[29] From this date onwards the free grammar schools began to decline in many parishes due to the appointment of most unsatisfactory masters and the tight hold that the church maintained.

One of these unsatisfactory masters was Josiah Younge who was stated to have neglected his school at West Kirby for the past three years, between 1686 and 1689, by frequenting alehouses, and was a 'drunkard and idle person' who rarely taught in his school. At the petition of Sir William Clegg and the feoffees his licence was withdrawn.[30]

Another unsatisfactory master was at Bedale in 1705 when the feoffees requested the Hon. Miss Sanderson, as descendant of Frances, Countess of Warwick, who founded the school, to ask the bishop to withdraw the schoolmaster's licence of Anthony Wilkinson. The grounds were that although after his appointment in 1695 the school flourished for four years, it then began to decline and now by his

> wilfull negligence & drunken Life, it is brought in a manner to Nothing, to the great Loss & extreme trouble of the inhabitants of the parish. That all means have been used for the Reforming of the said Master, both by publick & private Admonition & all promise ineffectual & he's growing worse and worse.

Unless measures were taken, the school would be ruined if he was allowed to remain, but consent of the patron was required before a request could be made to the bishop. The letter was not sent, however, because the master dismissed himself in a most unusual way: 'Soon after the date of this Paper, Mr. Wilkinson in one of his drunken fits Listed himself A common foot Soldier & so the school became vacant.' Clearly Wilkinson now preferred to serve under the Duke of Marlborough in the War of the Spanish Succession which had recently commenced and required a great many recruits.[30]

A petition was received from the feoffees of Hargreave school in Tarvin parish that Ellis Rycroft was an unsatisfactory master in that he had intruded himself into the office without taking the required oaths and obtaining a licence to teach. It is clear from the petition that he drank very heavily, for he 'was much overtaken with excessive drinking as appeared by your stammeringe in your tongue, excessive visible & disordered staggering & reelinge & vomiting & spewinge in the School & upon your Schollars there', which was regarded as a scandal to the 'Ministry & profession'. As if these charges were insufficient, further ones were made, for he was said to be 'a Great Swearer & blasphemer of the Name of God, a rayler & evil speaker of & against your Neighbors'. His attitude towards the pupils left a great deal to be desired, and seems to have been totally opposed to the foundation statutes: 'by unfitting corrections & blowes & by your bad Carriage . . . the Number of Schollars there which heretofore was numerous & great . . . is now reduced unto a very small number of five or Seaven

. . . to the great damage of parents & harme of their children'.
Having been excluded from the school, he then forcibly entered
the building by breaking a window, 'in a rude unwarrantable
manner'. Such a man could not be permitted to continue in office,
so his licence was withdrawn.[31]

George Buckley, the master of Frodsham grammar school, was
cited to appear at Chester consistory in 1698 on the grounds that

> he was an immoderate drinker of strong drink, a frequenter
> of alehouses, he neglected his school, and was abusive to the
> Schollars by unjust Corrections with sticks & unlawful
> weapons to the disabling of the schollars & endangering lives.

He was said to have told the boys that if he did not arrive by nine
in the morning they were to go home and tell their parents that
it was a holy day. Clearly he observed holy days not then
appointed to be kept in the Church of England, namely, 8
September, the Nativity of the Blessed Virgin Mary, and the 14th
of the same month as Holy Cross Day. He had also begun to turn
poor boys away from the school. In his defence Buckley stated that
the trouble originated with 'the Sicknesse of his wife which by the
hand of God befell her in September and lasted until February so
he had to be away from School'.

It is quite clear from the evidence of the witnesses that children
were severely abused at the school. Margaret Bannen said her son
came home and told the maid that the master had hurt him with
a thick stick: the child was about 12 years of age. Next morning
the maid reported the matter to his mother: 'stripping the childs
cloaths off shee shew'd her the marks of the blows given him
which had much alter'd the skin & flesh on his arm and shoulder
and was black & blew in several parts'.

Margaret Bannen immediately went to the school where she saw
Buckley and laid the blame upon him. He confessed he was rash
and begged her pardon. In spite of his entreaties, she removed her
son and sent him to another school. On another occasion her
eldest son said Buckley had struck his youngest brother, aged 7,
on the 'side of the head with a Ferule till the blood came'.

Another witness, John Grice, complained that Buckley had
refused to teach his eldest son English, whereupon he complained
to the feoffees who told Buckley it was part of his job to teach that
subject. On another occasion some of the boys had reported to

John Cooke that Buckley would not teach his son, and that he had 'whipt him so severely and imoderately that the Boy could not sitt down of severall daies and . . . he bid him go home and tell his Father'. William Robinson said that he had heard 'from his son and a neighbours daughter' that Buckley had knocked his child down three times in the school. He then warned Buckley not to abuse his child or he would report the matter to Mrs Witton, who had allowed £3 per annum to the master. One day his son came home from school crying bitterly and, when questioned, told his mother that the master had beaten him with a stick. When she examined him she discovered 'his right arm black and blew and bruised so that he could scarce lift up his arm to his head or put on his cloaths'.

Thomas Webster's son, aged 12, came home with his arm and shoulder black and blue from a beating. When Webster went to school to see Buckley about the matter he was unable to find him, but the boys told him that 'the Mr. had abus'd thy Son very much and beat him with the Ferula'.

Thomas Richardson, the joiner, desired that his eldest son should be 'a good scholar' so he sent him to Buckley. After three years he discovered that he had made little progress and from the evidence it appears that Buckley was incompetent in teaching.

> [He] put him to learn in the Greek Testament, particularly in St. John's Gospell and after some time . . . removed him to the Book of Acts . . . but brought him back to the Gospell of St. John . . . whence he soon apprehended Mr Buckley could not teach him further.

When Richardson moved his son to another school, Buckley neglected his younger son on the grounds that if he could not teach the elder he would not teach the younger one. Both the sons of John Platt and John Lathom had the same experience, and Buckley had 'broken a stick upon this deponent's [Lathom's] sons arm who indeavouring to save his head from the stroke put up his said Arm to guard it'.[32]

Corporal punishment is not a feature of the present day nor of the immediate past. It is part of the long tradition taken quite literally from Proverbs, 'spare the rod and spoil the child'.[33]

Probably one of the worst cases of child abuse came from Malpas in 1636. Roger Wakefield, schoolmaster in the parish, was charged by Thomas Morris of cruelty towards his son Thomas. In his replies Morris stated that, 'having examined his hurt in his members, and being burst he conceived that . . . his said sonne had received wrong under him . . . and he thought he was dismembered'. One witness, John Adlington, said he was in the fields with others, 'making Races and Thomas Morris was to run'. When Morris was stripped for the races Adlington and the others with him observed that 'his privy members had been hurt or bruised and were swollen'. Asked how he came by these bruises, Morris refused to say except that his mother had told him to say he 'had hurt them by striding over a dorrsill or with crying too much'. However Adlington was unable to identify whether the injuries were received before or after Wakefield had whipped Morris.

Thomas Morris, the father, said he looked to Wakefield for amendment for beating his child wrongfully. He added that many parents removed their sons from his school by 'reason of his barbarous cruelty and abusing of his schollers, and for other just causes as he hath credibly heard'. In the end Morris believed his son had been abused by Wakefield who had, 'smitten him over a form or two because he [the father] would carry him no coals or chips [firewood]'. While some witnesses supported Morris there were others who considered Roger Wakefield to be a conscientious master, who, in their opinion, 'would never committ such a barbarous act'. The depositions are in a very poor condition since a number of sections have been destroyed by damp, so an accurate assessment of the actual truth of the case is impossible to ascertain for no sentence survives. On the face of the evidence Wakefield would have been penanced and threatened with the loss of his licence but that appears to have been as far as the case went.[34]

Blackrod school is one that is well documented for the mismanagement of the school and its scholars. In 1696, two of the feoffees, Richard Holland and Adam Gregory, cited the then master, Adam Sixsmith, to appear in court and state why he had intruded into the office of schoolmaster without a licence. Also he was accused of immoderate drinking, haunting tippling houses, a lower type of alehouse, and neglecting his school. In addition he was guilty of the abduction of Elizabeth Vause in order to marry her. The feoffees obtained the withdrawal of his application for a licence and he was replaced by John Sumner.[35]

Unfortunately, Sumner proved to be no better than his predecessor for in 1701 he was cited to appear at Chester by the churchwardens of Bolton and Blackrod on the grounds that for the previous three years he had neglected to teach Greek and Latin, or to bring his scholars to church to hear sermons and then examine them afterwards on the contents. Furthermore, he did not use the Latin grammar 'sett forth by King Henry the Eighth . . . & none other', and he resided at a remote distance from the school. In the beginning he had tried to be 'industrious and assiduous in the discharge of your said Duty & Charge'. However, Sumner yielded to other matters:

> in that time your divertions, excess of idleness and the temptations of your Games have . . . drawn you in Sight of the said School, you have exprest an aversion to come into it, nearer than an Alehouse within the village . . . where in it is scituate.

Robert Rigby, a witness in the cause, confirmed that Sumner had attended his school once or twice a week, staying there about two hours and in that time attempted to examine one or two of the boys 'in their Learning'. Another witness, Robert Aynscough, who was a flaxman and kept a shop opposite the school so he looked directly on the school entrance, said he saw Sumner many times when he should have been in school, going on his pleasure 'with a setting dog along with him and sometimes with strangers or Gentlemen, some of which have carry'd a Gun, so that hee seems to bee upon his recreacion'. Although he was responsible for the care of the schoolhouse, he had grossly neglected to undertake any repairs:

> [it] is in very ruinous condition, the walls being watld and don with clay are broke or worn down by the weather, the slates or many of them are blown or faln off so that the school is scarce tollerable to . . . the scholars especially in winter and foul weather . . . also . . . snow and rain fall severely into it and so exposed that boys may easily enter it when the door be shut.

The witnesses did not approve of Sumner residing in Wigan or at Haydock Hall as both were some distance from the school. The feoffees pointed out to the bishop that he had failed to observe the statues of the school and also accused him of 'heinous immoralities'. Since the conditions inserted in the licence 'ad nostram vero bene placitum tantumodo duraturas', the withdrawal of his licence was justified.[36] In 1703 Sumner appeared before Bishop Stratford and was deprived.[37]

When Richard Woods, for the feoffees, preferred charges against Roger Walthew, master of Rainford school, in 1704, the bishop appointed a commission headed by Archippus Kippax, the vicar of Ormskirk, to take evidence on the charges that he drank to excess, neglected his school, and never attended the church. On this occasion he received a warning.[38] Two years later he again appeared in the consistory on the same charges but brought with him a certificate testifying to his good character from the parishioners and he was allowed to remain.[39]

It was otherwise with Matthew Holdford, the master of Goostry school, who neglected his school and was, worse still, 'illiterate in Latin'. Also he kept an alehouse where he tippled on Sundays with an assorted company and never attended church. He appeared before the bishop, who withdrew his licence to teach.[40]

Kirby Ravensworth school was an old foundation based on a proposal by the last medieval archdeacon of Richmond, William Knight, who became bishop of Bath and Wells before he could execute his plan. It was left to Dr John Daykin to endow the school with £240 to provide 'free instruction in grammar, rhetoric and verse, and bring them up in good manners and pious wisdom'.[41] By 1700 the school had fallen on evil times due to the incompetence of the master, William Horn.

The statutes of the school specified that the master must be in holy orders with the status of priest but, as Horn was not, he was unqualified to act as master. He was said to have obtained a licence by 'undue means and with false suggestions' though what precisely these were is never stated. It is however clear that Horn was not a scholar and had not the ability to educate the boys to a high standard. The result was that the school, under Horn's control, had declined in status so that several parents felt they must send their children to other schools.

It is apparent from the evidence that between 1694 and 1699 Horn had became 'an immoderate drinker of strong drink, a frequenter of Alehouses and an habitual drunkard', so that he neglected both the school and pupils.

John Heslop of Dalton said that Horn was often in the alehouse when he should have been in school but was so negligent that 'he left the Government of the school to some of ye Boyes who were reputed to bee of the best schollars tho' they were very short in learning . . . [and he was one] who never in his Life made a scholar or brought up a youth to any considerable degree in Learning'. Heslop's son had been at the school for eight years and made so little progress that 'he did not understand the Construction of the Book called Cato nor the rules of English Grammar', so parents removed their children elsewhere and the school decayed.

Another witness, Thomas Wilkinson, a cooper, who lived adjacent to the school and had a son attending it, stated that from his observations he knew the numbers attending were small, 'having sometimes about 15, other times about 5, others about 3 schollars there at a time'. Therefore the standards and discipline of the school had become 'low & mean'.

Horn's life was no credit to him. Instead of living in the schoolhouse, he lodged in an alehouse in the village kept by Christopher Cockfield, and Wilkinson had seen them both drunk, 'in a sottish and stupid condicion, very unfit to teach children, and that in the day time . . . severall daies in the week, for severall weeks'. Furthermore, he had drunk ale, 'sotting and dozeing' for twenty-four hours at a time. In fact, the usher had to collect the key, conduct the school, and return the same to Horn in the alehouse. In winter Horn could be seen accompanied by his former landlord, Michael Allen, coming together across the Green when 'both were full of drink, tottering and stumbling by chance helping each other toward the school'.

William Applegarth, when he was churchwarden, had seen Horn sitting in the alehouse besotted with drink and was informed that 'hee had been drinking and tipling all the Night'.

Although Horn attempted to make some defence, the sentence of deprivation was passed against him, whereupon he obtained a writ of prohibition for the cause to be heard at York. The cause was heard in the chancery court upon allegations that he was totally incapacitated and had wilfully neglected the school. The sentence was upheld and Horn was dismissed.[42]

Competition from a rival school in a parish was sufficient to create conditions that could and did lead to litigation in the courts.

In 1691, James Moore, master of the grammar school at Burton-in-Kendal, cited Thomas Wood, the parish clerk, for teaching a school in his own house without any licence which was, Moore stated, 'to the great Detriment and Obstruction of the publick & free Grammar Schoole of Burton'. It appeared that Wood was said to 'so farr indulge the Children to come to you by Spices and other allurements' so that when a boy was corrected at the grammar school, he left and went to Thomas Wood, 'to be fostered in all his Roguery & neglect of his Books & Learning to the great loss of time & utter Ruine of such Boys'.

As if these were insufficient grounds for a cause, it was said of Wood that, although not in holy orders, he had 'taken upon him the Office of a Minister of the Gospell and publicly to read Divine Service on Sundays and Holydays . . . to administer the Sacrament of Baptism and to celebrate Matrimony between several and many persons' in the parish church of Burton. Unfortunately only the libel of charges has survived in this cause.[43]

Another cause that is of interest was at Bowes, in Richmond archdeaconry, where the archives reveal that the school then bore a close resemblance to the infamous Dotheboys Hall, a century before Dickens visited the parish. Here, Joseph Taylor, who was both curate and schoolmaster, was charged with neglect of duty, absence from the school for six consecutive weeks at a time, receiving the salaries of both the master and usher, and not employing any to teach during his absence. He employed the boys, instead, to milk his cows in the church porch and do other labouring tasks.[44]

These causes from the Chester and Richmond courts are by no means isolated or unique, for parallels are found in the diocese of York. The master at Kirkheaton was accused of such cruelty towards his pupils that parents had removed them from the school:

> That Thomas Blyeth did make distinction betwixt children of some men from others and did not correct them equally according to their demerits and that the cruelty and neglect of . . . Thomas Blyeth was the occasion of the parishioners and Inhabitants sending their children to foreign schooles . . . and that those sent abroad . . . have profited more than those who continued at Kirkheaton.[45]

Joshua Smith, schoolmaster at Holme and curate of Woodhead

chapel, was the same type of man. He was accused of severe cruelty towards his pupils and for being drunk and disorderly. John Whitehead, among several other witnesses, stated that

> he [Smith] struck a tooth out of Reuben Armitage head, son of Enoch Armitage of Lidget . . . and broke his head. Nathan Whitehead my brother he broke his head and so abused him that he out run my father to Wakefield. John Bilcliffe son of Edward Bilcliffe of Cumberworth he struck him so on's head that he made him deaf to this day. Jonathon Battye son of James Battye he did same and John Oldham son of John Oldham he struck him so that he caused him to swell under his Chin that his father is afraid it should bred the Evill [King's Evill] and several others.[45]

On one occasion in the alehouse at Holme when he was refused any further ale, he picked up one of the landlord's daughters and threw her on the fire and she was badly burnt. On another occasion he attempted the chastity of several women by day and by night, especially one Sarah Beardsel whom he caught washing some yarn: 'he put his arms round her belly and said he would show her the difference between a real man and her husband whom he said was an old man'.[46]

At Cawthorne in 1619 the schoolboys were completely out of control. The school was taught in the church and on the occasion of a wedding the boys demanded twelve pence from the bride. When she refused they locked the church door and threatened to remove her 'left foote shooe' and make her walk the three miles to Barnsley for the dinner.[47] The cause led to the washing in public of no small quantity of dirty parish linen. Some of this was the forging of entries on the baptism register, marrying couples by moonlight in the ruined chapel at Midhope, theft, assault, and drunkenness.

These cases involving the schoolmasters present a sorry picture of education in some parts of the diocese. Seventeenth-century schoolmasters often behaved in much the same way as their predecessors. Although the founders of schools intended that education should train boys in the ways of honesty, right living, and strict morality without any deviation, these aims were never completely attained. During the seventeenth century inflation eroded the fixed income of the schoolmasters, so one finds the unlicensed, the double-duty men acting as schoolmaster and incumbent, the negligent, and the scandalous appointed to the post. In fact in many parishes the job of schoolmaster was considered suitable for those who could find not other more profitable employment. This is illustrated by the corollary 'he being unfitt for anything in common wealth except keping of scole',[48] which was applied to William Clark when he was elected schoolmaster of Wybunbury in 1637. It is possibly a fitting comment on the standards of many schoolmasters who appeared before the consistory.

Closely connected with the schoolmasters were the readers, some of whom held both positions, while others were readers only. The office of reader survived in the chapelries of the archdeaconry of Richmond and the diocese of Carlisle long after it had disappeared in the southern province. One reason for its survival was the reluctance on the part of incumbents to consent to the subdivision of their enormous parishes into smaller, more manageable units. This led to the creation of chapels of ease, a device that enabled the fees and emoluments of the incumbent's stipend to be protected. The stipends of those who served these chapels had to be provided by those assessed for poor rates, so these stipends tended to be low, in the region of £5–£10 per annum.[49] Therefore it was usually the reader-schoolmaster who could manage to eke out a living by holding both offices, to which could be added the small sums to be obtained for drawing up wills and conveyances until the Stamp Acts terminated these privileges.[50]

Chancellor Fergusson of Carlisle had a poor opinion of readers, for he wrote that they were 'tailors, cloggers and butter print makers'.[51] Some readers received emoluments in kind, such as 'clothes yearly' and 'whittlegate'. The former meant one suit of clothes, two pairs of shoes and one pair of clogs, while the latter meant being fed for a number of weeks or days in the houses of the inhabitants of the chapel. Since few families had more than two knives and fewer used forks, the reader brought his own cutlery or 'whittle' with him.[52]

One must pose the question as to what type of man would accept a curacy or reader's place in one of these rough, tough, remote, northern chapelries. The answer is found in their licenses and testimonials, as the majority were born and bred in the locality of the chapel they served.[53] Visitation returns and consistory court files reveal that the office of reader, or even permanent deacon, was by no means always a happy or even a rewarding one, for seventeenth-century parishioners could be as awkward and difficult as their twentieth-century descendants. Indeed, some inhabitants of a chapelry were not always prepared to support a reader. One such case comes from Old Hutton in Kirby Lonsdale parish in 1628 when William Walker, the reader, was cited to appear in court on a charge brought by William Whitwell that he was, 'given to drink and a troublesome man'. On these grounds Whitwell had refused to pay his proportion of 2s.8d. for the last twenty years towards his stipend. Walker had served as reader for thirty years, but while he remained, Whitwell intended to pay nothing.[54] The social life of many readers was that of the community whose lives they shared.

A leading parishioner could make life most difficult for a reader. In 1628, Leonard Fell had been reader at Lowick chapel for some forty years, when for some reason, which is not clear, John Ambrose had taken offence when Fell read prayers on Lady Day 1628, had laid violent hands on him, and had driven him out of the chapel. John Askewe said he had assisted Ambrose to 'carry out of the Chappell' the chest of Leonard Fell, 'in which he had nothing but his victualls' and all his other property so 'he was unable to read prayers that day'. The next day was Sunday, so Fell went as usual to read prayers and, to his amazement, found the chapel door open and one John Fell reading in his place. When Leonard Fell appeared John Fell withdrew into the chapel yard under an oak tree while Leonard read prayers in the chapel. Ambrose then returned into the chapel, totally ignored Leonard, and told the congregation that they ought to be in the chapel yard and that he intended to stop Leonard Fell reading prayers. Some withdrew but others remained.

The next incident, apart from a disturbance about the removal of a lock from the chapel door, occurred on Palm Sunday when Ambrose entered the chapel, removed the communion book and table cloth, and took them away.

On Easter day, when John Fell, who had been hired by the inhabitants, was reading morning prayer, Leonard Fell came into the chapel and offered to take the book from John Fell. A violent struggle followed with Leonard Fell trying to pull John Fell to the chapel door. At one point John Fell managed to return to his stall but Leonard snatched the Bible and hit him on the head, at which point Ambrose came between the two of them, 'and stood betwixte them duringe the rest of divine service, persuading Leonard to be quiet'.

On the evening of the same day, while John Fell was reading in chapel, Leonard Fell came at the beginning of the service and, taking a book, 'read alowde and lowder than he otherwise read', whereupon John Fell took the churchbook, the Prayer Book, and went into the chapel yard where he 'read service under an oak tree'. Ambrose followed John Fell out of the chapel, and said 'openly in the chapell, "go to whither you will"', and the greater part of the congregation went out of the chapel from Leonard Fell to hear John Fell.[55]

From the evidence presented at the hearing, it appears that Ambrose, one of the leading parishioners, and his father before him, had for many years taken upon themselves the duty of appointing a reader at Lowick chapel. Should the reader offend either Ambrose or any of the inhabitants, then Ambrose regarded it his duty to replace him in his office, a matter that was at the root of the case. The evil was that leading parishioners, such as Ambrose, regarded not only the chapel but also the reader as their property to be discarded when it suited them without any regard for the work they had done.

Had it not been for the loyalty and devotion of many of these schoolmaster-readers, the Christian faith in many remote chapelries in the north would have barely survived and would have become a folk religion. The existence of a permanent diaconate in Chester diocese, when it had disappeared elsewhere, enabled a strong Christian presence to be maintained in the small but remote chapelries.

Part 3

SIN AND THE LAITY

Chapter Seven

DRUNKENNESS

The diocese of Chester was much larger than many other English dioceses, and several deaneries within it were remote, difficult of access, and sparsely populated. During the sixteenth century in the northern part of the diocese, as in the rest of the north, feuds, murders, and affrays disturbed its life, but these problems do not justify the region to be classified as backward, immobile, and reactionary, an opinion that has been a historical convention for too long.[1]

Although there was a fairly liberal provision of grammar school education, the greater part of the laity left no records of their personal thoughts and attitudes towards authority, for the majority were still by and large illiterate.[2] Hence it was left to the gentry and those who were interested to record these matters. The lay folk in the diocese, as elsewhere in many parts of the north, did not live in a world free from mundane forces, where time was available for them to study the rival doctrinal systems of the period. Life was hard, material amenities were very few, disease was rampant, pain and suffering were widespread, violence was frequent, and anxiety was common. The laity of the sixteenth and seventeenth centuries did not resemble the desensitized members of modern industrialized urban society.

The population was never entirely static, although in some remote valleys in the Lake District men often lived like cabbages from birth to death. The vast expanse of moor and fell, of marsh and sand dunes, isolated many parishes from contact with their southern neighbours, but these never formed the majority. Somehow the circulation of ideas and the movement of people continued despite the impediments of geographical barriers, poor roads, and poverty. Influences and ideas were brought back to Chester, Manchester, Kendal, Lancaster, and Richmond by those who travelled to London and the more populous parts of the country.

The rapid series of religious changes that had taken place between 1545 and 1580 caused many men in the northern province to arrive at an unspiritual stage; their mood was cautious and materialistic as a result of the changes. Both Church and State failed to establish anything approaching a spiritual uniformity or to bind the laity as they bound the clergy. Elizabeth I never achieved the aim of an ideal uniformity, and whatever chance there was of attaining it was destroyed at the Restoration when Parliament made the Church unable to accept within its structure all who were Christians.

In an article on the social causes of the Industrial Revolution, Professor Harold Perkins has described the English as, 'one of the noisiest, most aggressive, brutal and bloodthirsty of nations', which two centuries later had been transformed into, 'one of the most inhibited, polite, prudish, orderly and (some would say) hypocritical in the world'.[3] It is an opinion that the consistory court files reflect.

The social structure of the seventeenth-century society was like a pyramid, with a small apex of rich landlords and the poor who formed a broad base living at or near the marginal level of subsistence. The landowners owned the land and they could exploit it as they pleased, either developing it for buildings, or exploiting the mineral wealth beneath. The lower orders were not peasants working small plots of land and paying feudal dues and services, since the remnants of the feudal system were abolished at the Restoration, but by and large were landless labourers or artisans earning wages. By the end of the century an ever-increasing number were working part-time outside agriculture, either in textiles or in metal trades. This was not a class society in modern terms for there was little elbow room in the seventeenth century for the broad antagonisms of class: Gregory King reckoned there were some eighty different grades from duke down to pauper and vagrant. The artisans, craftsmen, and yeoman farmers who could afford it dissented from the church of the ruling aristocracy as an expression of independence. Men were well aware of the inequalities of wealth and status. The important links were not horizontal ones of class, but vertical ones of dependency and patronage.

Attendance at church was not universal and had never been the custom in the past.[4] The poor rarely, if ever, attended church. Indeed the majority of those who were presented by the church-wardens for non-attendance were heads of households and artisans. The great mass of the unregenerate wished to pass the seventh day in idleness and debauchery. Therefore it was thought that the choice should not be left to them but that they must be compelled to come to church and be edified.[5]

Bishop Pierce of Bath and Wells was informed by some clergy that men who were deprived of 'their honest and lawful recreation on Sundays after evening prayer would go either into tippling houses and there on ale benches talk of matters of church or state or else into conventicles'.[6]

The reports of the Lancashire lieutenants reveal an attitude towards Sunday observance that was totally contrary to official policy, and to puritan denunciations:

> The multitude call Sunday their revelling day which is spent
> in bull baitings, bear baitings, bowls, dicing, carding,
> dancing, drunkenness and whoredom insomuch as men could
> not keep their servants from lying out of their houses, the
> same Sabbath day at night.[7]

In Lancashire and other northern counties legislation concerning observation of the Sabbath was commonly ignored as a report from a group of puritan ministers revealed:

> popishe Fastes and Festivialles . . . duely observed in all
> these partes and that with greater devotion than the Sabboth
> . . . Fairs and Markettes . . . are usually kept upon the
> Sabboth . . . Wakes, Ales, Greenes, Maigames, Rushbear-
> inges . . . Pipinge and Daunsinge . . . frely exercised upon
> the Sabboth . . . By great tumultes of the people remaining
> in the Churchyarde, Stretes and Alehouses in the time divine
> service. From whence stones are often throwen uppon the
> leades of the Churche and many a clamorowse noise and
> showtes geven out. . . . Fornication and Adulteries in all
> sortes shamefully prostituted. Drunkenness maintayned by the

multitude of Alehouses and unreasonable strength of Ale sould withowte size of Statute.[8]

The Reformation in the north-west appears to have advanced with difficulty and in a number of areas had made little impact, so the blame was placed upon the shoulders of those who were responsible for furthering reform. A report made to the Privy Council in 1591 about the prevalence of old custom stated that:

> Small reformation has been made there . . . as may appear by the emptiness of churches on Sundays and holidays and the multitude of bastards and drunkards. . . . Although their Lordships have often written to the justices for redress, small or no reformation has followed and cockfights and other unlawful games are tolerated on Sundays and holidays during divine service at which justices of the peace . . . are often present.[9]

Although puritan preachers fulminated against the old customs advocating enforceable legislation against Sabbath-breaking, rural communities, at all times, have resented official attempts to interfere with their social activities, often by open demonstrations. In July 1588, Joseph Rhodes of Aldborough had been one of a group of persons rebuked by the vicar for holding a rushbearing and entering the church in various disguises during divine service. According to the vicar this event had been accompanied by 'A noyse of pyping, blowing of the horne, ringing or striking of basons and shouting . . . that the minister was constrayned to leave off redinge of the prayers'. Rhodes was angered by the rebuke, and went to the alehouse where he gave 2*d.* to Richard Scruton that he might

> have a shott in his gonne and having charged the same gonne with paper came into the church . . . and discharging the gonne, aiming directly over the minister eyther to hit him or as was reported to affray him and the paper blew about the minister his ears.[10]

The whole body of offenders were sentenced to perform a public penance.

Frequenting alehouses was not a custom confined to weekdays but was a feature of Sunday observance both in the sixteenth and seventeenth centuries, and a habit that continued in Lancashire communities until the end of the eighteenth century.[11] However, for many respectable folk the alehouse seemed to pose a threat to family life since it proved to be an attraction for servants and young adults who could spend their time and money away from the watchful eyes of parents and masters. Members of families were encouraged to mix and drink with all kinds of company so that many alehouses came to serve as convenient meeting places for prostitutes where casual sexual relationships could be formed.

Judging from cases of drunkenness that came before the church courts and also quarter-sessions there appears to have been, on the whole, an increase in this type of case until 1670. No doubt the introduction of hops into brewing contributed to this, for the use of hops made a cheaper and stronger beer available. Also, many drinkers lived on a poor diet in which beer formed an essential part. As the century progressed there was a' trend towards less socially regulated alehouses so making them more public. Underemployment coupled with seasonal employment, and a high percentage of those under 25 years of age, also appears to have made some contribution to the disorder that often occurred in alehouses.

Despite the fulminations of puritan preachers, the populace clung to their old habits of playing at bowls, cards, and dice and holding rushbearings, and were prepared to defy the legislation against Sabbath-breaking. Opposition to restrictions on Sabbath customs caused James I to issue his *Book of Sports* in 1618, which once again permitted the holding of May games, Whitsun Ales, morris dances, and maypoles, accompanied by drinking, after divine service on Sunday.[12] Puritans do not appear to have objected to the drinking of alcohol as such but rather to the habit of drinking healths which, to them, deserved the judgement of God. No doubt the kind of health drinking that occurred in Chester in 1640 encouraged the strident attacks on health drinkers. In this case, Richard Broster accused John Edwards that 'upon his knees [he did] drink a health to the Divill or to Beelzebub the prince of the Divills' in Hugh Anderson's alehouse in Foregate Street.[12] Henry Prescott describes in his diary the drinking of healths in the Pentice, Chester, on Queen Anne's birthday, where 'each had his bottle before him'.[13]

The custom of spending part or indeed the whole of Sunday in the alehouse was not confined to any particular deanery nor to a specific group of parishes but extended throughout the diocese. Parishioners who were annoyed by Sunday drinking could report the offenders. In 1621 at Kirby Fleetham, three victuallers were cited for 'Selling drinke and keeping Drunkards in their houses on the Sabbath in time of Divine Service'. The offenders were ordered to pay 2s. each to the churchwardens for relief of the poor.[14] In 1627 victuallers from Wath and Richmond were penanced for permitting gaming and drinking in their alehouses on Sundays. Two of the offenders found themselves in court twice for the same offence since quarter-sessions had already dealt with the case.

> Thomas Pooley and William Brafferton were dismissed because Mr. Alderman who saw them drinking hath punished them for this offence. Nicholas Hudson saith he was in company with these men and did well repent of his dede.[15]

Askrigg parishioners were so annoyed by a persistent drunkard that they petitioned the Commissary of Richmond to take action.

> Pleaseth it your Worship to be advertised that there is one William Metcalfe of Cravenholme . . . in Askrigg which is a common drunkarde, Baracker and Railer . . . that he doth disquiet all men that is in his company and he is a verye great blasphemer of god's Name. When he is in his outragious drunkenness he will abuse all men and will in noe wise be persuaded.[16]

So the only course open, so it seemed, was to bring a case against him in the consistory which led to a humiliating public penance for the offender.

It was quite a common event for a man to spend the whole of Sunday morning in the alehouse and attend church in the afternoon, with disastrous results. At Winwick, Henry Hurst accused John Flitcroft of coming to church drunk and going out to be sick.[17] Such cases were common in Yorkshire towns, especially Leeds, where in 1627 'Edmund Saurer was drunk, at morning prayer upon a Sabboath day that he did vomite upon the Communion Table.'[18]

Manchester provides several cases of drunkenness with violence, but the outstanding case is that of William Pascall in 1663. He was said to be a common swearer and cursor with many profane oaths, 'as many as fifteen all at once and in one breath', which is no mean feat. When he became drunk it was his habit to

> discharge pistols, draw his Rapier and quarrel with his neighbours with quarts and potts and to break their heads with the same, swearing many times that you will kill & slay the next you meete though they intend you noe harm.

One witness, George Birch, confirmed his habit of swearing and cursing, stating he had been bound over at quarter-sessions and readily took offence. Birch also pointed out he was a nuisance: 'when he had been out late at night he would disturb those that lived neare him by his unruliness and sometimes discharging his pistol so late at night'.[19]

It was not only men who became drunk, for a number of women fell into the same category. In 1632 Margaret Knowsley of Broughton was charged with being 'so fuddled with drink that she brawled and railed at her neighbours'.[20] At Ashton-under-Lyne, Margaret Heywood was accused of being drunk and playing the whore. It appears that she had had intercourse with one William Day 'ten times in Cow Lane and she boasted about it'. William said in his defence that she drank so heavily that she could 'neither stand nor speak'.[21]

There were always women who encouraged others to spend money in alehouses with the inevitable result that quarrels arose. Elizabeth Barker, alias Ormishaw, was said to be 'a common companion and company keeper for severall persons both married and unmarried to spend their means in Alehouses' with the usual result that she became classed as a 'common sower of debate and strife betwixt man and wife and do usually go about to sett dissention and discord amongst your Neighbours'.[22]

Seemly behaviour and attention to the sanitary needs of those patronizing alehouses was woefully lacking. Bessy Clerk's alehouse in Sephton was the haunt of Marjory Bryanson where, in both 1678 and 1680, she was so drunk in the company of Marjory Fleetwood that 'she shitt under her'. Margaret Darwen, a witness, stated that Marjory Fleetwood had called at her house and informed her maid, Ellen Pennington, what had taken place. Ellen, when questioned, replied that the incident took place 'a week after Whitsuntide when Marjory Bryanson was drunk in Bessy Clark's house at the church yard side'.[23]

Occasionally there are references to alehouse songs with very definite sexual overtones. A good illustration comes from the Old Swan in Petticoat Lane, West Derby, concerning the landlady, Hanna Horrocks, and her daughter.

> There stands a House in Darby
> Not far from the Old Swan
> The wife will play at Tarly
> With Jos the serving man
> Old Mother Rump and her daughter plump
> They never will refuse it.

> But Robin the Baker, a man of round wit,
> He often goes thither to get a fresh bit,
> Old Mother Rump and her daughter plump
> They never will refuse it.

So the song continues through a number of verses.[24]

Standards in alehouses where songs of this nature were sung and gossip exchanged could lead to strained relations between husband and wife, for most men spent the bulk of their time in drinking with others of the same sex. Husbands who staggered home after a night's drinking often attacked their wives in a brutal fashion. When in 1630 Thomas Hough of Runcorn returned home after a day's drinking he attacked his wife Anna, 'beating her severely that her arms, legs and thighs were black and blew'.[25]

Drunkenness could also lead to adultery in the alehouse, as happened at Clayton-le-Moors where Henry Byare saw Mary Darwin commit adultery. Her husband was sleeping off his drunken stupor on the alehouse floor, and Mary went to another room where Henry saw her with a man on a bed from which he heard 'much puffing and blowing'.[26] Some women took offence when reports circulated that they were seen drunk. One of these was Alice Johnson who cited Catherine Fairclough for saying she was 'drunk in Jeremy Smethurst Lane where she lost her apron and had all the fashion of a whore'.[27]

Objections were raised in Christleton when Robert Wainwright accused Thomas Smith that he had openly said that Robert was 'drunk all the week and received Holy Communion on Sunday'.

It was now beginning to be considered that drinking all week and communicating on Sunday was most unfitting.[28] On the other hand, complaints were made against those who drank instead of being in church at divine service. In 1636 Peter Stubbs of Lower Peover was accused of drinking and tippling in Margaret Bradshaw's alehouse on Sunday and not attending church.[29] At Chester, William Hatton cited Thomas Benson for openly stating that William 'could go to church but went instead to alehouses although in his sickness and weakness he had one foot in the grave'.[30]

What drinking bouts could lead to is well illustrated by a case from Great Budworth where one Mary Hatton had made a wassail of ale and apples on the 14 November to which she invited ten persons, and the day was 'misspent in drinking, idle vain talking and other exercises not well becominge the Company or holyday'. To this party she invited Thomas Hatton, William Lawrenson, and Thomas Hough who later cited her into court.

In December 1669 she had gone to Jane Ingham's alehouse in Grappenhall near the church where she spent all the morning and 'afternoon drinkinge and tipplinge'. She was said, according to reports, to be a woman 'of a lewd vicious and wicked life & Conversation'. It was also stated that she had stayed at the house of John Longshaw and slept with him. In May 1669 she had gone to William Lawrenson's house and taken his son Richard to an alehouse where they 'tarryed till Midnight'. Instead of returning home, Mary went home with Richard Lawrenson and went into his bed to which she 'invited him to come'. She also invited John Hough to bed, but he refused 'your wishes and invitations yet hereby you expressed your lewd and lustfull desires'.

On another occasion, Mary was sleeping with Elizabeth Middlehurst after a party at which a gallon of ale had been consumed when Lawrenson and Hatton came into the room and threw themselves on the bed. As a result of this the parties concerned were summoned to appear before Sir Peter Leycester at quarter-sessions, where they were fined. Mary Hatton was also excommunicated by the church court for her actions, but later requested absolution after paying the appropriate fees.[31]

The churchwardens in the latter part of the seventeenth century seem to have been less willing than their predecessors to search alehouses on Sunday mornings for absentees from church who were drinking and making merry. Certainly their enthusiasm waned in those parishes held in plurality which made it impossible to hold more than one service each Sunday. Hence there was no point in rounding up the Sunday drinkers so that task lapsed to the constables and Justices of the Peace, whose energies varied considerably. The number of presentments fell as the century advanced. Cases brought into the consistory which involve drinking on Sundays and non-attendance at church have virtually disappeared by 1700. Immoderate drinking continued but those cases that arose out of visitation were dealt with by the correction court.

By 1714, there appears to have been a change in the company that resorted to the alehouse in general, although in centres of growing population they retained their former attraction as a place for illicit sex. Certainly the alehouses were becoming more respectable since the 1662 Act of Settlement had controlled the movement of population. After 1660 the causes that appear in the consistory arise from incidents in alehouses that involved defamation of character on the assumption that the alehouse was used for adultery or fornication.

Chapter Eight

DEFAMATION AND SEXUAL SLANDER

Defamation was not one of the seven deadly sins, yet it arose frequently from envy and wrath between people. In effect, defamation in the church courts became the equivalent of slander in the secular courts. In his account of the working of courts spiritual, H. Consett states that a cause of defamation or reproach was an action cognizable in church courts. He then defines such a cause as

> the word (*convitii* or reproach) is wont to be writ in every citation together with the word (*defamationis* or defamation), the reason is . . . because if the plaintiff doth not provide that the defendant uttered words which of their own nature were defamatory, yet if he proves the words were reproachful, he shall obtain the victory . . . the reason is because these words were uttered out of a malicious and angry mind, and against all fraternal charity.[1]

R. Burn, in his *Ecclesiastical Law*, discusses at some length the criteria that determined which court should properly have jurisdiction in such causes. Church courts could only prosecute if the slanderous statements concerned the moral character of the plaintiff, though they claimed to have cognizance in all cases where the clergy were defamed.[2] To call a man a bastard was regarded as a secular offence but causes under this heading were heard in the Chester consistory. To describe a woman as a bawd was to ensure citation into the consistory or correction courts but a charge that she kept a bawdy house could be a civil case (although was not universally so regarded).

Slanderers had a very rich variety of strong vulgarities, most of which usually imputed vice such as 'whoremaster', and so many cases came before the church courts on moral grounds. Many arose from the welter of parish gossip and intrigue based on reliable evidence, but were more often grounded on the less reliable evidence of 'common fame and report' or 'vehement suspicion'.

In the seventeenth century, honour was one of the leading themes of the drama of the period. It had become almost a religion amongst the elite of society, for honour, a good name, and credit came very close to their centre of ethical values. C.L. Barber concludes that after 1660 honour was a matter for the upper classes, since 'ordinary people cannot afford such a luxury and have no pretence to it'.[3] In the wider community, Dod and Cleaver, commenting on the observance of the ninth commandment, stated that 'every man is bound to have a charitable opinion and good conceit of his neighbour with a desire for his good name and credit'.[4]

The study of court records supports the view that among the lower orders, never mind the upper ones, a good name was worth having and being anxious about. In 1696, in the small village of Langcliffe, near Settle, Elizabeth Baxter, a spinster, hearing some gossip that another woman was pregnant, attacked the scandalmongers with strong words and declared that they 'may as well take her life as her good name from her'.[5] This case is of some interest for it reveals that a north-country girl had the same notions of honour as those in the upper strata of society.

Such an eagerness to defend one's reputation was something that ran from the top to the bottom of English society at this period. The seventeenth-century commentators who said that they lived in the worst possible world, beset by new symptoms of social breakdown and by increasing new ones, can now be proved correct. Both in the church courts and the civil courts, defamation suits increased rapidly and the accounts of society in the time of the later Stuarts can be proved at the lower as well as the upper levels of society. Moreover this feature in the study of society is still in its infancy, and several regional studies will be required before the correct picture of society can be drawn.

Allegations were frequently brought by one man against another or one woman against another and between a man and woman for uttering slanderous statements against them. In 1605 at Warrington, Dorothy Smith had called John Barnes, 'knave, arrant knave, rascall, white livered ladd, base fellow, base slave, base rascall' while he in return addressed her as a drab and the constable refused to apprehend Barnes and take him before the Justices of the Peace.[6] David and Elizabeth Rogers of Chester did not spare Alderman Ince, for they said he was 'an ass, a foole, a base fellowe', and 'May God look upon this myne enemie and poure thy plague or vengeance on him'.[7] At Lower Peover, Matthew Jackson called Margery Slathome a 'carted whore', and at Middlewich Ellen Becket was a 'whipt, carted and stockt whore'.[8]

William Thompson and Nicholas Moore had been members of the jury at Lancaster assizes in the case of Henry Caillie and John Copeland, but on their way home had quarrelled over the verdict when Moore called Thompson a 'false lyer, a lying knave, a false noughtie harlot and notorious knave and lyer'.[9] Again at Caton, Christopher Wilson called Thomas Bateson a 'burncast rogue, drunken bad fellow, rascall, rogue' publicly in the street.[10] In like manner at Manchester, Edward Chetham called Katherine Hargreaves a 'whore, a curtall whore and a common whore',[11] while Dorothy Wright of Tattenhall said that Charles Knott's wife was 'a cut jade, a queen and sick for a tarse [penis]'.[12] A Stockport woman was described as a 'strumpet, a brazen faced jade and brazen faced whore'.[13] Both John and Margaret Carter of Shotwick had a colourful vocabulary to describe Lawrence Swettenham who, according to their report, was 'a rogue, a whoreson Rascall and his wife a scurvie Queane and a scurvie cutt of a whore'.[14] John Wilkinson of Malpas referred to Rose Bentley as 'a brazen faced whore'.[15]

Another colourful description of Anne Edwards of Chester, St Mary, was given by Richard and Katherine Anyon when they described her as a 'shaven ars't and shaven tail'd whore',[16] but the most lively of all is the description that Cecilia ap Ievan gave to Katherine Dodd, 'a Sowe, a whore, a drunken jade, a drunken pispott, drunken sockett and drunken sowe' in 1601.[17]

Richard Hartford of the same Chester parish had stated that widow Alice Parre deserved 'a whip and cart for an old bawd' implying that she ought to be tied to the back of a cart and whipped through the streets as the legislation for dealing with vagrants prescribed.[18] The occupation of tallow-candle maker was by no means a savoury or pleasant occupation, as candle manufacture produced some strong odours, so when Margaret Burrows had taken issue with Robert Shaw, a tallow chandler in Bridge Street, Chester, and called him 'a stinking knave, a bull head, knave and bafflehead' he cited her into court for defaming both himself and his trade.[19]

When William Ashton of Manchester heard the verdict of the assize court at Lancaster in which Rebecca Sidebottom was involved, he remarked 'that Lord Chief Justice Wylde had made her a whore', enabling Ashton to get even with Rebecca Sidebottom for having stated that Ashton's wife had given birth to a bastard.[20]

In 1686 Margaret Goulden of St Oswald, Chester, had called Maria Touchett a 'whore and bastardly Tilling'. In the libel of articles forming the charge, the deputy registrar, Henry Prescott, defined a 'tilling' as meaning 'not only a whore but the grandmother of whores', implying that prostitution ran in families.[21] Dr Favour, vicar of Halifax in the early part of the seventeenth century, identified in the parish registers by a series of numbers from 1 to 4 to indicate four generations, that prostitution and bastardy ran in families.[22]

The annual wakes which are a feature of life in Lancashire and Cheshire could be occasions that presented opportunities for some defamation. In September 1694 Margaret Haslam had been to Congleton wakes, and while in town took the opportunity to visit Elizabeth Hobson. As she entered the house she saw William Whittaker standing near Elizabeth when suddenly, in a violent manner, he shouted 'God damn thee thou whore. Kiss my Arse thou damned bitch.' Ellen Swain, another visitor, said that she was already in the house when Whittaker arrived demanding a discharge. When Elizabeth asked for what purpose he required a discharge, he replied that he had 'come to pay her some money'. When she told him that it was time he did so, he shouted, 'Thou damned whore, thou damned bitch here is money for thee'. However, Elizabeth stood her ground and maintained that she was an honest woman both when her husband was at home and when he was abroad.[23] She had assumed that Whittaker was implying that she was free with her favours, which proved to be incorrect.

Since the widespread involvement of north-country women in daily work and social activities removed them from the house, confinement was useless, and protection was not enforced below those families in the upper strata of society. Reliance was placed on normal restrictions for it was through gossip that their behaviour would be commented upon and that would lead to the loss of reputation. Accusations of adultery and fornication are comprehensible in a world where sexual honour was of great importance, and gossip about the sexual conduct of one's neighbours was indulged in in alehouses, markets, and fairs where numbers of people gathered.

The cause between Sara Mottershed and Mary Banyon of Davenham in the summer of 1694 illustrates the way in which gossip could sour relationships. The two women walked together across the weir at Whartcroft Hall in order to gather crabapples, presumably for making into jelly. On the way they met Thomas Parker, Mary's brother, who told them they could not have the crabapples since he wanted them for his own use. Mary then left Sara and returned across the weir to her husband. Later Sara followed them, and upon meeting Mary Banyon turned to her and said 'Thou art a whore; she's William Kelsall's whore and Anne Bostock will confirm it'. Anne Bostock failed to do so.[24]

An innocent occupation such as cutting flowers in the garden could provide an opportunity for defamation. Elizabeth Harrison of Fishmonger Lane, Chester, was in her garden cutting flowers when she over heard Hester Street, in the next garden, speaking to Martha Woodward. Elizabeth interrupted the conversation by saying that Martha was 'a Lyer and Lancashire witch', but that she herself never bewitched young men as Martha Woodward did, for 'Martha staid at home and never went to Church on Sunday morning but drank brandy with young men'. Matters were not as straightforward as they appeared, for Sarah Massie, a witness in the cause, stated that she never heard Elizabeth speak any of the alleged words. However, Hester Street's maid gave the game away when she swore that she was given 'a gowne body and a whiske if she would swear for them that the words were spoken'.[25]

When Jane Wilding of Aughton accused Peter Leadbetter of Ormskirk of defaming her by calling her his whore, she dealt smartly with John Spencer of Lathom for attempting to confirm that the charge of being Leadbeater's whore was correct.[26]

Another case of backyard slander took place in Aldford two weeks after the Feast of All Saints, 1684. At that time William Brown and Edward Calverley were in their own backyards when they quarrelled. Brown was driving some geese belonging to

Calverley out of his yard when the latter turned and called Brown a rogue. Then, 'speaking to John Carden said, "Landlord, Landlord, bear witness that I call him a Rogue and I'll prove him one"'. Mary Barnes and Katherine Humpston, who were standing near, stated they also heard the words spoken, which earned Calverley a penance.[27]

Occasionally, an employee would defame his employer in strong terms. Thomas Martincroft defamed Sir Edward Stanley by stating in public that 'by the flesh and blood of God, I care not a turd for Sir Edward Stanley's service'. Being summoned by Hugh Hesketh and Edward Dickenson to complete his work 'he did fall into a great furie and did curse them saying . . . "the divell of hell take them go with them altogether"', and he also cursed Sir Charles Gerard, a relative of Sir Edward Stanley, and John Brook.[28]

Some defendants were not above offering an open insult to the court. In 1621 Richard Hartley, of St John Baptist's parish in Chester, cited Robert Whitby of St Michael's parish for calling him 'beggar drunkard and usurer'. Whitby had gone to court where 'he did publicly piss upon or near the table in Court, calling the defendant an old doting fool and that he would go mad'. For his abuse and attitude towards the court, Whitby was promptly evicted.[29]

Violence to children was commonplace, though frowned upon and dealt with if it took place in church or churchyard. The child of Richard and Dorothy Grundy of Manchester was stated to have been abused by Alice Beck when she 'did cast down Dorothy Grundie's childe in the durt and did trample it with her feete'. When Dorothy found her child so abused she said 'is this naballs [Naboth's] vineyard that you deny my child water and use it so and if this be naball's vineyard and if you be Jezebell, God send you the reward Jezebell had'.[30]

When John Houghton of Halton cited Margaret Cheshire into court for abusing her grandchild he was shocked by her brutality, for 'she had beaten her grandchild so severely that she made him unconscious'.[31] Trouble could and did arise concerning the ownership of a child's top. In Chester, the children of Elizabeth Wright and Sarah Crichley, whilst playing together in the summer of 1668, quarrelled as to who owned the top. Eventually the two mothers took sides whereby Sara called Elizabeth 'whore,

Bedward's whore and queane'. When cited into court she admitted that she had spoken the words in anger but was given a public penance to perform.[32] Edward Bebbington of Harthill accused Margaret Dodd of abusing the young Richard Harcourt by 'laying violent hands on him and . . . pulling his ears until they bled.'[33] Mary Whittingham of Middlewich had trouble with Mr Wadforth who refused burial for her dead child. In his charges he stated that in his opinion the child had been so ill treated that in the end it was virtually murdered. He also added that 'he cared not a turd for her' so implying that he had a very low opinion of her.[34]

During the time of war the task of pressing men to serve in the armed forces fell upon the parish constable as the representative of the law, and often he was the recipient of a great deal of abuse from the families of pressed men. In 1711, the constable of Heversham was ordered to press Thomas Pearson to serve in Marlborough's army in the War of the Spanish Succession. Christopher Ellery, the constable, was abused by the Pearsons who stated openly that 'Christopher and Anne Ellery kept a bawdy house . . . likewise their daughter Anne . . . is a whore, a common whore and they would cut her nose off her face and give Anne Ellery the whore's mark'. The words were spoken when Ellery conveyed Thomas Pearson to the justices to be 'turn'd over for a soldier'.[35]

As part of their duties, constables had to collect lays for the repair of the highways and relief of the poor. Those who disliked paying lays would offer abuse, as did Elena Scholfield of Littleborough, who openly said that John Milner, constable of Rochdale, collected lays to maintain his bastards; Jane Kay, for her part, called him a whoremaster.[36]

It was the custom when defaming some persons to refer to them as pimps (who replaced the prostitute who had already made an assignment and found it inconvenient to keep the date). Martha Morton, of St Oswald's, Chester, said that Judith Blenston was a whore, 'who got eight shillings in one night for standing pimp to Mr Bradshaw'. Doubtless she was envious of the money Judith earned from using a room in the Golden Lyon for her immoral earnings.[37] It was also possible to refer to an older person as a pimp, which was what Francis Eaton did when she said that Anne Taylor was 'an impudent whore who will be like the old pimp her mother and my husband must give her her morning draught', doubtless thinking and implying that her husband was satisfying her sexual needs.[38] Normally this type of defamation occurred between two women, yet in 1664, in Chester, Thomas Hough cited Thomas Franks for calling him 'a pimping rogue a coffee man and hangman'.[39]

Theft and debt were also incidents that gave rise to defamation. Richard Chadwick of Rochdale, was charged by Richard Ogden of stealing pork for his own use.[40] Robbing orchards was not a petty crime practised by boys, for in 1636 William Holle of St Oswald's, Chester, cited William Mosse and Robert Dennison for robbing his orchard, taking pears and crab applies. Elen Hignet who had seen them stripping the fruit said they should be 'whipt, stockt and sent to the Northgate, and confined in the Pentice'.[41] It was normal practice to place thieves in the stocks followed by a public flogging and then confining them in prison as a deterrent for the future.[42]

When Richard Leadbeater accused John Rogerson of Tarvin of 'stealing another man's sheep, he was laying himself open to a criminal charge before quarter-sessions.[43] The loss of Agnes Ellershaw's ducks led her to accuse Leonard Townson of Bentham of 'stealing our Ducks to feed his whores withal'.[44] In 1697, sharpeyed John Bateman of Bolton-le-Sands discovered the secret of Elizabeth Jackson's supply of cheese. He stated that 'she may well afford to sell Milkcheas for she milketh Lancelott Battersby's Cowes and stealeth his Milk and I have seen her do it'. In court Battersby confirmed that indeed this was the case.[45]

Suspicion that a person was in debt was sufficient to encourage defamation of the debtor. Richard Watt accused George Cottingham and Thomas Goldson of Woodchurch of defaming him by stating that 'he was soe far in debt and owd for the very clothes on his back'.[46] Indeed, an accusation of theft could lead to an assault if the debtor wished to avoid payment. In 1603, Francis Bellfield of Rochdale preferred a charge against Elena Milnes, wife of Thomas Milnes, when she took him by the arm and held him, saying 'dost thou charge me to have stolen hennes?' Giving him no time to reply, she pulled him into the barn where her husband was hidden under the hay. As soon as Bellfield and Elena Milnes were in the barn and the door closed, Thomas Milnes came from under the hay with 'a knife or thwittle in his hand and gave Francis Bellfield divers dangerous wounds in his arm saying he had been naughty with his wife and he would take him before the bishop'. However, the accusations of theft and also of committing adultery with his wife were secondary to the main reason, which was that Milnes was anxious to obtain the consent of Bellfield to cancel the debt of 46s.8d. Milnes owed him for a cow he had bought, and if he would agree then Milnes 'would let him go'. Attestations were produced in court to the excellent character Bellfield had in the parish, and the Milneses were penanced and fined in costs for defaming him.[47]

Usually the occasion of death is one for expression of sympathy with the bereaved but when the dead were defamed then resentment could be roused in the parish. In 1628 at Rochdale, on the occasion of the death of Francis Wolstenholme, his brother John had remarked that, 'he had gone to the devil and his bones were roasting in hell'. The churchwardens presented him for defaming his dead brother and he was penanced.[48] A similar cause came from Warrington in 1639 when widow Margaret Ireland cited Elizabeth Baron for saying that her 'dead husband was at the devil and during his life had been a damnable sinner to God and his neighbours' implying that his life had been far from respectable in the eyes of the community.[49]

An exceptionally forceful method used to slander a man was to refer to him as a cuckold, especially in cases where his wife was known to be involved with other men. In 1669, Elizabeth Costerdine cited Jane Bowker of Blakeley for saying that she 'made her husband cuckold with two persons in one night'.[50] William Mawdersley of Blackburn cited Robert Eastham for saying that he had three bastards by two women and had managed to cuckold twenty men.[51]

The insult of cuckold was rather more personal at Prestbury when William Davison said that Anna Mason had openly said to him that his 'mother's brother William is a cuckold and his wife a whore', so implying that William did not know about or ignored his wife's activities.[52] In Manchester when Dorothy Richardson said to Thomas Baxter, 'go thy way Cuckold to thy wife that dirty slut', she was associating her with the common type of whore.[53]

It was also quite a common term of abuse to refer to a man as a 'cuckold bird', which Ann Winstanley used towards William and Anne Ford.[54] Henry Rose, schoolmaster in Chester in 1628, confirmed that while walking down Common Hall Lane, he heard

Elen Wright call John Werman a 'cuckoldly witwardly fool'.

Ancient custom decreed that the emblem or sign of a cuckold was a pair of horns. Hence, to attach a pair of horns to the door or fence of a cuckold's house could be a far more humiliating experience than to use mere verbal abuse. At Great Budworth, Thomas Kitchen had shouted to Peter Lawrenson in the presence of his wife Anne, 'Ware horns, ware horns thou cuckoldy knave'.[55] Elizabeth Leake of Congleton expressed herself far more strongly when she said that Joanna Halliday was John Presbury's whore, and continued by saying to John: 'Get in at the dore thou Cuckoldy rascall, for if thou come forth and do not make thy dore wider thy horns will be so long thou canst not get in again.'[56]

Statements of this nature, frequent enough in the sixteenth century, gradually decline in the following one and by the last decades of the seventeenth century completely disappear from the consistory court files.

Closely connected to defamation was the practice of formal cursing, which in some aspects seems to be an activity having some connections with witchcraft. In his book, *Religion and the Decline of Magic*, Keith Thomas argues that in the early seventeenth century the 'real source of continuing belief in the efficacy of cursing lay, not in theology, but in popular sentiment'. The basis of the argument is that curses retained their efficacy when the curser's anger was justified.[57] Causes that involve cursing are by no means prolific in consistory court files, but those which survive do give the impression that being the victim of a cursing could be a horrendous experience. Dr J.A. Sharpe produces evidence of this from a cause heard at York in the early seventeenth century. John Wood of Wetherby reported that his neighbour, Helen Hiley, a widow, had come to his door 'and kneeled downe upon her knees and said, "a vengeance of God Light upon thee Wood . . . and all thy children, and I shall trulie pray this praier for thee as long as I live"'. In another cause from Leeds at the same period, John Metcalfe informed the consistory that Anne Dixon had called him

Whoremaster, whoremonger and harlott and did sit her down upon her knees and cursed and banned him, and his wife, and badd a vengeance light upon the wife of the said John

Metcalf and upon that whoremaster . . . her husband . . .
and prayed God that they might never thrive.[58]

Similar causes can be found in Chester diocese especially for the
period before the Civil War, though there are a few later survivals
of the practice as late as 1692. In 1601 a ritual cursing arose at
Tattenhall, when John Felkins cited William Mollineux for 'lifting
his hands and upon his knees saying, "A Vengeance might light
upon John Felkins and his wife and children with sudden
death"'.[59] Such a curse in that superstitious age was sufficient to
frighten those who were the objects of the curse. Again at
Stockport in 1603 a ritual cursing was given to George Hardman
by the Bensons who said on their knees that 'the vengeance of God
may light of George Hardman . . . and all the plagues of hell
might fall upon him . . . and you would so pray and desire at all
times'.[60]

Kneeling upon the knees was not the only method of performing
a ritual cursing, for at Egremont it was usual to stand with
upraised hands. In this instance, John and Maria Robinson cited
Eleanor Patrickson for 'lifting her hands and cursing Maria in the
time of her labour'. There would be the fear haunting the couple
that the new-born child would be accursed for the whole of its
natural life.[61]

The efficacy of a curse appears to have been a reality in Chester
in 1631. It appears that David Dobb had abused Katherine
Goodell by referring to her as a whore and complaining that 'this
is a hard case that a man cannot be at quiet in his own house for
whores and jades coming to pick quarrels of him'. Hugh Francis,
a witness in the cause, said that he heard Dobb call Katherine a
whore, his wife Marjery called her a runagate whore, and his
daughter Ellen called her an arrant whore. In retaliation Katherine
cursed the children so that 'they fell grievously sick and in danger
of their lives'.[62]

Robert Meacock of Upton cursed not only Emma and William
Basford but also their children, saying 'a plague on thee and thy
children'.[63] When Robert Collier of Plemondstall cited Elizabeth
Richardson into court for cursing him, he tried to place her firmly
on the wrong side of the law by claiming that she had not
'communicated for above four years'.[64]

In 1607 a cause was brought from Clitheroe, on the borders of the Lancashire witchcraft area of Pendle, when Richard Wood cited Ann Jennings for saying to him, 'The curse of God light on thee'.[65] A year later the same woman was once more in court for cursing Richard Mercer, a shopkeeper. Henry Riley, a witness, said that he was present when Ann spoke the words: 'I praie God neither thou nor anie thing or goods of thine may ever prosper neither by water nor land and I praie God that whatever thou takes in hand maie never go forward with thee.' Elizabeth Riley with John and Alice Usherwood and John Stanny confirmed that the words were spoken. Another witness, Anna, wife of Richard Dean, said she was in her house when Ann Jennings came in, for her house joined Mercer's shop, 'being but one slender wall to separate them', and heard Jennings curse Mercer. He came from his shop and called Anna Dean to witness the words spoken. Jennings then cursed him again, 'with an open voyce that all present might the better hear', and continued by confirming she would curse Mercer as long as she lived.[66]

Even the rector of Grappenhall, Samuel Eaton, was not above cursing Robert Massie when they had a dispute concerning the purchase of goods in his shop, saying 'the curse of God light on thee and thy wares'.[67]

In Chester diocese, especially in Lancashire, there was a strong witch cult flourishing and quarter-sessions took an active part in efforts to suppress the cult by conducting trials and hanging witches.[68] A most interesting and illuminating cause that involved a charge of witchcraft arose in Nantwich in 1663, between Ann Wright and Mary Briscoe, concerning the peculiar circumstances of the death of Wright's younger daughter. Over the previous eighteen months there had been several 'fallings out' between the two women. The symptoms described by Elizabeth Whitlowe are peculiar. She said that Ann Wright's daughter was about 12 years old when she was suddenly taken ill and for about thirteen weeks was afflicted in a strange manner:

> by fits and many times her eyes would hang upon her
> cheeks and roule up and down like two full bladders and she
> would say . . . Mary Briscoe pricked her to the hart with
> pinnes and needles and would have her hart and her life.

Cicily Winne saw Ann Wright's daughter playing at the door with some of Cicily's children when she became suddenly quite terrified and 'run into the house and said that Mary Briscoe had candled her eyes upon her like a cat as big as two saucers and presently fell into a long trance'.

Cicily confirmed the statements made about the girl's eyes and added that her body was very swollen. Elizabeth Jenkins confirmed that Ann's daughter had been bewitched, a belief later held by Ann, for the elder daughter had also died. Anne Ridgeway was quite convinced of Mary Briscoe's powers for she said that, when giving birth to a bastard child, 'she feared that Mary Briscoe had bewitched her when that child was got'. She also added that Ann's daughter was troubled with the King's Evil, 'and lay languising in a very strange and sad condition . . . before she died her eyes tumbled & rouled upon her brow very sadly'.

Mary Briscoe's husband confessed that his wife was a very high-spirited woman, and he was troubled by this case for 'he could not rule her and was afraid she would come to the same end that her mother did'. Ann Ridgeway was convinced that Mary Briscoe's mother was 'arrained and hanged at Chester for a witch'. This interesting and informative cause is the only complete example to survive in the consistory court files.[69]

Those who called down solemn curses and could bewitch people were believed to be in league with Satan who alone could give them such powers. Not only those who inhabited villages and rural communities, but also those who dwelt in towns, acknowledged and understood the corporal presence of evil in their midst. An illustration of this belief comes from Scruton, in Catterick deanery, in 1595, when Dorothy Jackson, alias Tait, was presented for maintaining that there were witches living in three or possibly five of the neighbouring houses in Scruton and 'she confessed herself to be ridden of a witch three times in one night, being thereby greatly astonished and upon her astonishment awaked her husband'.[70] Today this would be classed as sexual hysteria but no attempts were made to explain it in those terms at that date. On the face of it, it seems important that, of the Pendle forest witches, the first to be hanged was Jennet Preston of Gisburn. She had been into Lancashire to seek help from the witches to murder one of the Listers of Westby. She appears to have been successful for Sir Thomas Lister died accusing Jennet of being the cause of his death. Sir Thomas's son maintained that Preston, by cursing him, had caused him to lose a large amount of goods and cattle.[70]

Today there is still a strong witch presence in the Pendle area but it is difficult to penetrate this from the outside.[71]

The two causes that appear in the consistory after the Reformation were allied to a routine manner of cursing, arising from shady business dealings. In 1672 at Hankelow, John Wybunbury cited Ralph Vernon and his wife for saying 'A Curse of Christ light upon thee and thy family'.[72] The other arose at Sutton in the Wirral where Ralph Blagg cited Elizabeth Edmondson for calling him a 'cheating rogue' for depriving tenants of their livings and saying 'the curse of God light on thee, I hope to see thee rot above ground'.[73] On the whole, cursing and witchcraft were part of the folk lore and folk religion which the Church attempted to destroy, but it took a long time and even now is far from dead. The incidence of cursing seems to have been one of those facets of life where man's reactions are instinctive rather than intellectual or political.

Chapter Nine

FORNICATION, ADULTERY, AND BASTARDY

The Church realized that a struggle had to be waged against sexual and related sins; hence in the Book of Common Prayer this petition is found in Cranmer's Litany:

From fornication and all other deadly sins, from the world the flesh and the devil: Good Lord deliver us.

Fornication and its companion, adultery, between which the line of division is by no means crystal clear, were common sins in the seventeenth century and had been from time immemorial. When the Royal Commissioners visited Lancashire in 1535 to administer the Oath of Supremacy, they considered it their moral duty to order those Lancashire gentry whom they discovered to have abandoned their lawful wives to live with a concubine to return to their wives and maintain them.[1] In the long term an assessment of causes that came before the consistory in this field revealed that in many instances the efforts of the commissioners to impose strict moral standards failed.

Fornication and adultery were attractive sins in a society where young men were bound apprentice, under the terms of the Statute of Artificers,[2] which restricted their opportunities to mix socially with the opposite sex. Under the terms of their apprenticeship they could not marry until they were 21; and they were forbidden to commit fornication or to frequent alehouses, or to gamble at dice and cards. Under such restrictions many healthy young males were unable to resist temptation when an attractive woman, or perhaps some not so attractive woman, offered an opportunity for sexual release. Hence they yielded to temptation and fornicated, hoping their sin would not be discovered by curious observers or result in the birth of a bastard child.

Whenever indiscriminate or indiscreet fornication led to the birth of a child, parishes tended to be hostile. By law the putative father was responsible for the maintenance of his child but, on several occasions, the father could not be identified with any reliability. In 1635 at Halifax, when a young woman appeared before the consistory court on a charge of bastardy arising from fornication, she was unable to name the father because 'it was dark and she could not see his face'.[3] In the western deaneries of Richmond archdeaconry, it was easy for a putative father to slip across the sea to Ireland, where it was virtually impossible to find him, especially in the west of the country, and return him to England. In such cases the parish had to maintain the child from the poor rates and respectable parishioners disliked paying rates to maintain children illegally begotten.

Hence the church courts were concerned with scandalous living and not heresy as their prime concern. Authority demanded that Englishmen and women must be compelled by law to live what seventeenth-century society considered to be a Christian life. The vast bulk of office causes that came before the consistory court were concerned with licentious living, fornication, adultery, pre-marital pregnancy, failure to marry after a betrothal, or refusal to cohabit after marriage, together with some scolding, back-biting, and brawling between neighbours. These composed a goodly proportion of the court business.[4] Consequently, court officers became the objects of bawdy comments from parishioners, such as took place at Lamplugh in 1638. Henry Bowman, the apparitor or court summoner for Copeland deanery, cited Thomas Robertson of Winster for referring to the Commissary of Richmond's court as a bawdy court and Bowman himself as 'a cuntsomoner of the bawdy court'.[5] Such comments the court officials could not allow to pass uncorrected since they could lead to the authority of the court being ignored with impunity.

It is quite clear that as the seventeenth century advanced there was increasing concern with the sexual morality of the masses by the rulers of the land, for the number of morality causes that came before the consistory court after 1660 was almost three times the number between 1600 and 1640, especially those causes that arose from sexual immorality and bastardy. One has to remember that between 1642 and 1648 there had been two civil wars and a Commonwealth. During these intervening years, Dr Christopher Hill asserts there was a sexual revolution during which women gained liberation in a variety of ways. It took a long time to complete and may not even yet be completed in full. In one case, a woman stripped off at a religious meeting of one of the extreme radical sects and, raising her arms, cried 'Welcome the resurrection'. Christopher Hill also records one of the anti-Puritan stories concerning the Ranters, of a lady searching for sin in broad daylight with a lighted candle and finding it, to her great satisfaction, in a gentleman's codpiece.[6] Then, as now, 'sin' usually meant sex for Puritans. Certainly the pursuit of honour through the courts is a sign that the respectable poor of Stuart England wished to separate their conduct from that of the ungodly and disorderly poor, like the bawdy baskets and cony catchers whom the magistrates watched.[7]

Little wonder, then, that the evidence provided by the court records of the dioceses of Chester and York reveals a willingness to go to law in support of one's reputation, for a good name was an essential feature of the seventeenth century. The thinking behind many of the defamation causes concerning sexual matters was not that of future damage, but the implied allegations of past misconduct. This was the reason why Alice Shellin, wife of the vicar of Broughton-in-Furness, brought a cause against Alexander Danson for saying that Ferdinando Huddleston of Millom had 'carnal dealings with her in a chair in the bodiestead of the fire house', i.e. the living room.[8] In the past the Huddlestons had acquired a reputation for this kind of conduct, in that in 1580, Anthony Huddleston had been forbidden by the High Commission at York to travel within twenty miles of Millom Castle, for he would commit adultery and fornicate with any woman he met on his way. Hence it was desirable that Alice should go to law to protect her reputation.

The majority of defamation causes involve a female plaintiff who alleged she had been slandered by an allegation of fornication or adultery. Such cases give the impression of a world in which sexuality, so often a cause of adverse criticism, was in essence straightforward. An illustration of this type of slander comes from Dalton-in-Furness in 1717, when William Cragg was cited by Deborah Whinfield for stating in public that she 'was gott with a

Bastard Child by a Pedlar before her marriage whereupon the Pedlar over run his Country & would not marry her'.[9]

The nature and sequence of lovemaking was influenced by the style of clothing worn by both sexes in the seventeenth century. The male normally wore breeches that were loosely tied at the waist and the female had the lower part of her body covered by a smock and one or two petticoats. The upper part of her body was covered by a complex, tightly-laced bodice, therefore it was easy for the male, desiring to commit an act of fornication, to have immediate access to the woman below the waist. The single action of lifting the smock and petticoats revealed her naked thighs and legs below the waist. It was quite common to state in evidence that 'he saw her naked thighs'. Certainly, during intercourse the woman was always naked from the waist down. All that was required to be done to enable intercourse to take place was for the woman to 'pull her clothes' above her middle and to untie a man's breeches, whereupon his breeches fell round his ankles.[10] By these actions both male and female sex organs were easily accessible.

In every area there was no lack of those, of both sexes, who enjoyed peeping and prying into the activities of other members of the community, especially if sexual interests were involved. In 1606 Katherine Aldersey of Coddington cited John and Elena Prestburie for having openly stated that she 'was an arrant whore', who fornicated in a stable in Northgate Street, Chester.[11] Charles Holland and John Taylor were the 'peeping Toms' of Rochdale who had annoyed Ottiwell and Margaret Wylde by lurking 'under the walls of Wylde's house to see when Ottiwell would be naughty with Margaret'.[12] Being 'naughty' was a common term for sexual intercourse in Chester diocese at this period.

Places where persons were caught fornicating are frequently named. At Witton, in 1609, Thomas Percival said that he had seen John Walker, 'a lewd man', lurking in Julius Wynyngton's wash-house, 'disguised in a cloak with Thomas Rogerson's wife to be naughty'.[13] Jane Sharples, alias Fogg, of Manchester, admitted that she was 'naughty with Oswald Charlton on Salford Bridge',[14] while Anna Roscoe accused Elizabeth Massie of 'being taken naughty with James Hibbard at one of the clock in the morning in Market Sted Lane, Manchester'.[15] Even a ditch was not scorned as a convenient place: Jane Waddell said that she had seen Elizabeth Pemberton being naughty 'in a ditch in Woodcock Lane, Eccleston, on Palm Sunday morning 1637'.[16]

The morning of Christmas Day, 1664, also proved a convenient time to commit fornication. The constable at Warrington, making his way to church at nine in the morning, said he saw 'something white moving in the corn stubble in Wheatecroft field'. Upon moving closer to inspect, he saw that it was the white thighs of Jane Radcliffe with Peter Warrall, 'in his leather britches laid between her thighs'. He duly presented them both and in due course they found themselves before the consistory court for fornicating.[17]

Rumour played a large part in such cases, as did common fame. When Sara Pollett heard that Richard Drinkwater had informed Elizabeth Hay that he had seen Sara 'being naughty with John Dickson in Ackersfield, Pendleton', she brought a suit against Elizabeth for defamation.[18] Henry Hill of Hale confessed that he had taken Catherine Wright by her 'privities' in Holly Lane, where 'she stood as quietly to be done as his own wife and he would have been naughty but that his prick would not stand'.[19] Henry Byrom confirmed that Hill had told him this personally.

Even more precise was the account given by Jonathon Price of Handbridge of the place where Anne Parry had fornicated and that was 'between Percers and Baxters house with her belly and her thighs all bare'.[20] Anna Scarborough of Liverpool took offence in 1697 when Elizabeth Shields called her 'an arrant whore, pitt whore and that she rotted her hood laying it under her arse while she played the whore in the Butter Market'.[21] Occasionally, a resourceful woman could frustrate the designs of some amorous man, as did Christina Holt of Bowden when she was accosted by Isaac Ottiwell of Dunham Woodhouse, saying that 'he attempted several times to have kissed me and to have got me a great Belly, once in the barley field, once in the barn and once in the buttery'.[22]

In 1691 the behaviour of Joshua Horrocks aroused the suspicions of Humphrey Davenport who kept close watch when he saw them enter his shippon to be followed by Elizabeth Walkden walking softly behind him and 'hanging down her head'. His curiosity thoroughly aroused, he went to the closed door and;

> spying through a slit in the door . . . which was a quarter
> yard long and two to three inches wide saw Joshua and
> Elizabeth in a very Unseemly and obscene manner upon
> some Grass or Hay in a Cow Boose together for he was laid
> upon her body . . . and they appeared to be in copulation.

Horrocks then waited quietly to see what followed, and eventually
'Elizabeth came out, she had grass, hay or straw hanging from
her' and Joshua had 'altered in colour, black and trembling in his
lipps and faltering in his speech'. Thomas Rothwell, who had
joined Horrocks in looking through the slit in the door, said that
'he saw her naked thighs and the said Joshua upon her betwixt her
leggs'.

Evidently Elizabeth was not the only woman in Joshua's life, for
Hanna Wolstenham said that Joshua came to her house in the
evening of 1 May, her husband being absent. He laid hands on
her and 'drawing her back upon a stool saluted her on the lipps
twice. He then showed his privy member', which she declined.
She turned and went into the parlour and buttery, followed by
Joshua who 'did by strength force her hand so farr that she felt
his privy member with the back of her hand, upon which he asked
if shee would have it to which she answered, "No"'.

Another witness, Dorothy Ratcliffe, said that on Saturday evening towards the end of April, she met Joshua in the road when he
offered to kiss her. He 'showed his privy member' to this witness
and asked her 'whether she would have it'. One Sunday morning,
shortly afterwards, Joshua called at her house on his way to
church, and finding her by the fireside, took her by the middle
and 'then discovered his privy member to her' which she refused.
The following Saturday he made another attempt, but without
success. Joshua was a man of some resourcefulness, for when the
cause came before the consistory he had managed to obtain a
certificate of his good character signed by more than one hundred
parishioners, which enabled him to avoid a humiliating
penance.[23]

At Ormskirk, Ellen Spencer accused Anna Bushell of spreading
a report that James Carr had had the use of Ellen's body on a
malt sack, and William Fletcher at the 'side of a table'.[24] Mary
Hatton of Budworth Magna, who was notorious for enticing men
to her bed, fell foul of William Lawrenson for seducing his son

Richard, saying that she had come to the house at night and removing her clothes had entered the bedroom of Richard. Mary had also said that when Richard came to bed he 'had nothing standing but his ears'.[25] She had a reputation in the parish for her lewd and drunken conduct.

Jealousy could play a part in a fornication cause. Anna Brooke of Bunbury, who was clearly friendly or rather more than friendly with Henry Hare, had no alternative but to commence a suit against him for threatening 'her ruin and her life' by forcing her from her land for her relationship with John Mason. Hare kept an inn in Anna's house; since he expected to marry Anna in due course, he was angry when on entering the bedroom he found Anna and John Mason, 'naked in bed when the bedclothes were pulled off'.[26]

The display of a male sexual organ to a woman, accompanied by manipulation, was usually an indication of illicit sex. Sometimes it was a substitute for and at other times preliminary to copulation, but in alehouses it was part of the merry-making of peasant company. One case of this nature arose in Wigan where William Eccerson reported that he had seen John Wilkinson with Ellen Laithwaite for three hours 'handling his prick and he had his hand on her plackett'. He then 'reared her up against the wall and had carnall knowledge of her'. A short time after, Eccerson saw them get undressed when Wilkinson 'laid Ellen upon a chair or stool in an indecent manner and was naughty with her a second time'.[27] Another cause of a similar nature took place in a Macclesfield alehouse, when Edward Chantler stated that he had seen Samuel Elcocke with his hand up Sarah Whamley's clothes, 'holding her commodity', while 'she had her hand in Samuel's codpiece, it being reputed in the area that Samuel was well given and people scandalised him on that ground'.[28]

At Woolton, Elizabeth Bushell accused Catherine Lyon of being 'naughty' with her husband James Bushell 'six times and on the seventh she fell over backwards and his prick was soe sore she had to lapp it in his handkerchief'. Behind an alehouse was often a convenient place for intercourse.[29] In 1672, at Holt, Anna Hurst cited Henry Birch for saying that Robert Holdsworth 'beconn'd thee to the back of John Lees and there kissed thee and mossed thy belly and put that into thy bellie thou cannot shake out'.[30] Public exposure of genitals by both men and women occurred, and although G.R. Quaiffe asserts it was rare for woman in Somerset to do this, it was not a rare event in Chester diocese. At Childwall, William Lavrocke accused Jane Cook of being in the alehouse when she 'did pull William Holts prick out' and when he seemed angry she pulled up her clothes and said, 'does not this now give thee satisfaction'.[31]

The manipulation of the male sex organ by a group of women was not exceptional. In 1683 at Leighton Elizabeth Massey of Peverhouse cited Thomas Potter for stating in public that 'she did get Jack of Cobbs an idiot or natural fool into a house and rub his privities till she or they made it stand'.[32] On the other hand, Mary Smith of Runcorn swore an affidavit that Thomas Peacock 'took up her cloathes and drew his yard', meaning that he intended to have sexual intercourse.[33]

It is quite clear that many older men were not past their sexual prowess at an age younger men believed they ought to be. Likewise, many parents were alarmed when they discovered that their son was showing his sexual urges at an age they considered to be far too young. Alice Burgess of Bowden was disturbed and annoyed with Ellen Alcocke and cited her to court for enticing her son John Burgess to sleep with her, and went on to state that 'John had layn with her soe long that hee was made soe weak hee could scarce eat fried eggs'.[34]

Some men when frustrated in their attempts to have sexual intercourse devised an alternative method, as occurred at Macclesfield in 1671, when Rebecca Blacklach cited George Booth for saying, when caught by the mayor, 'I gott my hand under her Apron and could nott gett any pricke stand but took out my knife haft and put it into her breach and could have finished my work but Mr. Johnson came in'.[35] Even more drastic was the action of John Watkinson of Dean whom Anna Edge cited for stating that he had;

> shaved her privity twice and put peppins [long apples] in
> and put a white candle up her body. Once doing with a
> candle you were disturbed and Anna rushed out, the candle
> fell from her body melted almost to the wick.[36]

Even an incumbent was not above asking to be assisted to obtain sexual satisfaction. The rector of Doddleston, in 1697, was accused by Dean Fogge, the patron, for committing adultery with Jane

Harris, Mrs Barlow, and Betty Yates (who was considered to be a woman of ill reputation), of St Mary's parish, Chester, and asking Jane Sinclair who kept an alehouse in the parish if she could 'help him to a little cunt'. She seems to have introduced him to one Anna Lach whom he told that 'he would not hurt her for his prick was not too thick for her'.[37]

The precise point at which fornication becomes adultery is vague and no clear definition is provided. The term used by the court tends to be that of 'incontinent by fame', that is by public report or rumour of such misconduct. Often it is expressed in direct terms that couples were 'loose livers', that they had been 'naughty together', meaning they had met together for illicit sex. Alongside this charge went the one that implied pregnancy by stating she had 'a great belly'. By no means is every case laid against the man, for in the consistory, unlike the civil courts, women often accused other women or a woman brought a charge against a man or even one man against another. When church-wardens presented them it was customary to present the woman on the grounds that she was a bawd.

Joseph Ottiwell, the vicar of Wrenbury, was not above making an attempt to have intercourse by force. Alice Edge cited him for attempting to commit adultery with her in Wrenbury schoolroom, where 'he pulled out his genitals and tried for one quarter hour to have carnal knowledge till at last he fowled her garments with his nature'.[38] He was penanced with costs.

One simple method of stopping the male who was intent on sex was to offer verbal abuse and, if that did not work, to cry out. At Newchurch, in Pendle, the churchwardens presented John Cook, the parish clerk, for coming to Henry Cooke's house where he saw Cooke's wife Isabel carrying hay into the barn. He followed her into the building and then, according to the libel 'he took up her clothes, took her by the privitys to have carnal knowledge but she being with child her screams made him runaway'.[39] Again he was frustrated in his attempts to have carnal knowledge of Grace Lancaster after evening prayer on Sunday, 2 February 1703.

When Samuel Wilson of Rochdale accused Emmanuel Tompson of adultery with Grace Ogden, Wilson said that 'he caught Tompson in Grace Ogden's house with his britches down to his knees on a bed and clapt him on the buttocks'. For this, Tompson took Wilson before 'Mr Fell the magistrate' who promptly committed him to Rochdale dungeon when he was, 'unjustly bound over' but Wilson brought Tompson before the consistory on the grounds of defamation.[40]

The case of Isabella Ashcroft and Robert Sydebottom is of interest because it took place during the day in Thomas Robinson's alehouse in Bredbury, Stockport. William Milles, one of the churchwardens of Stockport, brought a cause in the consistory upon the report of William Thornily against Robert Sydebottom, a married man, and Isabella Ashcroft of Ashton on Mersey Bank for suspicion of adultery on 15 August 1663. Thornily had called at Robinson's house, being an alehouse, where he found Sydebottom and Ashcroft engaged in sexual intercourse, as the 'words of Robert . . . then & there uttered did hold out'. Thornily described the scene:

> Robert Sydebottom . . . then & there had his breches downe
> & Isabella Ashcroft . . . had her coats & all upp to her skin
> & the said Sydebottom . . . driving at her & Isabella haveing
> her face & eyes upon . . . William Thornily . . . spoke to
> the said Robert some words but what they were, she spoke
> so low, they were not understood but it is believed it was to
> have Robert know of because they were seen. But what ever
> the words were, that were spoken . . . Robert Sydebottom
> then & there to the aforsaid Isabella replyd [with an oath
> viz:] Gods wounds, I will fuke out my fukeing if the king
> come: upon which William Thornily went away being
> ashamed to see them there to do the evill as aforesaid.

The constable presented a certificate with the result that Thornily was absolved and a further cause commenced against Isabella Ashcroft for adultery with Sydebottom on the churchwardens' presentment, when she was given a public penance to perform.[41] Another allegation of adultery arising out of the constable's presentment was at Sandbach in 1663, when Maria Leadbeater cited Jacob Bailey for stating that 'Maria had all her clothes up and Yarwood his breeches down'. Ralph Kennedy, the constable, brought her before Justice Mainwaring at Warrington, but the cause against Bailey was changed to one of defamation.[42]

A parallel case came from Cheadle Heath in 1670 when Judith Hooley, the witness in an adultery case against John Bate, said that in the previous year she had called at Thomas Walmisley's house, entered somewhat uncertainly and inside found 'the said Walmisley's wife reared with her back against a post and all her clothes up . . . and John Bate come hastily from her with his prick in his hand . . . which thing she was much ashamed to see'. On looking round Judith saw no other persons in the house except the two engaged in adultery and a little child, adding that there was a common fame and rumour that they were naughty together. However, the night after the incident, Thomas Walmisley's wife asked John Hooley, Judith's husband, to say nothing of what she had seen by John Bate. Evidently Ellen Walmisley told Judith that Bate offered to be naughty with her and 'promised that if he got her with child he would give it a new coate'.[43]

In many cases money was exchanged or offered either as some compensation if bastardy might result or else as a bribe to prevent an action. At Malpas, Ellen Holford accused Mary Russell of being 'an arrant whore, who robbed her husband of five shillings at a time to give it to the miller of Whitchurch and hath played the whore with a man of Shrewsburie'.[44] At Nantwich, Richard and Alice Brown cited Alice Cowper for saying that Alice had offered 5s. to Thomas Marchant to 'be naughty with her'.[45] Again at Warrington, Grace Holland demanded payment from Thomas Hilton and because he 'had not sixpence to be naughty with her, it would be a good thing to burn the house over her head'.[46] At Over it was the other way round, when Anna Burnscoe cited John Withingham for saying that 'if his son had given her sixpence more he could have been naughty with her'.[47]

Anne Bourne of Wrenbury presented John Savage for committing adultery with Joyce Bramhall and a cause commenced in the consistory when Anne Bourne reported that she had seen 'a woman lying on her back where all the broom was high with all her clothes up for this deponent to see her smock up and her naked thighs and a man upon her betwixt her leggs in a very unseemly manner'. Joyce knew that they had been seen so she demanded £5 in order that she could give 40s. to Anne Bourne to hold her tongue, but this he refused to do.[48]

Joyce Bramhall was not the only one to have problems of this nature, for in 1633, Jane Hurst of Blackrod cited George Brown for stating in public that 'she was naughty with Edward Dughtie in a wood and she gave Henry Coiter's wife money to keep quiet but that Tom O'th Nook told Brown this was correct and what was more he could find sufficient witnesses to prove it'.[49]

Two years later, George Livesey and James Whitelegg cited John Cooke, vicar of Northenden, for attempting to commit adultery with his maid servant, Ann Savage. According to their evidence, Cooke proceeded

> to pull up her clothes and put down his breeches and lying with his naked belly on her naked belly did endeavour to get between her thighs and enter her body. . . . He had his hand under her clothes twice or thrice a day . . . he told her he had a herb growing in his garden which he would give here and she would be free before morning.

The danger of contracting venereal disease was an ever-present one where over-sexed women conducted themselves in a very free and open manner before males in alehouses. It was unfortunate that John Cooke became involved with Ann Savage for she was described by a witness, George Lingard, in the following terms:

> Ann Savage is a woman of lewd and vicious and lascivious behaviour and talks in public company very filthy both in his [Lingard's] own and other public houses . . . to pull up her clothes and show her nakedness before several persons & clap her hand to the bottom of her belly.

Even worse was the account that it was her custom to run up to men, 'whinnying like a horse and say, "Take him Ruffe"'. It was her habit to approach men, take their hands, and put them to the bottom of her belly. Not satisfied with this approach she was known to put her hand into men's breeches, pull aside their shirts, and 'handle their members & shake & commend some of them very beastly and bawdy'.

In one instance she had enticed a man into the barn where a number of women were engaged in spinning when she removed his breeches and proceeded to 'pull his privy member', causing him so much pain that the other women present had to rescue him. On another occasion three of Lingard's maids were sleeping in one bed and Ann Savage in a truckle bed when, suddenly, Savage jumped into the large bed and 'disturbed the other three so that they thought they were about to be ravished' and, running for Lingard, who came to them in his shirt, Savage immediately proceeded to 'handle his member violently' and he had to be rescued. Cooke was condemned in costs and suspended whilst Savage had to perform a humiliating penance.[50]

It is clear from other sources that a knowledge of methods of procuring an abortion by using herbs was known in areas other than Chester diocese.[51] A cause from Holt chapel in 1667 names the herbs used for this purpose. James Bowrey brought a suit against Margaret Royden for saying that, 'they lay under the hill at the crabtrees in the moonlight' and committed adultery. Fearing she was pregnant as a result of her indiscretion, Bowrey had given her a drink made from bearsfoot and water germander (black helibore) which, it was said, 'would cause a mare to drop its foal and a woman her child'.[52]

When Alice Greenhalgh of Bury cited John Scott for saying publicly that 'his leather britches had been between her legs and he got her with child and she took geere [sic] to kill it', he meant that she had drunk a similar potion which appears to have been the common method to procure an abortion in Chester. In 1612 Alice Butcher gave information that it was possible to obtain such potions from the apothecary of Warrington.[54] In Somerset it seems that it was the custom to drink a mixture of bearsfoot and sea wormwood or savon boiled.[55]

There is abundant evidence which reveals that a number of men were quite ready to boast about their sexual prowess. In 1630, John Roger of Knutsford boasted that he had occupied Mary Shothill 'five times in one night in Roger Nicholson's alehouse',[56] and at Stockport Isabella Thompson cited Alexander Fallows for stating that he had 'occupied her as oft as he liked'.[57] Margaret Owen of Budworth cited Thomas Janyon for proclaiming that he could 'have the use of her body in the day time as her husband did at night'.[58] Thomas Tarleton of Liverpool cited Richard and Katherine Higginson for saying that Tarleton and Henry Boden's wife 'could not get enough in the night but most go to it in the day',[59] while Anna Harrison commenced a suit against Elena Bridge for stating that 'William Bridge rides his mare, meaning Anna Harrison, all day and all night'.[60] Maria Darwen of Leyland cited William and Margaret Pincocke for stating that she had committed adultery with Captain Bayard, 'on a bed in the loft', presumably in the alehouse, 'laying under him like a pack of wool and they saw them at it'. To be described or compared to a pack of wool implied that Maria was of some considerable size.[61]

Curiosity on the part of some women who considered others were obtaining illicit sex aroused their envy, especially in a small community. At Tattenhall, Dorothy Wright accused Ellen Huxley of implying that she was the woman involved when Huxley said that she 'had seen a man and woman together and the man was as deep in as ever man was in a woman'.[62] Robert Lowndes also boasted that he took Anna Woods 'by the privities three times and could have had to deal with her but that someone had six in doing before you'.[63] Peter Bathom of Wigan had said to his wife Margaret that he 'could have taken Elena Barton upon the nest', and a woman like Margaret who spread information found herself in due course in court for defamation.[64] In much the same manner, Seth Ashton of Ashton-under-Lyne had said, concerning Mary Walker, that a 'man had loosed thy garter and laid the legg over'.[65]

Many men who were sexually motivated and keen to fornicate were reluctant to fornicate with women who by no means regarded cleanliness as a virtue. Jane Fairclough of Wigan cited Henry Prescott for stating that 'I might have had thee but thou art so very filthy between the legges I might not find it in my hart to use thy bodie carnally'.[66] A woman who was offended by such comments was quite capable of administering some rough justice on the offender. When Elizabeth Minshall of Malpas had been abused in a similar fashion by Edward Weaver she took her revenge. Waiting until he had gone to bed, Elizabeth climbed into the loft over his bed and, pulling up the floorboards, 'did piss on him'.[67] For James Houghton of Prescot it was otherwise, for he desired the body of Elizabeth Hey and during the absence of her husband had called at Elizabeth's house; he was told:

> your prick did stand and that it was seaven yucks long and that you asked her for help to measure it . . . and you said to Elizabeth that she could have five yuckes of it and that you would keep two for your own wife . . . she gave you five pence for your labour out at the window as you went away.[68]

So by his remarks he had implied that Elizabeth committed adultery with him and the Heys brought a cause of sexual defamation against him.

The village smithy has always been a centre where local

inhabitants have gathered to chat and gossip. In 1712, there was much gossip circulating in Whitegate, concerning Sydney Lee's wife. One Alice Jellicoe was reported to have said about Lee's wife that 'she wants a pinkle and a pinkle she must have so she went a whoring to London and was arrested by the watch and put in Bridewell'.[69]

The yards at the rear of many inns and alehouses were convenient places to fornicate or commit adultery and even a table tombstone in a neighbouring churchyard would serve equally well. Sara Badrett of Chester was furious when she heard that Catherine Moulson had remarked that Sara was 'common of a whores breed and wert caught whoring in St. John's churchyard; having left the inn of widow Kirk, The Pigeon, in Eastgate, Chester.[70] So Sara commenced a suit in court to protect her name. Frodsham Inn was another convenient place, according to Joseph Page, who said that he had seen Mary Cook of Mickle Trafford 'committing adultery on a sheaf of vetches with John Cook's man, at the back of the King's Head'.[71] Another favourite place was the Road Eye in Watergate, Marbury, when Hugh Wicksteed accused Jane Taylor, alias Ryder, for committing adultery which had resulted in a bastard child.[72]

An alleged adultery cause from Whalley highlights a tragic event. In 1699 Jacob Shackleton was at Margaret Shaw's house when Jeffrey Wilkinson, his neighbour, called and invited him to come over the following evening. After dark he went to the house where he saw, 'in the dwelling or fire house, a bed in which Wilkinson lay with Margaret Shaw'. There were several neighbours present and Margaret and Jeffrey appeared to be married. Another witness, John Tempest, said he had been present the same evening when 'he helpt the said Jeffrey to undress him and saw Margaret Shaw, alias Wilkinson, in bed with him'. As he went away he saw several neighbours on their way to make merry. Tempest said the events of that night enabled him to recollect the proceedings, 'from the sudden and unexpected death of the said Jeffrey which happened the same night . . . for he saw him layd out dead in the same room about nine of the clock next morning'. James Hartley suspected this was not a wedding but a case of adultery, so he commenced a suit. Margaret was unable to produce evidence that she and Wilkinson were married so she was penanced and condemned in costs.[73]

The churchwardens of Holy Trinity, Chester, walking in the parish one evening in 1699, reported that they had stood and watched Peter Stringer commit adultery with Mrs Alcock on 'widow Burroughs' stall in Eastgate Row in company with Thomas Booth and John Wisham, a shoemaker'. They swore on oath that the charge was correct and both were penanced, with costs.[74] Much earlier, in 1635, a suit was brought by William Massie against Thomas King for stating that he 'caught Massie with Hester Jacks at midnight, suspiciously together in Rowe'. Massie was evidently anti-Puritan for King was alleged to have 'taken hold of them saying if Hester had not been a puritan he would not have said so much'.[75] The Puritans' attitude to sexual matters was strict.

A very unusual place in which to fornicate must have been a privy, or house of easement. Privies were usually constructed to seat more than one person and it was in such a privy that Randle Taylor of Davenham said he saw William Goodier commit adultery with Samuel Lee's wife when 'he put his head through a hole in the said house of easement'.[76] A butcher's shop could serve when convenient. In 1632, Robert Evans of St Bridget's, Chester, stated that when Elizabeth Case came from Ireland she stopped at Broad Lane near Hawarden at a butcher's house; 'and there she fained herself to be sicke and called for a chamber and spake for a possett and laid her down upon a bed and that an Irishman did lye with her upon the same and were naughty together'. When the serving man, Turner, brought the possett, Elizabeth opened the door and Turner was convinced they had committed adultery and told Robert Evans about the incident, hence the cause in the consistory.[77]

In 1634, Thomas Lawton, who had come to be the 'minister of God's word' at Adlington in Prestbury parish, became involved with Mary Beech, with whom he lodged until his family came into residence. According to Elizabeth Johnson, she had heard John Blackshawe state that he had seen Lawton and Mary Beech, 'very unseemly together in a barne through a hole out of a henn house', and his wife Maud Blackshawe said she did 'see them in the house in a very indecent & unseemly manner in a chair & that she heard the chair cracke, she looking through a hole in the house'. Anne Blackshawe said she saw Mary Beech after she had put the children to bed go into the room where Lawton slept, and 'put out the candle & afterwards went to bed to the said Mr. Lawton'. One Hugh Brodhurst of Adlington alleged that Thomas Lawton and Mary Beech were 'Tusslinge in a chair and heard the same Creake exceedingly' in Thomas Blackshawe's house. Anne Blackshawe then called her sister-in-law Maud Blackshawe to come and see it, Maud called her maid to come and look, and the entire party saw 'Thomas Lawton with his breeches down between the naked thighs of the said Mary Beech'. Afterwards Mary Beech became pregnant and all believed that Lawton was the father until Mary in her labour declared the father was William Podmore of Mow in Staffordshire, an announcement that led to some reversal of opinions.[78]

A person's reputation for sexuality could be used to plead that he or she was unfit to act as a witness in a cause on the basis of their reputation in the community. In 1701, William Maddock's aunt, Anne Heighton, was involved in a case at Lancaster sessions. One of the witnesses was to be Helen Ingham of Woodplumpton, Preston, who was to testify against Maddock's aunt. He promptly stood up in court requesting that no credibility be taken of her evidence because 'she was a woman of bad carriage and that he could bring on oath that there was a man in towne that was naughty with her one Hundred Times since the Sessions began'. The justice then asked: 'Pray Mr Maddocks what man is there in towne that is soe brisk and mettle to perform such a feate?' to which Maddocks replied 'It is Captain Crichley'. In defence of her character, Helen Ingham had to commence a suit against Maddocks for defamation.[79]

One person could encourage another to commit adultery by inviting him or her to touch their body. In 1616, at Chester, the churchwardens of St Mary's cited Richard Davies and Ann Lloyd for adultery. According to Robert Chambrell, clothworker, he looked from his garden where his men were working on tables, into a stone quarry, or mason's yard, where John Addie was at work. He enquired of him what he knew about getting a child on the body of Ann Lloyd, to which he replied that he had seen Richard Davies and Ann Lloyd sitting on either side of the fire. He heard Davies say to Ann, 'Show me thy privities and I will give thee some bread and cheese'. John Addie stated he had been sent by Thomas Field, his master, to ask Davies to come and have a meal with him since his wife was away. When John returned he said to Katherine Field, 'Dame, I wold to God you had not sent me for Richard Davies for I saw such a sight as I never saw before. . . . Richard Davies upon Ann Lloyd and saying to her, "Let me see they privities and I will show thee my pillocke".' Evidently Ann did as requested and was rewarded with bread and cheese.[80]

A similar case came from Macclesfield when Ann Hobbes, wife of Richard Hobbes, was presented by the churchwardens for committing adultery for five years with James Heys, when she 'did desire him to feel your limbs and the state of your body' to which Heys had said that she 'had a leane rumpe and that he touched that and your other parts'. She was penanced in expenses for her five-year period of adultery with Heys.[81]

Jealousy could play a major part in a charge of adultery. It is clear from the evidence that William Clayton had been very familiar with Beatrice Boulton, wife of Lancelot Boulton, and eventually they quarrelled. Clayton then called her

> 'Batholome Barker's whore and hast plaid the whore with
> John Crommock and Thomas Greenfield . . . and I did
> find John Hothersall occupying Beatrice . . . he did
> commit adulterie with her' then losing his temper shouted
> at the top of his voice, 'Let her come out for by gods
> bloud she hath been my whore anie time these three years
> gone and I have had my will and the pleasure of her in
> everie room of the house & at everie apple and plumm
> tree in the orchard'

so announcing to all around that she was free with her favours.[82]

A false accusation could conclude with the plaintiff receiving a humiliating public penance as it did for Bathsheba Halton of St Bridget's, Chester, when she acknowledged that she had enticed her lodger, John Longford, to commit adultery so that she could marry him.[83] The consistory court had a long arm and passage of time was no guarantee that the offence would be overlooked. In 1637, Elizabeth Hulme of Wigan was cited to appear, upon presentation of the churchwardens, that she had committed adultery or fornication with Titus Marshe some twenty-four years previously and had given birth to a bastard child. That was not all, for some twenty years before she had done the same thing with Richard Rownson. She admitted that the charges were correct and was ordered to perform a public penance, bare-foot and in a white sheet, in the churches of Blackrod and Bolton.[84]

One consequence arising from illicit sex was the ever-present danger of contracting some form of venereal disease. Judging from the reactions of witnesses in such cases, the disease appears to have aroused in the seventeenth century as much fear as Aids in the twentieth. Dr M.A. Waugh notes that while there are a number of works on this subject from continental Europe, there is no authoritative modern history of venereal diseases in England.[85] Gonorrhoea appears to have been of early origin but there is little doubt that syphilis was a disease brought back to Europe by the Spanish explorers from the West Indies and South America. It made its first appearance in England around 1503 and was known as the French or Spanish pox. Syphilis spread in England like wildfire and aroused a great deal of alarm. Within three years of receiving reports of the arrival of the disease, steps were taken to close and demolish the ancient brothels in South-wark, an area within the jurisdiction of the bishops of Winchester. St Bartholomew's Hospital rapidly became the centre for victims of syphilis, where 75 per cent of the beds were occupied by sufferers. It was claimed that fifteen out of every twenty admissions were of patients suffering from the pox. At first the treatment for the disease was for the patient to drink a potion made from guiacum bark imported from South America. Later this treatment was replaced by fumigation to which Shakespeare refers in *Timon of Athens*, in 'tubs and baths'. He also uses the verb 'to burn' meaning to be infected as in the *Comedy of Errors* where he writes, 'light wenches will burn, come not near her'.[86] The earliest reference to venereal disease as burning occurs in Guy de Chauliac's book, *Chirurgia Magna*, which has a section on the 'heating and filthiness' of the penis 'for lying with an unclean woman'.[87]

In 1604, Cicily Aldersey of Nantwich cited William Bottock and Thomas Gilling for saying that 'she had a worse disease than the plague from playing the whore for she had the pox'.[88] Alternatively, a woman could blame a man for having the pox as Anne Wright did at Chester when she accused Thomas Hulme and Ralph, his son, of 'being laid with the pox and she hoped to see the plague amongst them'.[89] When Thomas Broster of Audlem cited William Tunstall for calling him a 'pockie ladd, a pockie knave', he continued by stating that he had caught the disease at the 'house of one Jarvis in Clow Heath, Shropshire'.[90]

Burning was the term used at Macclesfield in 1637 when Thomas Orme cited John Higginbotham of Macclesfield Park for openly stating that he 'was burnt by a woman and his member was swollen as big as his arm'.[91] David ap Hugh, alias Pue-emyll, of Chester was really brutal not only in his comment that Ursula Martyn had committed adultery but also in saying to her 'Thou art a pocky Queane and thou hast the pockes in thy throat'.[92] When John Bennet of Backford discovered that his wife had committed adultery he dealt with her most brutally by beating her severely for contracting the French pox; he admitted that he was drunk at the time.[93]

A case of venereal disease that gave the occasion for William Halliwell to slander Peter Leigh by stating that he had caught the disease in Dublin gave rise to another charge that Leigh had been involved in dealing in brass farthings. From the evidence, it appears that Leigh, Halliwell, and Thomas Cook were apprentices under Arthur Harvey, wet glover of Dublin. During this period Halliwell said that Leigh dealt in bundles of brass farthings which were used in Chester as small change by householders, freemen, merchants, shopkeepers, tradesmen, and 'persons of good quality'. After they returned from Dublin, Peter Leigh was in business in St Michael's Lane and Halliwell was in Bridge Street, Chester. Halliwell told Edward Ashton of Clayton Lane, while drinking in widow Wicksteed's alehouse in Bridge Street, that Peter Leigh was a 'burnt pricke knave' by which he understood him to mean that he had been naughty with some woman in Dublin. During that time in Dublin, Leigh, Halliwell, and Cook lodged with the Harveys, as was the custom with apprentices, and slept together in one bed. Eventually Halliwell and Cook were compelled to go into another room by reason of 'the said Peter Leigh showting & skreeching with the pain of the Infirmity he then did undergoe'. The two apprentices meanwhile had to make do by sharing, or attempting to share, a 'very little bed'. The following morning when Halliwell and Cook entered Leigh's bedroom, he threw off the bedclothes and showed them 'his swollen member as thick as his arm' and begged them to obtain the services of a surgeon. When the surgeon was informed of the details of the case and its nature, he refused to come near, 'nor would he meddle with him'.

However, they were put in touch with a Mr Bell who came and dressed it, remarking that 'he had only arrived just in time', for any longer delay would have meant death. Halliwell said that both Leigh and the room 'stank of the pox' and Mrs Harvey, his landlady, turned him out and made him find fresh accommodation. Peter Leigh, who brought the charge of slander against Halliwell, was eventually condemned in costs and to perform a public penance at the High Cross on 11 February 1664 for his fornication and attempted fraud with the brass farthings. It is a lengthy case which contains several letters from Dublin from Arthur Harvey about the events during their apprenticeship, which also throws light on life in Dublin.[94]

BASTARDY

Bastardy was also an offence that could be dealt with by the magistrates in quarter-sessions, when offenders could be sentenced to be whipped or sent to the House of Correction. Both church-wardens and constables were expected to present offenders at the visitation and if necessary to pursue the case through the consistory court. Since the church could not, after 1641, impose a prison sentence or order a public whipping, it was limited to the use of public penance or excommunication as punishment. Those who had funds to support a suit made use of the consistory court, until the suit was determined or the funds ran out.

George Harrison of Ditton confessed to adultery with Jane Evans but made an allegation of seduction against her with some success. When Harrison first met Jane Evans he was unaware that she was already married to one Gowen Evans, but knew she had acquired some notoriety. Three years previously, in 1695, she had travelled from London to Wales, and there craftily set her plans to obtain a fortune by proclaiming that she was the daughter of Mr Clayton, a Liverpool merchant, and so Gowen, falling for her charms, married her. A few months of married life and she left her husband under the pretence of visiting an aunt who resided in Chester but went instead to Ditton. Here she met Harrison, but six months later when she gave birth to a child she threatened to lay the blame on him unless he handed over a substantial sum of money. The case came before the Lancashire Justices of the Peace, when what was revealed of Jane Evans' past life cleared Harrison of all blame. In revenge, or in expectation of achieving it, Jane Evans threatened to pursue him through every possible court and bring him to ruin. In his confession he begged the Chancellor to issue what order he considered suitable since he felt he had been deliberately seduced. In the end he obtained full absolution from Jane's counter claim that he had seduced her.[95]

Holding the office of parish clerk and schoolmaster was no guarantee that the holder would avoid a charge of bastardy. One such was Robert Barrett of Barthomley, cited to appear before the consistory court in 1693, on a presentment made by the church-warden, Isaac Ridley, for committing adultery with Margaret Skerrett of Baulterley in Barthomley parish. The case is of interest since Barrett was involved in a similar case in more than one parish.

Zachariah Cowdrey, rector of Barthomley, stated that Margaret Skerrett's mother came to see him some six months prior to the cause and told him:

> the said daughter after she had been some time at school
> with Robert Barrett to learn to. read told her that the said
> Barrett had abused her & lain with her, and that she was
> afraid she was with child by him.

Shortly afterwards, Barrett's brother-in-law came to Cowdrey with a request that the rector pay a visit to Barrett and his wife. Cowdrey did so and 'found them both in great sorrow and tears'. Barrett believed he was guilty and became penitent for his acts, so the rector prayed with the Barretts for the grace of God.

On 3 February, Margaret Skerrett declared before Cowdrey and other witnesses that Robert Barrett had indeed had, 'carnal knowledge of her body several times'. Furthermore, Cowdrey received a letter from Mr. Mainwaring, vicar of Wybunbury, in which he said that Barrett,

> having debauched a servant of his both in point of cons-
> cience towards God and credit to the world indeavoured a
> satisfaction to the one and vindication to the other . . . got a
> friend to discourse with the woman's parents . . . From them
> he learned the news that Barrett had lain with her many
> times and in several places and had not spared the church
> and most of the best credible persons pews therein.

In small communities rumour and fame quickly spread so there was a common report prevalent in Barthomley that Barrett had committed adultery with Margaret Skerrett and the churchwardens had presented him to the rural dean for the same. In consequence of this he had no alternative but to withdraw for some time from his office of parish clerk. Mr Crew of Over, the patron of the benefice, sent the churchwardens to Barrett to ask for the church keys, which he surrendered and so ceased to officiate for six months.

On 4 February, Barrett came to church and went into the clerk's seat, whereupon a number of the congregation objected. Cowdrey, upset by the disturbance, ceased to read prayers and summoned them to meet in the vicarage. At the meeting, the churchwardens and sidesmen requested Cowdrey to draw up a petition to the bishop of Chester that Barrett's licence be withdrawn, and at the same time Cowdrey advised the church-wardens that for their own security they ought to present Barrett for correction: all present subscribed to the petition.

Thomas Cheyney, yeoman, said that on 15 February Margaret Skerrett confessed at Chester that Barrett had 'the carnal use of her body 7 or 8 times and named the places where'. It was in view of the common report that he, as one of the churchwardens, together with his opposite number and sidemen, made a present-ment against him. Barrett then handed over the church keys and ceased to exercise the office of clerk. Therefore, 'a great many of the neighbours were offended and scandalised at the foule report that went of him'. As a result, Barrett promised that he would never attempt to officiate again without the consent of the rector, churchwardens, and parishioners. Cowdrey admitted that he had subscribed his name to Margaret Skerrett's confession drawn up by Mr Woods, a neighbour.

The evidence turned on events in the alehouse kept by Humphrey Holland, a glover of Barthomley. His wife Dorothy stated that Margaret came to her house on an errand and in the course of conversation admitted that Barrett had had the use of her body and she thought she was with child by him. One week later, Barrett came to some company drinking there and shortly afterwards Margaret Skerrett came and asked for some 'barme' (yeast). Having remained a while, Barrett saw her depart and immediately she had gone out 'he paid his 2d and went after her'.

Some two hours later, Dorothy thought she heard voices in the room over the back room and, on going to investigate, found Robert and Margaret 'privately there together sitting upon the side of the bed, they having come up a private back way into the room'. They remained in the room until seven p.m. and then left together.

When Dorothy spoke to Barrett about Margaret's fear, he said 'he must confess he could not say he was free from her'. There was also a report in the parish that he committed adultery with other women, including some at Wybunbury.

Joseph Pickering of Baulterley, a button maker and former churchwarden was cited to give evidence. He confirmed that during the time that Barrett was clerk at Wybunbury, there was a report that he was 'naughty with' a young woman there and as a result had lost his place. Three years ago during the time he was churchwarden, Barrett came and asked for the job of parish clerk, but because of reports from Wybunbury, neighbours did not want him. However, in the end he prevailed upon Mr Crew, the patron, and obtained his consent. Later, with some difficulty, he obtained the consent of Mr Cowdrey, the rector, and was duly appointed clerk, 'upon his continuing good behaviour'. He had promised that neither he or his family should be chargeable to the parish and gave bond to that end, a bond which he never completed. Information had also reached Pickering's ears that between leaving Wybunbury and coming to Barthomley, Barrett had been for some time parish clerk at Keele and there the same reports of his conduct with women circulated as they had done at Wybunbury.

Thomas Richardson of Baulterley, a mercer, said that Margaret and her mother came to his shop before the court hearing and asked him to draw up a note of confession that 'Robert Barrett had had carnal knowledge of her body seaven severall times'. He wrote it out and gave it to her. He had also heard that Barrett had a child fathered on him while he was parish clerk at Wybunbury and for that reason he gave up his job as parish clerk.

Anna Whitgreane, of Barthomley, said that a year previously she had been in the fields on two occasions when Robert Barrett and Margaret Skerrett came from under a hedge together 'where there was no high wayes neare'. She acknowledged the existence of a common report about their adultery. It appears that Barrett was anxious to do his best for Margaret, for Marjery Boughy of Baulterly said that Margaret Skerrett acknowledged that Barrett had had the use of her body:

> the first time that he had so was in the school house . . . and in private and suspected places for that purpose and afterwards in the fields. . . . Barrett said that if she was pregnant then he would have her mother send her away to some private place and he would be at part charge to maintain it & if she had a child he would take it off her & it should never trouble her more, for his wife was a good women & had promised him that what lay in a woman to do she would do it for that child . . . what she has done amiss we must not see her cast away now.

Edward Mainwaring, vicar of Wybunbury, confirmed that some ten years previously Barrett had been schoolmaster and parish clerk there, at which time 'one of Mr Mainwaring's servant women was gotten with child and she . . . named the said Barrett to be the father of it and afterwards fathered it on him in her labour and likewise before a Justice of Peace upon her oath'. In consequence, Barrett was confined to Stafford gaol for eight or nine weeks. Mainwaring wrote to tell him to clear himself, otherwise the clerkship would become vacant. Barrett replied that if he did not clear himself in one week the office could be disposed of. Shortly after another man was put in as parish clerk.

Finally, James Moate of Barthomley, tailor, said he had known Barrett for twelve years, and in all that time 'as to women wherever he lived he was in a bad name . . . & that a woman in Wybunbury did father a child on him and there was a report they committed adultery'. Moate said he was present in Barthomley church when Margaret Skerrett performed her penance for the crime of adultery with Robert Barrett.[96]

The women always came off the worst in an adultery case, on the grounds that the men fell because they were seduced. A cause from Whalley in 1639 saw the woman sentenced to be punished while the man escaped since he was not identified. Edmund Bowker, a churchwarden, said that Maria Hodgson was 'a woman of low life and conversation, said to have . . . folowed a Jugler up and downe the cuntrie and to have had a bastard child'. Like Margaret Skerrett, Maria was found guilty by the magistrates at

Lancaster and was publicly whipped for her misdemeanours.[97] A pattern appears to have been followed, that the whipping did not conclude the case but the church court dealt with the offence as one of adultery and so a public penance was extracted from the offending woman.

The parish of Rochdale had, early in the century, acquired a reputation for bastardy. In 1608 Charles Holland was cited by the churchwardens for living with Jane Wylde as man and wife for twelve months while not married so they were guilty of committing adultery. In addition Holland was also charged with committing adultery with a number of women, especially Anne, daughter of Edmund Fielden of Castleton, Jane, daughter of Robert Butterworth, and the unnamed daughter of Robert Turner, 'all begotten with one or more children'.[98] The women were penanced together with Holland.

A second case in the same year concerned Robert Ashworth of Middleton, a man who had been married for eight years and said to be a 'lewde, licentious incontinent liver' who had committed adultery with Sara Bury, Ann Haworth, Jane Heywood, and Lee's daughter of Rochdale, all of whom had borne children. Ashworth did not appear in court and was declared contumacious and excommunicated. Later, when he found the sentence inconvenient, he appeared in court, made his confession, and received absolution.[99]

Occasionally, a man would attempt to avoid the charge that he was the father of a bastard child by attempting to lay the paternity claim on someone else. Ellen Greenhalgh of Winwick was under suspicion of being pregnant, so when Enoch Houghton and James Cash were travelling together to Wigan from Haydock, Cash remarked to Enoch, 'Thomas Houghton and I are free from Ellen Greenhalgh for they say she is not with child'. The remark was premature, for Jonathan Blackburn of Tildesley stated that 'Ellen had fathered her child on Thomas Houghton', he knowing this because he was one of the justices at Ormskirk sessions when an order was issued to Houghton to maintain the child.

Thomas Houghton made a detailed defence, so it was essential for Ellen to be brought before quarter-sessions by warrant. Upon her appearance she was warned not to commit perjury, and confessed that the father was James Cash, her former employer. During the evidence the bench detected that Cash planned to involve Thomas Houghton in the case by means of the following plan. Very late one evening, Cash contrived that Ellen should take 'his plow irons' to Houghton's shop for repair and 'use the occasion to draw Thomas Houghton into the snare'. Very early next morning Cash said he went to Houghton's shop where he found Houghton and Ellen in bed together.

The plot failed, for Ellen Hill, who kept an alehouse near Burtonwood chapel, said that James Cash came Good Friday evening pretending that he had a letter for John Dunbabin for whom Ellen Greenhalgh was now working as a servant, having left Cash. Cash gave Ellen Hill a penny to send her son to fetch Greenhalgh and she returned with him. Cash and Greenhalgh then went into a far room. The affair was complicated by a meeting of the town officers and constables who were discussing town business in the next room, so it was impossible to get to the far room since it meant disturbing the constables' meeting. Eventually John Hill, the landlord, did get to the room, where 'he saw James and Ellen on the bed laid down though their feet and leggs were off the bed to the floor in a familiar loving manner kissing and snugling together'. Hill left the room but returned later to find them in the same position except that James had laid his right leg over Ellen. He reported what he had seen to the constables who went to look through the window, but the noise they made disturbed Greenhalgh and Cash.

Maria Harper, alehouse keeper, for whom Greenhalgh had once worked, said she asked her to leave her service for she feared she would bring disgrace upon the house.

When the magistrates had heard and assessed the evidence, they dismissed the case against Houghton, and Ellen was punished by whipping. Thomas Houghton then brought a suit against Ellen in the consistory for alleging adultery and bastardy, which was in reality defamation. She was penanced, not only for the allegation, but for being with child a second time.[100]

Katherine Eaton kept an alehouse in Tarporley where, in March 1679, John Gregory of Huxley was drinking ale with John Whalley when Katherine asked if they had any news concerning John Hough. A country alehouse, then as now, was a good place to hear local news and gossip. When John Whalley said he had no news, Katherine told him that 'Mrs Brassie was gone out of Chester into Wales to spin blew wool', which was a local saying about any woman who had moved from her home into another place, especially Wales, which meant that the woman concerned was expecting a child and had gone there to give birth. Katherine appeared to know the precise location which she said was 'near Harding' (Hawarden). Katherine found herself in court for sexual defamation and she was condemned in costs.[101]

A comparable case comes from Chester in 1638, when a jealous wife, Margaret Greene, had said publicly that Margaret Jones was her husband's whore, that he had been naughty with her, and when she was pregnant sent her away 'to Oswestry or twelve miles further'. She also added that 'Margaret Jones has been abroad to empty her caske & was come back now she had emptied her and her husband had laine with her and they had been naughty together'. In the end Margaret Greene was condemned in costs when the suit came up for hearing.[102]

Richard Bennet, draper of Chester, was cited by Anna Boswell for stating that he had, 'got a woman with child who wore a Canvas Smock and a Linsey wolsey petticoat', and swore the accuracy 'in wyne & drink'. His remarks earned him a public penance.[103]

Weather conditions were blamed for encouraging John Stonier and Ellen Wold to commit adultery, resulting in bastardy, according to Hugh Slade who promoted the case against them. During 'the great snow' in the winter of 1635, Stonier escorted Ellen Wold from Nantwich to her home at Wybunbury. In his confession Stonier admitted that when they left Nantwich they arrived at his father's house in Shavington where they remained for two nights. Ellen slept on the rushes covering the floor of Stonier's chamber for the better part of two nights as she wouldn't go to his sister.

Continuing their journey towards home they called at Widow Gilford's alehouse in Wistaston where they stayed that night and the next. During the second night he had carnal knowledge of Ellen's body 'three several times', and she would not be 'persuaded but that he had gotten her with child'. The night in question was Tuesday before New Year's day. She believed her pregnancy could have happened when Widow Gilford came into the room where they were sleeping and could have taken them 'in the act'. However, Ellen said Stonier had promised to marry her to make her an honest woman, but he never came near her for at least a year.[104]

The churchwardens of Rochdale noted carefully the activities between John Milnes and Alice Shaw, a spinster, with whom he committed adultery. He was said to have kept company with this woman by 'following her from alehouse to alehouse and spent time with her in the barn and sent her money and tokens when she was great bellied ready to drop the bastard'. Both had public penances to perform.[105]

Occasionally the court was used in an attempt to enforce payment for the maintenance of a child. In 1638, Catherine Akerley cited Henry Cookson for failing to pay £20 in maintenance money.[106] The only other comparable case comes from Malpas in 1604 when Margaret ap Robert attempted to obtain payment of £6.6s.6d. from John Jenkins for maintaining Randle Jenkins whom John 'got upon her body'. The total sum claimed was for five years at 23s.4d. per annum.[107] There is, unfortunately, no indication of the extent to which these appeals were successful.

An excellent illustration of the way in which gossip could influence incidents of adultery and bastardy comes from Giggleswick in York diocese in 1716. It is quite clear that Robert Newhouse had said in Settle market that Ena Mary Spark was a whore and that a 'man in a blew apron was upon her and in active business by the wayside between Long Preston and Settle and her smock was as high as her teeth'. He had also added that she had a bad reputation in the part of Lancashire in which she resided. When Thomas Lawson, gentleman, reported to Newhouse that Ena Spark intended to sue him he replied that he had but repeated what William Salisbury had said. Nevertheless, Lawson believed that her name was slandered and she had been injured by the remarks. Ena Spark then commenced a suit against William Salisbury for saying that 'he saw such good sport as he never saw in his life that a man in a blew apron was on a woman in a black quilted petticoat with her smock high'. One young witness, Richard Clark of Long Preston, was present in Settle market on market day, in company with his father, when Salisbury came up and asked if it was he who was 'kissing' the woman on the wayside this side of Long Preston, but Clark vigorously denied this.[108] Market-place talk of this kind, of being active in fornication, adultery, and bastardy, often lay behind a cause for defamation.

When an examination is made of presentments recorded in the Comperta Books for Copeland and Furness deaneries, it is clear that many cases of adultery and bastardy were not taken forward to the consistory, and one suspects that the cost in court fees would be prohibitive in a majority of cases.[109] Also it was no easy route from the north either to Richmond consistory across the Pennines or south to Chester. Punishment by public whipping and imprisonment handed out by the civil magistrates was far more severe than that handed out by the consistory courts where a public penance and excommunication was the maximum punishment for the laity. Naturally, it seems unfair that it was usually the woman who was found to be the guilty party and that the male was dismissed, and more so when the woman had to appear before the consistory on a charge of adultery leading to bastardy, having been previously punished by the civil court.

On the whole the majority of bastardy cases are fairly straightforward and follow a pretty traditional pattern over the entire diocese, but there are variables. In 1683, Rachel Paughton of Chester cited Edward Bridge for calling her a 'bastard bearing whore who would have flung her child into an house of office if people had not been present'.[110] It was not unknown for unwanted children to be killed by throwing them into the privy shortly after birth. At Marbury Elizabeth Stockton accused James Dean of stating that 'she had a child by John Stockton and was his concubine for sixteen years before he married her'.[111]

At Stockport, Anna Astall of Bowden had openly stated in a very offensive manner that Mabel Bradshawe had given 'two pieces of gold to William Oldham to christen her child "Bastard"'.[112] The court took action against those clergy in remote Pennine and Lake District parishes who churched women without presenting them for bastardy. In September 1637 Thomas Crichloe, vicar of Clapham, had churched Anne Burton who had borne a bastard and was excommunicated in Clapham church but the churchwardens asked him to forbear publishing the sentence, and in 1638 he was penanced for the offence.[113]

In an attempt to hide a bastard at the time of the birth, the woman was often lodged with a friend in expectation that the churchwardens or constable would not discover the incident. In 1623 the court took up the cause of Margaret Warburton of Bunbury, 'whom the churchwardens believed that George Rawlinson had made pregnant and was lodged with Rafe Powall'. However, in her labour, under pressure from the midwife, she named George Spurstowe as the father, which then meant a new presentment.[114]

Not all adultery offenders performed a penance, for at Waverton Peter Dutton and Anna Hunston were able to commute this to a money fine of £20, by no means an insignificant sum in 1633.[115] There is, as should be expected, an overlap with causes that involve matrimonial disputes where adultery is often the reason for seeking separation or divorce.

A useful contrast with Chester can be found in the Halifax area in York diocese. In 1633, Anne Whitby reported that 'the said Anne Nicholls was a whoore and that she kept other wives husbands . . . a couple at a time in secret places a woman of lewd character committed the crime of fornication with other wives husbands'. Luke Horsfield accused George Holgate in 1692 of being

> a fornicator, adulterer and incontinent . . . with Catherine
> Jenkinson and that he . . . got her with child, and 3 weeks
> after she had had the bastard . . . Holgate had carnall
> copulation with her; he then promised her 19 pounds if she
> fathered the bastard on John Broadbent.

During the same year, Martha Hardcastle had called Ann Mitchell

> a whoore, the greatest whore in Towne (meaning the Towne
> of Halifax) and further said that the said Ann Mitchell kissed
> with one James Robinson for a great time . . . and also said
> that her brother John Hardcastle could not be kept at home
> at night nor day for going to whore with her.

One witness, Dorothy Hill, said Mitchell was 'a common sailors whore . . . and that she was kissed against a cupboard, against a mill stone and in Mr Bentley's swine coate'. The same Bentley bragged to his friends that he had kissed Grace Noble twenty times in the hayloft.

On 25 May 1611, Thomas Hall was cited to the consistory on the grounds that two years previously he and Ruth Rishworth had been 'naughty . . . and had been so several times at Hollins Top to be naughty'. A further witness stated that Hall and Rishworth had been naughty between the houses of Edward Northend and

Edward Balsey in the presence of Pheobe Bentley, who also had her children with her. Ellen Pickering said that while she was working in Hall's house she heard him tell his sister that 'he had been with Ruth Rishworth whilst she was making butter . . . and he asked her for the use of her body there and now . . . she said . . . "Nay if we are to have it, we should have it upon the bed . . ."'.

In the course of his dissertation, Steven Hughes looks in detail at one particular family to discover attitudes to morality. At the beginning of the seventeenth century, this family, the Barracloughs, lived in Southowram and Halifax, but in later generations spread into the parishes of Elland, Lightcliffe, and Illingworth. The Barracloughs' reputation was widespread. For several generations they were churchwardens, constables, and even High Constables. However, each family has a black sheep in it and the Barracloughs had more than others.

Three were presented in 1613: one for keeping company drinking during service time; another for adultery with Richard Brooke of Woodkirk, Leeds; and another sister, Elizabeth, was presented for fornication twice, once in Shelf and a second time in Halifax. In 1636, Alice was presented for fornication and ante-nuptial fornication, and her three brothers, William, John, and Leonard, were found responsible for forcibly burying a suicide by night at Elland. The following year, John was cited for making Grace Brearley of Illingworth pregnant, and so the saga continued.

It can be argued that fornication as a moral and social offence was an actionable act since it encouraged bastardy, and to bring a child into the world without provision for its maintenance by tying down the father, was unquestionably an anti-social act in a parochial society with very limited resources upon which to call.

Part 4

MATRIMONIAL PROBLEMS

Chapter Ten

CHILD MARRIAGES

Marriages, even in the Middle Ages, were a source of endless problems and disputes that provided much business for the church courts. Many of the difficulties arose from the fact that marriage, besides being a sacrament, was also a legal contract. It was the existence of this contractual factor that was so very often used to promote a marriage for purely secular and worldly purposes. In its attempt to codify and regularize the law concerning matrimony, the Church had to take account of a number of factors.[1] These were

> partly inherited Jewish traditions to which was added the ceremonial observances prescribed in Roman Law and the different types of marriage therein allowed; and also the tenacious Germanic customs that varied in each tribal area. . . . Outside and above all these, was the Church's conception of marriage as a mystery, a sacrament and a symbol.[2]

Well into the eighteenth century, and for many years before, marriages amongst landed families were usually arranged between the parents of bride and bridegroom designate. Often these arrangements were made when the children were quite young, and later the wishes of the children were completely ignored. Property, especially landed property, was the motivating factor either for combining the landed estates of two families or for acquiring a substantial sum of money as a dowry. These were the prime considerations.

Legislation was required to regulate the solemnization of a marriage with penalties attached for performing clandestine marriages, in alehouses and elsewhere, for totally unworthy reasons. Canon 11 of the Council of Westminster (1200) ordered that the banns of marriage between two parties should be published in the parish church of each of the contracting parties on three consecutive Sundays prior to the marriage, during divine service. This piece of legislation was intended to circumvent marriages between minors and those adults who were within the forbidden degrees of relationship. Canon 18 of the Council of Eynsham (1009) regulated the hours of daylight during which marriages could take place; these were between eight in the morning and twelve noon in the parish church attended by either of the contracting parties, as long as no impediments existed.[3]

The Reformation brought changes in Christian doctrine, making some modification to medieval canon law desirable, and the Canons of 1604 contain the amendments. Canon 62 states that marriages are to be solemnized in the parish church either after publication of banns or on the production of an episcopal licence, issued by the diocesan registrar, authorizing the marriage. Canons 99–101 specify the conditions under which a marriage could be contracted. The publication of the Table of Degrees of Affinity (1563), attached to the Book of Common Prayer, forbade any marriage between parties below the age of majority (21 years) without the consent of parents. The prohibitions made by this canon were avoided by contracting a marriage outside the Church, during hours of darkness in private houses, or clandestinely in some remote chapel by an obliging curate, to conceal evidence of ante-nuptial fornication or to avoid parental objections. In 1619 George Whittaker, vicar of Cawthorne, was cited to appear at York for marrying persons by moonlight in the ruined chapel of Midhope on the Pennine moors.[4]

Certain incumbents of peculiar jurisdictions acquired the right to marry people without banns and could grant a licence for a marriage in their church.[5] The penalty for any incumbent who deliberately broke regulations concerning marriage was suspension for three years from his benefice.[6]

By Canon 109, churchwardens were required to present all persons in the parish 'who committed adultery, whoredom, incest and any other wickedness like cohabiting unmarried', to enable the diocesan authorities to take action.[7] This canon also involved all divorced persons who lived with a member of the opposite sex, husbands and wives who lived apart, those who sheltered and fed pregnant single women, and unlicensed midwives who operated in the parish.

In 1653, under the Commonwealth, marriage was removed from the clergy and handed over to the civil magistrates, when after twenty-one days of public notice given in the parish church or in the market place on three successive market days, a marriage could be solemnized between eleven in the morning and two in the afternoon. Alarmed at the increase in sexual immorality, Parliament passed an Act in 1650 to 'suppress the abominable and crying sins of Incest, Adultery and Fornication wherewith this land is much defiled and Almighty God highly displeased'. The penalty for incest and adultery was to be death except for any woman whose husband had been absent for three years. Fornication meant three months in gaol and a bond for one year's good behaviour. Brothel keepers were dealt with very harshly, and were whipped, put in the pillory, branded on the forehead with the letter 'B', and gaoled for three years. If they were convicted a second time the penalty was death.[8] The Restoration in 1660 saw the end of this brutal legislation and the restoration to the Church of the right to solemnize marriages, with disputes being heard in the consistory court.

The legal position of men was superior to that of women. If a woman murdered her husband she was to be burned, but if the man did the same to his wife it became only a hanging matter. Woman had to occupy an inferior position in church for they were not allowed to share their husband's pew if it was near the chancel.[9] In parts of Yorkshire wife-beating was taken to be a serious offence in which the community handed out some rough justice, as the following case from Appleton-on-Wiske, in York diocese, reveals.

Several men were involved: Robert Buttrie, John Brunton, and John Steward; also William Rowntre, John Rowllee, William Johnson, and Robert Taylor, the churchwardens, William Hodson, Robert Eden, and Ralph Stockdale; also John Rimer, Thomas Bratton Jennett Hodson, James Timworth, and especially Thomas Ward, who was the moving agent in the affair. The ceremony known as 'riding the stang' was a popular method of expressing disapproval, especially where wife-beating was involved. The stang was a cart shaft, or failing that a long pole, upon which the offender sat astride. He was then carried round the village, followed by the mob, while those who carried the stang bounced him violently upon it. The offence took place on Sunday, 20 September 1635. The organizer, Thomas Ward, hired William Steward to play his bagpipes and walk in front. The narrative continues:

> all the parties before mencioned did fetch William Hodshon from his owne house and did carry him upon a stang to the churche and about the churche and the mob dancing before him and soe carried him into the church and about the Font and set him in his stall with the piper playing before him all that time and that was done the Sunday . . . named in the time of Divine Service. And Robert Taylor a churchwarden did not only goe himself but lent a stang to carry the same Hodshon on and being asked why he did soe he answered in great derision that he would do the like again if it were to doe.

The cause commenced in 1635 but dragged on due to opposition from certain parties in the cause. On 25 October 1637, Rimer appeared for himself and Bratton to swear that neither party was involved. The next hearing was 5 April 1638, when James Timworth appeared and swore that 'he was not consenting to the said disorder but only light on the company in his going home when he left them'. He was dismissed and the rest were penanced and had to seek absolution. The performance of the penances and absolution extended over three years,[10] the law operating no quicker than it does today.

By 1650 there was some improvement in attitudes towards women, for wife-beating had become an offence, and to call a woman a whore meant she could bring an action against the defamer in court. On the whole, the actual position of women was in fact better than the theory, for the law had not yet caught up with the economic changes that were taking place. The increasing advances, with the desire to impose severe penalties for adultery, were all part of the battle that was being fought to release marriage from a concern based solely on property to one based on marriage purely for love.[11]

In his study of Lancashire in the sixteenth century, Dr C. Haigh has pointed out that marriage was treated lightly in the higher social groups, but the consistory court files have revealed that the same attitude prevailed at lower levels. Certainly the instability of many marriages was due to the young age of persons joined in matrimony.[12] The evidence in the consistory court files confirms Dr Haigh's statement that many marriages were used as means to forge alliances and bind settlements. Although F.J. Furnival collected into one bundle the child marriage causes, this collection is by no means complete, for a further thirty have been found for the seventeenth century during sorting and listing.[13] Peter Laslett is of the opinion that child marriages were rare in England,[14] but the social structure of Lancashire and the evidence in the consistory court files show the contrary, and child marriages were a feature of Chester diocesan life throughout both archdeaconries.[15]

It was the law that minors must get consent of parents before any marriage could be solemnized, but in several cases this was avoided with unexpected results. In 1663 at Christleton, there was a cause concerning the marriage of Hannah Crofton to Robert Williamson. On 13 October, Thomas Carter had gone to the registry to apply for a licence for a marriage to take place between Hannah Crofton and Robert Williamson of Shipbrook in Davenham parish, for whom he was guardian. Carter swore an oath on the gospels that the consent of parents had been obtained and that there were no legal causes pending in court to stay any proceedings of matrimony, and had subscribed to the same. He also entered bond for £100. However, Zechariah Crofton, her father, said that Hannah was not above 16 years of age. When the case came for hearing, Carter admitted that he had not obtained parental consent for a licence. He had also stated that he could write his name, but when presented with the bond he only 'set his mark to it'. The judge decided that he had committed perjury in arranging the marriage between two minors and that his bond was forfeit. In addition, Carter had to stand in Davenham market-place when Zechariah Crofton had to announce to all what Carter had done. He was also condemned in costs.[16]

Catherine Nicholson of Stidd was heiress to a reasonable estate, so Richard Moody, senior, decided that it would be a sound idea to marry Catherine to his son, Richard Moody. The marriage eventually broke down and Maria Moody, a witness, said she remembered the marriage of the two, and that Richard Moody, senior, had by 'fair inducements and by tender language and sometimes by threats' tried to create a situation 'not found in the mutual inclinations & affections of Catherine & Richard'. Indeed it seems that even before she had reached the age of 12 Catherine had often expressed her dislike of the marriage and repented and renounced it. Edward Sherborne remarked that since Catherine attained the age of 12 he

> heard and observed Catherine declare against, disowne and renounced the marriage and refuse & deny to own Richard as her husband and had spoken also to her neighbours that, 'she would never own him or come in bed with him'.

The couple had been married when they were 11 years old, so the final sentence was that the marriage was null and void.[17]

Quite different was the marriage between Henry Davies and Margaret Manley at Doddleston in 1667. Henry Davies was believed by George Manley of Lach to have inherited a good estate and be under the guardianship of Henry and William Binley. Manley's approaches for a marriage were resisted for some time, but 'by continual solicitation' they finally agreed and a marriage was arranged. On 8 June 1663, when Henry Davies was 11 years of age, having been baptised on 24 July 1653, the marriage was solemnized, not in church but in George Manley's house in Lach, by Samuel Lloyd, rector of Aldford. Also present at the marriage were Margaret Manley, mother of Margaret, Alice Manley, William Burgery, Jane Edwards, and two young girls, according to the evidence of the rector of Aldford. After the marriage, Manley became guardian to both children by an order from the Chester Exchequer Court, but by the summer of 1667, Henry's former guardians were having second thoughts about the marriage. In an attempt to get the parties to agree to a petition for nullity, Joseph Binley, Henry's uncle, and Susan Cowley, his mother, now remarried, called at the house to speak with Henry and Margaret. Both were in bed when the visitors arrived so the two adults went to the bedside, and in reply to their questioning Henry replied that 'he had marryed his sayd wife and would live and dye with her'. There was no petition for nullity, but the parties were penanced for permitting marriage in a private house and the rector of Aldford was penanced for taking part.[18]

In other cases, some people went so far as to organize an abduction of one of the parties in order to obtain a marriage with prospects for the children. In 1673, Ellen Plant of Tottington was cited into court on a presentment for abducting Samuel Bury to marry her niece Maria, between March and May, in the house of James Bordman of Prestwich. The Plants knew that Samuel Bury, an only son and heir to a considerable estate, was at the time an apprentice in Manchester. The evidence reveals a well-laid plan to secure the marriage of young Samuel to Maria Plant.

Evidently Ellen Plant, 'having a design upon him and his Estate, which he is likely to enjoy', had the assistance and agreement of William and Alice Plant and several other persons for the preferment of both Maria Plant and her parents. James Bordman offered his house for the marriage and the Plants obtained the services, illegally, of William Hilton, curate of Pott chapel, to marry them. Ellen and the others had 'invited and inticed Samuel Bury from his master's service and procured a minister clandestinely to make a show of marrying them'.[19] Ellen Plant was found guilty, given major excommunication, and sentenced in costs as well.

In 1628, Thomas Willin of Upton, near Prescott, cited Margaret Lawton of Farnworth for breach of a marriage contract. It appeared that Margaret was born in 1614 and married in 1625 below the age of consent, so the marriage was declared null and void.[20] Another example comes from Cartmel where the churchwarden's presentment cited Anne Breres, alias Tyllesley, and Thomas Tyllesley, for entering into marriage when Thomas was 14 years of age. Since the parents had not consented to the marriage, it was declared null and void.[21]

The marriage between Isabella Mason of Lea and Robert Walker of Garstang, which had taken place in 1590 when both were 11 years old, lasted until 1615, when the parties requested divorce which was granted in that both were below the age of consent when the marriage took place.[22] Similarly, the contract between Thomas Rathbone of Woodchurch and William Ball, guardian of Alice Tottie, for Alice to marry George Ball, son of William, was declared to be of no value since both contracting parties were below the age of consent.[23] John Barlow of Doddleston asked for a divorce from Martha Clegg on the grounds that he was married to her before he was 14.[24]

Undoubtedly some child marriages survived, for the only ones to appear in court were those where divorce or declaration of nullity were the only and obvious solutions to the problems that had arisen. Child marriages do not appear to have been a feature of Essex society, nor of Somerset, at this time, according to F.G. Emmison and G.R. Quaife, but were prevalent in Chester diocese.

It was the social structure of northern society, the relatively small population, and the geographical structure that seemed to encourage child marriages. The evidence points to the fact that it was among those families, including the gentry, who had property rights to protect that child marriages were common. It became the custom to permit a child marriage on the grounds that if the relationship proved unhappy or the families quarrelled and were not on speaking terms, then the contract would be null and void. The entire matter was based on the nature of what constituted a matrimonial contract.

Chapter Eleven

MATRIMONIAL CONTRACTS
AND DISPUTES

The study of child marriages brings into focus the matter of a betrothal contract. Any study of church court act books reveals a constant stream of men and women who were involved in failure to marry after a betrothal or repudiation of a contract to marry. In courtship during the seventeenth century and before, love was not the paramount factor. Society at this period was concerned with the acquisition of property in the shape of lands or goods as prosperity increased. The selection of a bride was influenced for many men by the possibility of bringing some small estate or property that could be developed or even inheriting at some future date a considerable fortune. Therefore a contract to marry was considered to be of a firm contractual nature enforceable at law.

There appear to have been two distinct methods by which a couple could enter upon a contract to marry. One was by speaking what were known as 'verba de fururo', where a man would say to the woman in the presence of witnesses, 'I will take thee to my wife', and the woman replied in the same words. In such a case, the contract was not considered sufficiently binding since no firm date was fixed for completion. This type of contract one usually finds made in alehouses where the mock marriage was often followed by the not so mock consummation afterwards.

The second method was by using the 'verba de presenti', where the man said, 'I take thee to my lawful wife', and the woman replied in the same words, so giving the incident a firm contractual nature, sealed by breaking a silver coin, which led, if the contract broke down, to a cause in the consistory court on the grounds of breach of promise, which tended to be successful.

In 1632, at Macclesfield, Alice Johnson cited Philip Orme for

169

breach of contract, stating that in July 1626 the two had made a contract by 'verba de presenti' in the house of Ralph Broadhurst in Sutton, where 'they did break a piece of silver between them in ratification of the said contract of Matrimonie'. The night following the sealing of the marriage contract the two slept together and 'he did carnally know her and begot a child upon her body as he believes they were married and she bore a male child'. It also appeared that a contract had been made between Philip Orme and Joanna Smith at the time when he was only 15 years of age. Philip was convinced that he was made to contract matrimony against the will and liking of Joanna. Incidentally, Alice Johnson was 16 years of age and the breaking of the piece of silver was taken as evidence of a firm contract and it was upheld. It was the custom to regard the parties as virtually married as often there was a definite sexual relationship between them. In this case a pregnancy followed.[1]

A cause from East Witton in 1606 reveals that Elizabeth Croft's mother was opposed to her daughter's marriage to Thomas Richardson, and when the latter brought a suit for breach of contract he claimed that 'Elizabeth had been his handfast wife since St Ellenmas last . . . and that he had th'use of her body . . . the same day her mother clipped her sheep'.[2]

One cause for breach of promise was the opposition from parents and friends, for with such formidable opposition if the parties went ahead with marriage the end could be economic ruin, so marriage to a pregnant girl in the face of opposition was extremely hazardous. Other breaches resulted from the man being involved with another woman, or the marriage portion being too small. Financially, marriage with an insufficient dowry was no more attractive than the cost of maintaining an illegitimate child. Unscrupulous men would extract high dowries from the father of the pregnant spinster in return for covering up the family's shame. However, the sensible ones took care of this aspect before committing themselves to betrothal.

Since marriage depended on the ability of the husband to make a sufficient living to enable him to maintain a wife, it often meant that eldest sons could not marry until their father, and sometimes their mother, died. Occasionally younger sons could not marry until the eldest brother was dead. The only real security a girl had was to have the promise recorded in a formally witnessed contract so that she could rely upon a legal enforcement. In some cases a man refused to marry the woman until she was pregnant.

In 1623, Dorothy Nuttall of Manchester cited Charles Nuttall of Bury for having made a solemn promise to marry her. One night Charles went to the house of Elizabeth Nuttall, a widow of Rossendale, where he found Dorothy in bed. He called for someone to pull off his boots and said that he would go to bed to his wife. Dorothy awoke and offered to get up, but he said the 'he would be with her and it should be in confirmation of their former contract and if she refused it should be on her conscience'. Dorothy said that he had obtained a licence from the registry to the curate of Manchester for a marriage and gave it to her, 'to allure her to yield to his desires and swore and protested he would marry her'. It appeared that Dorothy had given him sums of money, namely £7, on two occasions which Charles said he would use to buy her wedding garments and linen for his own use. He also affirmed that he would accept as part of her marriage portion

> one capp wrought with gold worth xxx shillings, one pair of boothose worth xii shillings, handkerchiefs wrought with gold worth xxxvi shillings, two gold hatbands worth xxi shillings, three gold rings worth xliii shillings, two pairs of gloves worth xix shillings.

He had also written letters to Dorothy to procure her love and affection.

In his defence, Charles said that he would marry Dorothy

> so soon as she shall contain with child, I will make her my lawfull wife. Public marriage is but a ceremony of the church but the contract is a true and lawful marriage before God for Joseph and Mary were contracted before they were married.[3]

Juliana Vernon and Richard Croxton of Middlewich had entered into a contract to marry by 'verba de presenti' exchanged between them. Richard had said, 'Juliana thou knowest that my love is toward thee and none other', and then, taking her by the hand, said, 'I give thee my faith and troth and do promise that I will marrie thee'. He went on to state that 'he could not marry her during the life of his mother' and asked Juliana to delay official marriage until his mother died for they were both young and could afford to wait, but that they were now secretly married.

Richard Croxton continued to pursue his suit to Juliana's parents for marriage. Randle Vernon, her father, was suspicious about the whole affair and feared that Richard would not 'deal well with her', so he rejected his proposal and forbade Richard to come to the house. A quarrel arose so Richard told Randle that Juliana was his wife. Her father replied, 'if she be thy wife, take her to thee but first goe forth of my house and she shall not tarrie longe'. Richard would have taken her to his mother but Juliana persuaded him to go without her, saying that she would remain with her father until his mother died, 'which she hath done accordingly'.

Randle Vernon, gentleman, said that four years previously Juliana had had a child and Richard Croxton was the reputed father. Richard denied it and refused to support or maintain it, so Juliana's parents kept the child while it lived. Although Randle had forbidden Richard from entering the house he found them together one night, said 'it would serve Richard right if he gave him as many strokes as he could bear', and ordered him out of the house.

A witness, Marjery Smallwood, said that one night, four years before, Juliana Vernon had knocked on the window of her house and her mother, hearing the knocking, arose and let her in. Juliana said her father had turned her out and asked to stay the night. However, one of Juliana's mother's servants came and said she was to return home, so she immediately left. Marjery said that she had heard there was to be a marriage between Juliana and a Staffordshire man some five years before, but that her father had refused to agree to the marriage; for what reason we are not told.

Jane Buckley, another witness, stated that some three years previously Richard and Juliana were in Cyprian Venables' buttery when Juliana accused Richard of avoiding her company in favour of Elena Highfield's. One source of trouble was the fact that Juliana had already given birth to a child, and while her family tried to lay the blame for this on Richard Croxton, Juliana stated that he was not the father.[4]

It was possible for the man to promise marriage and then take the woman to his house to work as a servant whilst all the time delaying marriage. A good illustration of this type of behaviour comes from Colne in 1605 in a cause concerning breach of contract between Margaret Walker and John Hargreaves. Margaret Walker stated that John Hargreaves of Colne sent James Hargreaves to the house of Ambrose Greenwood in Widdop, Heptonstall, in Yorkshire, where Margaret lived, to request her to go to Lancashire to John Hargreaves' father's house and then 'he wold marrie her'. One Sunday a short time afterwards John Hargreaves went to Heptonstall, and meeting there with Margaret 'so far [did] prevail with her in hope of marrying, she left her friends and came from thence' into Lancashire to the house of James Hargreaves, John's father; here John kept her, 'using her at bedd and bord as his wife for the most part of one whole year then next following'.

Some while later Margaret was anxious to view her property, 'some ground which she took to be hers', so John Hargreaves sent a man with her in his name as husband to Margaret, 'to claim, take hold and keep the possession of the said lands lying in Yorkshire'. Upon marriage a woman's property became that of her husband, hence the eagerness of John Hargreaves to lay his hands upon it. The messenger, we are told, did not

> only enter upon the lands but broke open a door where the goods of the said Margaret were, viz; brass potts and pannes bedding and other ware of material value, the same goods and bedding to the value of £20 more or less . . . and the same goods did take away and were brought by them . . . to the house of John Hargreaves where the same or some of them remain unto this day . . . all this under the cloke of the said marriage.

On a later occasion when the two of them went to Widdop, John '[did] use the said Margaret in all respects as his wife'.

Isabel Loundes, wife of Henry Loundes, a witness in the cause, said that John brought Margaret from Yorkshire to his father's house, but 'whether to be a servant or to what other purpose or end she knows not'. Nicholas Hargreaves, John's brother, '[did] bydd Margaret fetch playne household stuffe of hers thither & she did bring thereupon playne bedding, wood vessells & other things which she thinks are in the house there yet but what value she cannot depose'. Another witness, Laurence Manckinowles of Colne, said that John Hargreaves confessed to him as constable that he 'had of the same Margaret ten shillings in money and likewise divers other things of hers in sundry places of the house which he would have had the constables take away'. John Hargreaves then added if she 'will go to her friends & bring him fourtye markes he wold marry her', to which Manckinowles replied, 'if she bring twenty pounds you shall marry her'. John Hargreaves confirmed that in this matter he would be ruled by Manckinowles decision. Two of John Hargreaves' father's servants were sent to Yorkshire to collect Margaret's goods but when they returned one had his head broken. He believed that John Hargreaves brought Margaret to be his father's servant.

Edward Stevenson, a hired servant to Nicholas Hargreaves who worked in the loom shop and was another witness, said that Margaret and John lived in the house together and 'Laye in several chambers there being a partition of cords between and two doors for passage from the one to the other', but he did not know if they shared the same bed. He knew nothing of any sum of money that John received from her but he heard him say that, 'whatsoever he owed he either had or wolde pay her'. He also told how one day, when he was in the loom shop, 'John entered the shop where Margaret was, having in his hands a purse, and saying to Margaret, "here is thy purse and all that I owe thee is in it"' and she refused to take it but added that Stevenson slept in one of her blankets. When John offered the purse to Margaret she gave it back and would not received it, at which John took her in his arms; then 'a boy came with a hand cuggell & struck the same Margaret either upon the head or shoulders and shortly after she complained of head ache'. He also heard Nicholas Hargreaves say to her, 'what wages I owe thee I will pay thee' and offered her money, which she refused, saying, 'I came thither for an other interest and purpose viz; marriage'.

It is certain that some violence was used towards Margaret, as Martyn Dyckson, another witness, stated that 'whether she was beaten, strucken or violently put forth of the house or not he knoweth not', but he found her crying in the fields near the house one day about Whitsuntide or midsummer. John Hargreaves was also there with his father, who wondered whether she either intended to burn his house or make away with herself. He then urged John Hargreaves to marry Margaret as he had done on other occasions. Not long after this event Sir Christopher Nuttall, clerk, was at Hargreaves' house when Dyckson found Margaret in a stable there, and since he was the constable he 'took her by the arm until she had spoken with Sir Christopher Nuttall who did tell Hargreaves that if he had made her any promise of marriage he must perform the same'. Later he found Margaret in a 'close near the foresaid house sitting amongst certain owlers and bushes in the cold'. The witness then turned to John and said 'John this will not doe – you must marry her'.

The result of this cause is in some doubt for no sentence has survived to indicate if the order was obeyed, but knowing the force of the law in these disputes, John Hargreaves would have found it difficult, if not impossible, to refuse to marry her.[5] The cause has been dealt with in depth as an excellent example of what could happen under certain conditions when a promise to marry had been given.

A contract to marry was not always fulfilled with the eagerness with which it was agreed. At Holt in 1600, Anne Powell brought a suit against John Bathoe, claiming that in 1598–9 and again in 1600 he had promised by 'verba de presenti' to marry her. Anne made the like promise to John, 'and gave their hands either to other upon the same'. Since handfasting, or contracting to marry, meant that in the sight of the community they were married, sexual relations were allowed, so it is no surprise to find that John 'did allow the said Anne to commit fornication with him, after he made promise to marry Anne and did beget her with child'. When John realized that Anne was pregnant he began to deny any agreement to marry her, whereupon her father, John, and some of their friends of both sides, met together and had a conference concerning the marriage. The upshot of the conference was that John was to marry Anne before midsummer.

Anne's father agreed to give £16 as Anne's dowry to John, of which £8 was to be handed over on the wedding day and a further £8 at Michaelmas. John did receive part of the first sum, £4, but it is clear from the libel that Anne's father had a difficult task to raise the money, for he 'sold his kyne and made other hard shifts to provide & make ready the sum of eight pounds which was to be paid on the wedding day'. The court enforced the contract as legally binding, but John attempted to avoid honouring it since he would then have a child to keep and would be liable to face a court presentment on the grounds of ante-nuptial fornication.[6]

An act of fornication could cause a contract to fail. In 1672, John Pickford of Adlington, in Prestbury parish, who was the owner of 'great estate', sought the hand of Mary Higginbotham in marriage. He appeared to have a rival, however, one John Cotterill. When John Pickford learned of this he ceased to pursue his affection to Mary and on one occasion stated that 'Mary Higginbotham would never have any child let whosoever will marry her and that he would undertake to keep all the children begotten on her body for two pence'. Since the above words were spoken in the presence of witnesses, Pickford meant that Mary Higginbotham had committed fornication with his rival John Cotterill or some other person. Mary, anxious not to lose a wealthy husband, tried to enforce the contract, but failed because of fornication with another person.[7]

A delayed marriage licence following a contract could and did create trouble. Margaret Beesley of Ingalhead chapel in Broughton, a widow, was annoyed by some scandalous words said to have been spoken against her by Hugh Barrow, vicar of Lancaster and rural dean of Amounderness, and Thomas Jepson, the parish clerk, to the effect that she had married or 'layne with' George Grayson of Fulwood in an alehouse in Preston. Hugh Barrow, by virtue of his office, had issued a licence to John Wilkinson, vicar of Lytham, to marry George Grayson and Margaret Beesley. Unfortunately, Barrow had cited Margaret to the correction court for ante-nuptial fornication with Grayson and imposed a public penance for her to perform on three consecutive Sundays in the churches of Preston, Garstang, and Lancaster. Margaret, being a resourceful woman, brought a suit against Barrow for false accusation.

It appears that George Grayson and Margaret Beesley were contracted some three months prior to the marriage. Margaret paid for the licence but some of her relatives removed the licence from George's breeches which prevented the marriage being solemnized. Margaret paid for a second licence and they were married in widow Swanley's alehouse at Ashton Bank on 7 April; they had visited the house three times that week to arrange a private marriage.

John Wilkinson confirmed that he had married them in the house of Alexander Swansey during canonical hours and Swansey was one of the witnesses. Margaret, however, admitted that she and Grayson slept together after the marriage was contracted and while waiting for the second licence. The penance for ante-nuptial fornication was not lifted.[8]

In the parish of Halifax, in York diocese, matrimonial matters were on much the same lines. In 1637, a child marriage took place at Sowerby between Ruth Fourness, aged 12, and Jeremiah Briggs, aged 13. In the depositions of Fourness, Ruth said that after the marriage they were taken to Richard Briggs', Jeremiah's father's house, but two days later her father came and took her back to Halifax. However, two nights later, when Ruth's father was absent, Briggs, his son, and three friends came

> with drawn swords and pike staves . . . and dragged her from the said father's house . . . and took her to Richard Brigg's house . . . and the two were made to lay together for two days during which . . . nether had any knowledge of each other's body.[9]

Oliver Heywood in his diary records cases where wives were stolen: 'John Mitchel stole away Abraham Walker's daughter and married her Feb.16 she being fifteen years old'.[10] He then refers to a marriage between an old woman and a young man: 'Mr. Shuttleworth of Clitheroe married Mrs Sunderland (78) of Fairweather Green, Bradford, Oct.8. Her husband left her £5,000 in money and £80 in land, he is a wanting man of twenty-four years old'.[11] Oliver Heywood, as a Presbyterian, was highly critical of the low moral and sexual standards in the parish of Halifax, where he remarked that there was an increase in fornication and bastardy, 'and many to their great shame do marry'. Where morals were concerned, conditions to the east of the Pennines were comparable to those on the west.

Chapter Twelve

CLANDESTINE MARRIAGES AND DIVORCE

It was by no means unusual for couples considering marriage to arrange for it to be clandestine. This practice was quite common in Chester diocese, especially in the archdeaconry of Richmond, where there were facilities easily available. Such marriages were entered into to avoid the objections of parents, or to conceal the fact that the bride was pregnant, an event that could easily lead to a presentment charge of ante-nuptial fornication, or to avoid the restriction laid down in the Table of Kindred and Affinity in the Prayer Book.

In the archdeaconry of Richmond there was a peculiar jurisdiction where such marriages could be solemnized. This was at Middleham, a collegiate church founded by Richard III to mark his marriage to Lady Anne Neville. Archbishop Rotherham, by a charter of 1481, exempted the church from all archiepiscopal, metropolitical, and other ecclesiastical jurisdiction. The status of the college was finally confirmed by a bull of Pope Sixtus IV. In the seventeenth century the dean was successful in maintaining his right to solemnize matrimony without banns first being called or licence obtained; this right lasted until ended by Hardwick's Marriage Act.[1]

After 1660 there was a second convenient church in which to marry on the same basis as at Middleham, and that was the manorial peculiar of Arkengarthdale, where the curate claimed the right to marry without banns asked or licence obtained.[2]

Sometimes an obliging cleric would solemnize a marriage for a good fee, and in 1684 Richard Bainbridge, vicar of Bedale, solemnized such marriages on the basis of having a dispensation from the dean and chapter of York granted during a 'sede Vacante'.[3]

Marriages by night were not unknown, and in the remote chapels and parishes they were not easy to detect. In 1665, 'Christopher Bates and Lucy Gayles of Spennithorpe, were married in the night time by the Ministry of Mr. Christopher Beverley'.[4] The vicar of Thonton Steward was cited to the Richmond consistory for solemnizing clandestine marriages in 1698 and 1699

> in a dwelling house by candle light in the night time . . .
> betwixt Christopher Tiplady of the parish of Bedale and his
> wife, Francis Hammond and his wife, and several other
> persons . . . before eight of the clocke in the forenoon and in
> the night time without the Consent of Parents or licence
> granted.[5]

In 1690, William Dunbabin of Great Sankey married John Hatton of Winwick to Ellen Tickle in a private house in Warrington without banns or licence. Dunbabin confessed that he had married the couple in violation of the canons of the church, 'for which he is heartily sorry and submits himself to the Law and Judgement and Mercy of the Court'. A penance was imposed upon Dunbabin.[6]

A clandestine marriage in which a considerable amount of money changed hands in alleged fees was solemnized in May 1637. James Crickloe of Clapham married Edmund Bentham and Jane, his wife, without banns being asked or a licence obtained. Crickloe alleged that he had a licence from the rural dean of Kirby Lonsdale and received 16s. in fees from Bentham. He agreed that if Bentham was presented for a clandestine marriage and excommunicated, he would receive a dismissal. Bentham was excommunicated and the vicar failed to get a dismissal. In the end, Bentham returned the sentence of excommunication for his marriage, was denounced in church, and was forced to obtain his own absolution. In all, Crickloe had received £6.8s. from Bentham to keep the matter quiet, but to no avail.[7]

An interesting clandestine marriage took place in 1628 at Rossett Green chapel and was obviously a hastily arranged one. Some time earlier, John Bruen and Matilda Smith had exchanged tokens in sign of a contract and agreed to marry. The arrangements were that 'John was to goe to the Colepit beyond Chester and willed her to meet . . . and stay for him & bee ready in a lane that leads towards Pulford & Rossith Gogh'. In the meantime he would be driving a cart and cattle and when he had sent them on their way he would come to Matilda to ride with her to Rossett Green chapel and there be married.

It is clear that the parties were afraid of John's mother, because John refused to allow a friend of Matilda to act as a witness 'for fear that she would disclose the marriage which he wanted keeping from his mother'. John Evans, the curate, was found in the Red Lyon alehouse and a request was sent for him to come and marry the couple. Since there was no one to give the woman away to her husband, John Evans sent for his son, Hugh, a boy, who gave her away. The couple were without a wedding ring so a message was sent across the road to the Red Lyon for the loan of one. After the ceremony the couple consummated the marriage and Evans went back to the alehouse where he '[did] bragg and affirm what money he had gotten', for they had paid him well. Francis Griffiths reported the event in the alehouse and, when questioned, Evans stated that he could not (conveniently) remember if he had married them but that 'he did marry two young folks'.[8]

James Finch had discovered that Jennett Mell had desirable property and so did John Barnes. He was angry when he discovered that Finch and Robert Waring had colluded to obtain the services of Edward Tempest, curate of Holland, to marry Finch and Mell in a private house, and brought a suit against Finch and Waring.[9]

In two cases the office acted when the couples were presented at the visitation. In 1613, Edward Birtles had married Maria Jackson in George Shrigley's alehouse, and in 1669, Charles Whalley of Christleton had married Mary Parlington in a private house.[11] They were penanced for an irregular marriage and had to pay fees to have the marriage regularized. George Brook, curate of Sephton, was presented by the churchwardens for marrying John Tarbock to Ann Morton without banns being called.[12] In 1690, James Bagdall, the schoolmaster of Winwick, confessed that he had married Joseph Lawton to Jane Thelwall in the schoolhouse without banns or licence. He had a public penance to perform.[13]

Problems could arise concerning the relationship of couples intending to marry. The Church prohibited any sexual intercourse between persons who had a close relationship either by blood or through spouse kinship, but it was not regarded as a secular offence by the State. Christian teaching, based on Genesis 2:24, that a man and his wife became one flesh, had extended relationships by affinity into the same importance as consanguinity. Those who were literate were expected to know the Table of Kindred and Affinity printed at the end of the Prayer Book. The church regarded cohabitation by those closely related as incest, since it presumed sexual intercourse.

Dr A. MacFarlane, dealing with the matter of marital and social relationships in seventeenth-century England,[14] suggests that the common people did not regard incest with any horror and that it seems to have been entirely absent in Tudor and Stuart England. However, in Chester diocese there are cases of incest between fathers and daughters. On the whole incestuous marriages seem to have met with little disapproval outside the church. Canon law forbade marriages between first and second cousins because the Church of England considered such marriages inadvisable on genetic grounds, but civil law accepted marriage of first cousins. There is no evidence in the Chester consistory court files that incest led to the birth of diseased children or to a lack of male heirs.

In 1692, when John Withnell of Euxton, in the parish of Leyland, died, his widow Elizabeth married his brother Thomas Withnell, whereupon he was cited in court and penanced for his act of incest.[15] In the same year, Sarah Ryley of Accrington committed incest with John Ryley, son of Dennis and her stepson. In 1693 she was ordered to perform a public penance 'to stand at the cross in Blackburn on market day in October with a notice back and front, "For Incest with my Husband's son" and on the 19th November in Altham Chapel'.[16]

An intriguing cause involving incest is one from Whitegate in 1669 between William and Dorothy Darlington, whose marriage broke down after six months. Ellen, wife of Richard Birtwisle, said in evidence that a year before, John Evans the carrier had visited Richard Birtwisle's house where he lodged a few nights. During his visit he told the Birtwisles that the previous August he had lodged at Dorothy Darlington's who had informed him that 'she was not well and gave him her water to goe to some doctor with it'. Evans took it to Mr Minshall of Stoake, telling him that the water was that of his own wife and not Dorothy's. Dr Minshall told him that the woman 'was with child and had a wash in her back'. Evans later took the same water to Dr Walley of Nantwich who told him the same and gave him a plaster for her back. Evans said that the plaster 'gave her ease and she soon sent to him that she was with child and laid him down a bagg of twenty shillings in money on the table and told him to take what he wanted if he would be true to her'. Another witness, Margaret Minshall, said that some eighteen months after Dorothy Darlington and her husband had parted she was conversing with Dorothy who told her a secret, namely that 'she had borne one child to her father before she was married and that she was with childe to him again'. At that point Margaret said she hesitated and added that 'it was got away'. There was, it seems, a common assumption that Dorothy, both before and after her marriage, had committed incest and adultery with her father and several other men.

William Richards of Minshall added the further information that a year previously John Evans had lodged with him for a time, and during a conversation had informed him that Dorothy Darlington had sent for him and requested that he would 'stick to her or she was undone'. She had told him that she was pregnant, and trusted that Evans would know a convenient place for her 'to lye in' and have her child. He then rented a room for her in Liverpool and brought clothes and other essential items for her some 'two or three times'. Evidently he faced some difficulties, as he said 'he had many a doe to get her thither before she was delivered she was so neare her time'.

John Evans admitted that he made all the arrangements for Dorothy to go to Liverpool, and they only arrived just in time as the child was born that same night. In order to protect Dorothy from a charge of bastardy, Evans claimed that the child was his and said that Dorothy was his wife. He arranged for the child to be baptised and the mother to be churched. Dorothy begged him to go with her to Ireland, usually a safe place of refuge in such cases, but he refused. While he remained in Liverpool, both mother and child wanted for nothing as 'he took her fifteen shillings and was given a good suit of clothes and a pair of boots'. Evans admitted that he shared the same bed with Dorothy but 'never touched her'. He then left Liverpool and when he returned to look for her some time later she had gone away.

Anne Carter, widow, sister of William Darlington added further details. She stated that when William married Dorothy they lived together in her father's house at Darnall for six months. Then William noticed 'some grievous behaviour betwixt her and her father so he took a house at Coddington'. William requested Dorothy to go with him but she said she would not leave her father so long as he lived.

William Darlington admitted that 'she has sometimes gone out of bed from him and gone to bed to her father and he had found her in bed with her father at other times', so he left her and never lived with her afterwards. It was evident that since William had parted from her that she had lived a scandalous life with her father and others, and had 'committed the sin of incest with her father & adultery with him and others'. Furthermore, she had one or more children before her marriage to her father, or to 'Thomas Kelsall with whom she was very familiar . . . & doth now live with one Hugh Robinson'. William also admitted that he believed Dorothy had tried to poison him, and 'given him something intended to kill him'.

John Darlington, William's brother, confirmed that William and Dorothy were married some nine years before but only cohabited for six months as she had committed incest both before and after her marriage. For this she had been 'arrained and tryed & found guilty of incest with her father (who is since dead) before the Judges at Chester and they were charged not to live or cohabit any longer together'. Despite this sentence, Dorothy and her father continued to live together until he died. John also added the fact that, six months after the marriage, William had come to see him and had sworn that Dorothy had given him

> A Mease of milkmeate wherein he found a spider . . . and he feared that he was poisoned for having drunk it he swelled very much upon it and afterwards was very sore and broke out in botches & byles [boils] for two or three years afterwards.

He refused to live with her any longer (the divorce case was not heard until nine or ten years after the marriage).[17]

Dorothy was not the only woman to make an attempt to poison her husband. In 1603, in St Mary's parish, Chester, Margaret Burnett, alias Barrowe, had attempted to poison her husband Richard, on the grounds that

[she] not fansieing the said Richard her husband hath made
. . . a possett of milke and drinke in which the said
Margaret had infused or putt in some poyson . . . and gave
the said drinke being so mixed with infection to the said
Richard . . . and presently after drinking felte a great heat
and distemperature in his bodye.

The information given in the libel states that Margaret had said
'she would rather lye with Doggs or swine than lye with the said
Richard', and that a knife had been discovered hidden under the
bedclothes which Margaret had placed there with intent.[18] Unfortunately the remainder of the cause is lost, but following court
practice a public penance would probably have been imposed with
a separation at bed and board.

The case of a dancing master and his relations with his said wife
reveal the problems of marriage to a man whose work took him
to several towns. In 1703 James Watson, described as a 'chor
didasculus' or dancing master, cited his wife, Grace Watson, into
court for adultery and desertion. Ellen Wroe, wife of John Wroe,
a feltmaker, knew the Watsons because she and her husband
cleaned and looked after his house during his absence, 'he
frequently being abroad at other places' – towns in Lancashire and
Cheshire where he conducted dancing schools. James Watson, it
appears, had lived for many years in Manchester before his wife
Grace came to him. The couple were married at All Saints,
Newcastle-upon-Tyne, in 1690. When Grace arrived in
Manchester, James received her with kindness, and maintained
her with clothes and other things 'according to her degree and
condition'. The couple continued to live together for some ten
weeks which ended in January 1701. (The case does not reveal
what happened in the period between their marriage and Grace's
arrival in Manchester.)

However, James Watson discovered one day, and Grace
confessed, that she had 'conveyed as well his as her own cloaths
away, out of drawers where they used to ly and out of the House',
and a quarrel broke out between them. On the next occasion that
James Watson went to conduct one of his schools in Liverpool,
Grace, during his absence, returned to Newcastle with the consent
of James and at his cost. On her departure Grace had said that
'she would trouble him no more & that she would not come again'.

No more was heard of her for some sixteen months when suddenly one Sunday in May 1702 she returned to Manchester 'big with child', to the Angel Inn and the next day she gave birth to a daughter. No one in Manchester believed for one moment that James was the father, for they had not seen each other for sixteen months. When James Watson accused her of adultery before the magistrates, Grace confessed upon oath that the father was not James but one John Garth of Middleham in Yorkshire, and that the child was got in the house of Dr Christopher Faucet in Richmond on Holy Cross Day (14 September), when the fair at Richmond was held. The cause ended in a divorce.[19]

Bigamy was not unknown, as a cause between Jonathon and Elizabeth Butterworth of Rochdale reveals. Jonathon was a soldier in the Thirty Years' War and fought in the Netherlands and Germany as well as other places. On his return to London he was promoted to the rank of Captain by Colonel Ashton. It was stated in evidence that Jonathon Butterworth of St Olave's, Southwark, and Elizabeth Hill, of St Sepulchre's, had been married, according to the parish register, at Islington parish church. They lived together for some time in St John's Street, Clerkenwell, where they consummated the marriage and slept in one bed. They were by no means a poor couple for they 'kept servants'. However, Jonathon had a brother, William, who at the time was living in Bridgerow, London, where he had a drapery business. Jonathon, for some reason that is not clear, wanted his marriage concealed from his brother so he gave instructions to Elizabeth and the servants not to speak of the marriage to his brother.

Some time later Jonathon returned to Rochdale where he met a woman named Elizabeth Simms and obtained a licence from the dean of Manchester to marry her. Two other witnesses, Dr Theodate and his wife, who now lived in Chester, said that the Butterworths 'had dined, supped and had diet, room and bed in their house in London', so the marriage to Elizabeth Simms was bigamous. A prohibition was granted and the cause transferred to the duchy of Lancaster court.[20]

Cruelty between husbands and wives was not a rare event. Marriages that were arranged, and rarely based on love, could break down and lead to court. In 1675, at Dunham on the Hill, Margaret Savage cited her husband for cruelty when he threw 'a skillet and tongs at her' for her adultery with Thomas Stevenson in 'a backhouse or kiln and also in a hen hurdle for gloves and money'. Another man, Ralph Calkin, admitted that he had fornicated with Margaret Savage 'several times and in several places within the township of Dunham and parish of Thornton'. He submitted himself to penance by the court and the Savages were separated.[21]

Margaret Forster of Sandbach cited her husband Laurence Forster for divorce on the grounds of cruelty. After a marriage of five years, Laurence evidently turned against his wife and admitted that he had 'beaten the said Margaret with a bull's pisle and that he hadd got a rodd for her that would not breake' when he used it to beat her, for his behaviour was said to be both savage and cruel. He also made her swear on the Bible not to reveal or disclose that he had beaten her, for he 'did give her such a blow in the eye with his fist that her eye was black & blew a long time after'. Finally he turned her out of the house and sent her back to her father with a letter saying he was willing to be separated from her.[22] Marriages in the seventeenth century could be as shortlived as many in the twentieth.

In a further cause from Sandbach, Grace Royle cited her husband Samuel for 'uttering scandalous words to her'. In return Samuel ordered her to 'goe where she had lived for two nights before'. She went away and Samuel then sent her to her mother-in-law's to be maintained, sending money for her 'maintenance and keeping' and highly satisfied to be rid of such a scolding wife.[23]

The marriage of a young woman to an old man was likely to break down if anything happened to the elderly husband through accident or serious illness. In 1639, Catherine Jepson cited Francis Jepson on grounds that he was impotent. In his defence, Francis said that he was 'now a very aged and impotent man of eighty'. Some years previously he had married Catherine, 'beinge a poore young woman for comfort and help in his old age'. Within the last six months Francis had received 'a great and dangerous hurt in his body by the fall or slipping of a tree', when some of his ribs were broken.

It appears that 'during his weakness and cure', Catherine had neglected him, and had not provided such things as were essential for his recovery. She had not fed him or provided such things as were required for his injuries but instead had 'often & frequently upbraided him with his old age & infirmities & continually abused him & vexed him with churlish, harsh & unquiet language'. The attitude of his wife caused Francis to leave his house in Mobberley, taking with him both his own and his wife's goods. He went to live with one of his sisters until he was cured and his ribs healed. He said that, because of his ill-treatment by Catherine, 'he was in danger of his life', and that compelled him to go to live with Margaret Musadic, his sister, until his cure was completed. Meanwhile he left Catherine his house and lands in Mobberley. He admitted the marriage had not been a success, for she had 'wasted his estate and his goods and by her abuse and neglect forced him to go elsewhere for his own peace and quietness'.

He was not a poor man by the standards of the day for he admitted his personal estate was valued at £1,341 and that he had lands worth 60s. that brought him in rents and service some 30s. annually. The couple lived apart but he provided some maintenance for her.[24]

A petition for divorce on the grounds that her husband was frigid and unable to copulate was presented by Elizabeth Jackson of Runcorn. In evidence it was stated that he suffered from some physical defects:

before any . . . marriage was solemnised betwixt the said Humfrey Johnson and the said Elizabeth Jackson alias Johnson the said Humfrey Johnson was hurt in his privie members or some part of them and was diseased in that parte of his body so that . . . some phisition was consulted touching his cure . . . and did applie some potions or medicines unto him.

Humfrey Johnson and his father, Rafe Johnson, confessed that a

Phisition hath . . . ministered unto the said Humfrey and hath taken out of his yarde a quart of Corrupcion . . . By reason of the Injuries and by other imperfections in the body of the said Humfrey Johnson . . . his privie member is so disproportionable that he is not able and is unfitt to have the Carnall knowledge of any woman's body.

It had been reported that if the marriage could be dissolved, then Elizabeth's parents could marry her to 'a gentleman or a better man'. In the end the marriage was declared null and void since he was unable to consummate the marriage.[25]

The above is an exceptional cause, but beating and desertion provided considerable court business. In 1632, Charles Knott of Tattenhall was cited by his wife, Ann, for turning her out of the house and swearing, 'by the Lord's Blood he would kill her if she returned'.[26] Thomas Hey of Prescott was cited by his wife Elizabeth for 'beating her with a cudgell and turning her out all night',[27] while Robert Martin of Nantwich forced his wife Ellen to, 'sleep naked on a brick floor'.[28]

It was not unusual for severe brutality to be used, as at Marbury in 1640 when Thomas Taylor was accused of beating his wife Sara 'with a shoe on the face and threatened to kill her as well as stabbing her several times with a knife'.[29] Another husband who drew his dagger at his wife was John Higham, when he 'forced her to beg her bread and milk from her neighbours which he has done since 1590'.[30] On the other hand, a woman could retort with violence if provoked, as did Isabella Green of Leigh who struck her husband with a spit and 'thrust it at his breast and threw his doublet on the floor'. The sentence was separation at bed and board.[31]

Most adultery causes ended in divorce as at Walton in 1623 when Elizabeth Fox cited Edward Fox for alleged adultery with Margaret Wright. Roger Watmough, a witness, said that they had indeed committed adultery together for he had seen Margaret Wright and Edward Fox in bed together and 'occupying her as his lawful wife'. Edward told Margaret that he would never leave her and since that time they have 'lived continually together as man and wife'.[32]

It was not unusual to have four persons involved in a matrimonial dispute. In 1681, Henry Roby of Upholland, father of Margaret Roby, cited Robert Halliwell on the grounds that he was 'keeping company with the said Margaret upon a proposal and offer of marriage between them with the knowledge and desire of both parents and neighbours' who understood that a 'marriage would be shortly consummated betwixt you and her'. They drew this conclusion because, as they pointed out to him, having gained her affections, on many occasions and in many places, 'then you perpetrated and fulfilled your evill desire to violate the Virginity of the said Margaret Robie by your carnall knowledge of her

Bodie'. Afterwards he had added to the offence by 'boasting to several persons of the crime to the evil example of others'.

Robert Parr also cited Margaret, for he too was pursuing his interest in her but discovered that she had committed fornication with several men and, what was worse, she was now pregnant. While she was encouraging Parr, Margaret wrote letters to Halliwell asking him to meet her 'at unseasonable hours in secret places, and used several ways and endeavoured to entrap & ensnare him using uncivil & wanton gestures & actions to him, she being young'.[33] The offenders were condemned in costs and penanced.

A most interesting divorce cause arose in Chester in February 1625 involving quite a number of the citizens of varying ranks in society, and it throws light on the social life of Chester. The cause concerned the activities of Elizabeth Case of Bridge Street, Chester, whose husband, Thomas, wished to divorce her for her drunkenness and other misdemeanours with young men. The first witness was Christopher Walker, aged 25, who stated that in 1624 he and Edward Johns went to the tavern of Henry Trafford to seek John Mottram whom they found sitting there. They had ordered a 'quart of beare' when Elizabeth Case came in to their company so Christopher Walker invited her to have a drink. She accepted and promptly sat down with the three men. Later the three agreed to go and drink a pint of wine, and 'they did goe to Samuel Robinson's, Lane End and there did drink only one pynt of wyne'. Later the three men decided to go to the Swan in Foregate Street, a tavern kept by Thomas Jones, asking Elizabeth to accompany them. She indicated that she would follow them and come in 'to Enquire for her husband and saie she had been paying 5li for Leather'. This she did, affirming that she had been paying for leather, whereupon the rest of the party asked her to join them and drink; she promptly accepted and remained an hour with them.

Edward Johns, a sheerman of St Martin's parish, aged 26, confirmed that he and Walker went to Henry Trafford's house to find John Mottram whom they found there. They sat down beside him and 'called for a cuppe of beare'. When Elizabeth Case came in they asked her to drink with them to which she agreed and remained sitting with them as long as they remained in the house. When Walker decided to go to the Swan, Elizabeth refused to accompany them but said, rather, that she would follow and come in declaring that she had been to the Tanners to pay for leather and that 'they should entreate her to sit down'. All went according to plan and she sat with them drinking 'until tenn of the clocke in the evening', and although she had consumed a quantity of drink 'did speak directly and did goe of herself', meaning she was able to walk unassisted.

Another witness, Margaret, the wife of Thomas Knowsley, aged 38, had some derogatory comments to make about the Tavern of Henry Trafford. She said she had heard that it is a place where

disordered Company do meet and hath heard evill and scandalous speeches given forth by divers against Henry Trafford's wife . . . and that she for some faults and misdemeanours had been sent to the Northgate by the Mayor or officers of the Cittie of Chester.

The Northgate was the city prison. When she had been at Trafford's house she saw Elizabeth Case 'very much distempered with drink who carried herself very idely'. Of late Elizabeth had lived in St Peter's parish.

On another occasion, when the wife of Thomas Tyas was sick, Margaret together with the wives of William Jones, Robert Daniels, Roger Wilkinson, and others were attending to Mrs Tyas when she saw Elizabeth Case come into the room 'very much distempered with drink'. When she had finished washing Mrs Tyas's hands, Elizabeth immediately drank up the same water. It was also alleged that Thomas Case had been 'unthrifty and neglected his trade for some time' (he was a shoemaker). Further it was said to be common knowledge that Thomas Case and his wife fought and beat each other.

Elizabeth Garfield, wife of John, aged 29, confirmed that Mrs Tyas had told her that Elizabeth Case was 'fowlie distempered with drink at her husband's house' during the time she was ill. One evening, one or both of her maids brought her back to Garfield's house about ten at night when the Garfields were in bed. Elizabeth stayed the night and left early next morning, but when Elizabeth Garfield went to the room where Elizabeth had slept she found it 'in a filthy Manner defiled by Castinge [up] or Spueinge', which Elizabeth Case confessed was her doing.

Thomas Cowper, shoemaker of St Bridget's parish, aged 33,

confirmed the reports about Henry Trafford's wife and said that one day he and John Minshall were on their way to Thomas Jones' house when they met with Elizabeth Case, 'who did there drinke a quart or two of beare with them'. She left them there but later when the two men were walking up the Row, Cowper saw her in her husband's shop. She called them over and asked if they would 'have or take anything', meaning a drink. They replied that they would do either so they went to the tavern of William Conwaie where Elizabeth came to them. After two or three pints of wine had been drunk, Elizabeth left them. The same evening they again met Elizabeth who asked where they were going, to which they replied, 'to Thomas Percivall's Taverne'. Later she joined them where they drank two or three quarts of wine and sat drinking until eleven o'clock, by which time Elizabeth was 'somewhat spent in drinke'. Cowper offered to take her home, but she refused saying 'she scorned to be brought home'. However, Cowper followed her to the Lane where he met Thomas Case who asked if he had been with his wife. When he replied in the affirmative, Case requested him to call and see what state she was in. He entered and found her sitting on a stool in the house, 'being distempered in drinke', and having hurt her face, presumably having fallen.

Cowper also added that Thomas Jones reported that John Crewe told him that Thomas Myles' son had committed adultery with Elizabeth. Meanwhile he was convinced that reports about Elizabeth were true, for he had played at tables (a version of backgammon) with Case in alehouses and taverns.

John Minshall, ironmonger, aged 29, was then called to give evidence and he said that three years before, 'come St Gregories daie' (3 September), while he and Cowper were at Thomas Jones's to have a drink with him, Elizabeth Case came in, 'being sent for by Thomas Jones'. She drank a cup of beer and left. Later passing up The Row, where Elizabeth was in her husband's shop, she asked them if they would take a pint of wine but they replied that they were on their way to William Conwaie's tavern and if she came she could drink with them. Some fifteen minutes later she arrived and spent two hours with them playing at 'Shovel Board'.[34] They themselves left shortly after she had left and went towards Thomas Percival's tavern, but going along The Row they met Elizabeth. Since she had bought them a pint of wine at

Conwaie's they though it only right to invite her to come to them at Thomas Percival's. Elizabeth said that as soon as she had closed the shop she would come to them. An hour later she came and then they drank 'a quart or two of wyne'. She remained with them some two hours until ten in the evening by which time 'she was overseen in drink for she was merry & went her waie herself'. When she arrived home Thomas had locked her out.

At this point in the hearing, the city watchmen were called in to give evidence. One, Samuel Baswell, a silkweaver aged 44, of St Oswald's parish, said about Henry Trafford's house that it 'is very much suspected to entertain bad companie and those persons that are of unhonest behaviour and they doe keep . . . disorder in the nyght time'. Samuel, as one of the watch, had been given the charge, with the rest of the watch, over the same house but could not discover any disorder. On one occasion during the night, he and the rest of the watch met Henry Trafford and his wife, accompanied by others. When the watch demanded to know who they were, they immediately began to fight them, whereupon Henry Trafford's wife, one other woman who was a stranger, and Mr Thomas Hartley were 'arrested and taken to the Northgate and the time they were taken was two or three in the morning'.

Samuel and other members of the watch had been standing at the Cross in Chester 'tending the watch' one night during the previous year, when at about eleven at night Elizabeth Case came up Bridge Street towards them. They demanded to know who she was, although they knew her, and requested her to go home for 'she had drunk too much and did talk idely'. Samuel recalled a charge given to the watch by Peter Drinkwater, the late mayor of Chester, that if Elizabeth Case was taken 'abroad at any inconvenient tyme she should be brought to the Northgate'. To his knowledge she had never been arrested nor had he heard of her drunkenness or that she kept bad company.

Another member of the watch, Edward Roberts, a butcher aged 33, said that during the previous Christmas he was a constable going on ward with the deputy alderman and others when, passing near Martin Ashe in Chester, they met with one Hampton and demanded what business he had there at that time of night, for it was about ten or eleven. Hampton replied that he was going about his master's business, but they saw Elizabeth Case walking along the opposite side of the street, and suspecting there would be some suspicious dealings between Hampton and Case he followed them into The Row where Elizabeth and Hampton walked hand-in-hand along The Row until they came The Lane. Hampton stayed there and Elizabeth went to her house in The Lane. Roberts remained to see whether Elizabeth would return to Hampton but after thirty minutes Hampton left, and although Roberts watched for a further thirty minutes, neither Elizabeth or Hampton returned.

On another occasion he and Richard Knee, also a constable, were approaching the door of Thomas Case's house when Elizabeth came out 'in a very distracted humor', and told them there was someone in her chamber for 'they had put their hand to the bed in which she lay and that one of them that was in the Chamber counterfeited his [i.e. her husband's] voice'. Elizabeth then asked Knee to light a candle, so Roberts waited at the door with Elizabeth until the candle arrived. When they entered the room with the candle they found only Thomas Case present.

Richard Shaw, a silkweaver aged 55, of Holy Trinity parish, said he had seen Elizabeth Case come out of Henry Trafford's alehouse where she confessed she had been merry in the house during the night and also at other times. Shaw affirmed that he had heard 'that the said Trafford's house to be a suspected house for to entertain those that give themselves to women & drinking'. Indeed he knew that Margaret Trafford had been in the Northgate for misdemeanours committed in the night time.

One Saturday night during the previous Christmas, Elizabeth was at his house at about seven o'clock. Later in the evening, hearing 'some Russellinge in the kitchen he went to see who it was'. There was neither light nor fire in the kitchen so he called out to ask who was there. One of those present, Peter Taylor, said, 'there is no bodie here but Bessie and I' (meaning Elizabeth Case). Shaw said that she would not get away with it, sent for her husband, and promptly evicted them from the kitchen. The two went out through the back of the house towards his garden, but there was a door in the wall of the garden that led into the street, so he made Elizabeth come after him and he turned her out into the street about 'nine of the clock in the night'.

Earlier that same evening, one Widow Isecca came into the house and, seeing Elizabeth, accused her of adultery, saying 'god save you Mistress Case you that occupied with three men and plaie or laye with the fourth at night. Ah! you whore that put your husbands shirt on while your smock was washing' (the remainder of the document is damaged and torn away). Shaw had also heard the report that Elizabeth had been drunk with four persons: 'the Night Bellman was one, Elizabeth Case's husband another and Peter Taylor and his wife the others, with more names that he cannot specifie'. He pleaded inability to distinguish between fame and report, saying: 'a fame is either a good or evill report & saith that he cannot distinguish between report and fame & saith for a Rumor that he doth think the same to be a more noted and publick report.'

Robert Minshall, tallow chandler of St Oswald's parish, aged 39, said he had heard reports that Henry Trafford's was a disorderly house but he did not know the place. However, one day during the last half year, he had been with Arthur Holland drinking in Widow Basand's house when Elizabeth Case coincidentally entered and, as she came in, 'she did flirt her fingers at this witness and the rest saying, "I care not for thee" or "I care for thee" with such idle gestures'. He was uncertain whether Elizabeth was drunk or not for she 'did speak and walk directly and that was as much as he saw'.

Thomas Jones, a clothworker aged 42, said he heard that Elizabeth Case 'as well by daie as by night hath comforted herself with the wife of Henry Trafford and there hath been Carowsinge and Swaggeringe with companie in the same house'. He had also heard that Margaret Trafford was suspected for 'her ill behaviour for the night and daie time' and was for this committed to the Northgate. Jones appears to have been well versed in the gossip associated with the case. He had heard that Edward Johns and Christopher Walker confessed that Elizabeth Case persuaded them to enter the alehouse first and she would follow making an excuse that she had been paying money at the tanners for her husband. Then, as they both afterwards confessed to Thomas Jones, 'they did then make her foule drunk'. More than this, Jones had a lodger, one Thomas Myles, who one night went to bed as usual but arose later and went out to meet John Crewe and the two went together to Thomas Case's house. When they arrived at the door together, Elizabeth refused to allow Myles to enter so they continued to the Lane end. Myles himself then went down to the third house, and since Crewe did not see him return went back home and later said that 'about three or four of the clock in the morning, the said Thomas Myles returned to the said John Crewe's house and told him that . . . he had dealings with the said Elizabeth Case saying he occupied her twice with a hoult & once after'. When he went to Myles's room he found him in the bed in which he first slept. Jones could affirm that Elizabeth was frequently drunk.

The last witness was John Crewe, the alebrewer of St Michael's parish, aged 41, who knew all the reports about the state of Henry Trafford's house and how Elizabeth Case was often in the company of Thomas Hutton in the same house. Crewe said that one day the previous year Thomas Myles, who had previously lodged at Thomas Jones's, came one night in his stockings and, knocking at his back door, asked him to lend him a pair of pantofles (slippers) and 'goe with him to the door of Thomas Case in the night. . . . Some two hours and a half later Thomas Myles came back where he continued till morning'. Myles confessed to John Crewe that 'he had had that night the use of the body of Elizabeth Case twice or thrice' saying he 'had tickled her twice with a holt & once after' and then returned to Thomas Jones's house from where he first came. John Crewe, for all that he was a brewer, had never heard of the drunkenness of Elizabeth Case until Thomas Cowper confessed she was drunk at his house.

In the end Thomas and Elizabeth Case were separated at 'bed and board' or, in effect, divorced.[35]

This cause has been treated at some length for it is a good example of the way in which evidence was collected and heard in the consistory. It also throws light on the artisan class in the city. Naturally the evidence which was taken down verbatim contains a great deal of circumlocution and repetition, but by careful analysis it is possible to extract a coherent account. The characters in this divorce drama are all from the artisan and lower-middle range of Chester society. Judging from other causes, many Chester alehouses, as elsewhere, were pretty rough places where adultery and fornication often occurred. The corporation disliked the reputation these places brought to Chester, so attempts were made from time to time to impose some discipline by confining offenders in the Northgate, the city prison. But the native cunning of many offenders made it most difficult for the authorities to impose full control on society in the towns and many rural parishes.

Part 5

SOCIETY AND THE CHURCH COURTS

Chapter Thirteen

THE ATTITUDES
OF SOCIETY

It is clear from the preceding causes that church courts were unpopular, and what made them unpopular was their attempt to enforce moral standards of conduct. When Robert Harrison proposed their abolition in 1604, Stoughton recommended that they should become secular courts, that civil lawyers be appointed to hear and determine ecclesiastical causes, and that no officers of these courts ought to have the right to excommunicate anyone.[1] From the mid-sixteenth century there was a steady increase in correction business dealt with by the church courts, a move that continued into the seventeenth century.

This arose from the desire of central government to enforce some of the wider aspects of the Reformation. Basically, the view was that church courts ought to be concerned with ensuring that people attended church each Sunday and feast day, and to enforce religious conformity, morality, and discipline upon the members of the Anglican Church. However, by the late Middle Ages, and even earlier, the church courts gave attention to sexual morality, drunkenness, indecent behaviour in church, and defamation.[2] According to Dr J.A. Sharpe, the inclusion of these offences as indictable before a church court meant that the State desired, through the Established Church, to regulate and to some extent control the lives of those whom it rules from cradle to grave.[3]

Prosecution of a cause in either the archdeacon's or the consistory courts were, by and large, the result of pressure from below, for the majority of actions were brought by a person or persons offended against. Their effectiveness and success depended entirely upon the willingness of neighbours in a parish to mind each other's business. Detailed study of the depositions quoted in the early pages of this study reveal that neighbours were quite willing to mind each other's business and to report, often with much repetition and circumlocution, what they had seen. It was actions of this kind that led to the phrase 'common fame and report' being part of the heading of the libel of charges. Certainly, dismay was felt by many respectable parishioners at instances of sexual misconduct and the willingness of others to report the matter. So the courts were not repressive, but depended entirely upon the active co-operation of people at large.

Between 1561 and 1640, the church courts had the support of High Commission and Star Chamber, but it is difficult to assess with any accuracy the extent to which the High Commission at York interfered in the archdeaconry of Richmond. One thing is clear, that the Chester High Commission was by no means as efficient as the court at York. The evidence at present available reveals that causes and appeals from Richmond were heard at York and also obstinate causes from Chester, such as that from West Kirby.[4] Comparing the numbers of persons cited to appear at York with the numbers that actually appeared before the High Commission indicates that its full authority never penetrated the remote deaneries of Kendal, Copeland, and Furness.

A cause heard before the Durham High Commission in 1632 records a Durham man who was reported to have described the church courts in this manner: 'You officers have gotten a trick to call many poor men into your courts and . . . to excommunicate them. . . . Their courts are but bawdy courts and merely to get money for themselves'.[5] Christopher Hill also quotes references to the use of the term 'bawdy court' by an Aylesbury lady in 1634 and some Cambridge litigants in 1639.[6]

It was not entirely due to Puritans that there was opposition to church courts. This is illustrated by a play put on at the Red Bull in 1639 which 'scandalised and libelled the whole profession of proctors belonging to the Court of Probate'.[7] Dr Marchant has pointed out how ineffective the church courts were at ferreting out Puritans in York diocese because they had no detective force at their disposal. If churchwardens and individuals did not present or bring a cause, then the courts had to rely on accidental information or mere rumour.[8] Overall, the impression gained is that processes in the church courts were an irritant for the industrious sorts of people, with time-wasting and costs involved that were totally out of relation to the suit in dispute. It was the ineffectiveness of courts that added to the costs, especially in those causes concerning tithes, which have not been covered in this study since they properly belong to the economic field.[9]

The existence of two types of court, one dealing with civil and criminal law and the other with canon law as it affected the Church, gave rise to endless possibilities of counter-pleading. It was inevitable that at some stage the situation would have to be clarified and rationalized. The common law judges claimed to have sole jurisdiction in cases that were connected with the rights of property. Such cases involved the execution of a will, matrimonial causes, right to present to a benefice, a charge of simony, payment of tithes, church rates, and even the ownership of a pew. Cases could be removed from the church to the common law courts either by a writ of *quare impedit* or the issue of a writ of prohibition by common law judges.[10]

By the early years of the reign of James I, the common law courts were becoming increasingly independent of royal control, yet at the same time the church courts were becoming more amenable to it. Hence prohibition, originally used to support royal policy, was now used to oppose it. No matter how self-interested lawyers may have been, they were not alone in wanting to remove some kinds of legal business from the control of both Church and Crown, whose policy seemed to be increasingly out of touch with the commercial spirit of the age. The propertied classes in the country had the same aims as the commercial interests, so an alliance was forged between the House of Commons, the Puritans, and common lawyers. Meanwhile, the church courts slowly declined in effectiveness after 1639 for the simple reason that they had lost the co-operation of the laity.

On 9 October 1646 Episcopacy was abolished and it was declared that 'all issues triable by the ordinary or bishop shall be tried by jury in the usual course'.[11] Alongside this went the transfer of matrimonial and divorce causes to quarter-sessions or the assizes, which was 'a considerable judicial and social revolution'.

The Commonwealth failed to establish a Presbyterian style of discipline so the matters under this heading were left to be decided by the uncontrolled consciences of individuals, since the Justices of the Peace did not seek to become or act as residuary legatees of the church courts. So sin was now distinguished from crime, a fact which, according to Christopher Hill, accelerated an intellectual and moral revolution which church courts had previously retarded.[12]

What had taken place during the Protectorate could not be undone. When the Church was restored along with the monarchy in 1660, a clause was inserted into the Act of Uniformity that neither 'this act nor anything in it be construed to abridge or diminish the King's supremacy in ecclesiastical matters.[13] So for the future, prohibition ceased to be the weapon that it had been before 1640. The divine right of the church courts had gone, and prohibition became the device for giving effect to the overriding control and supervision of the canon law judiciary by the common law judges. Political developments after 1662 eventually changed the supremacy of the king over the Church into the supremacy of Parliament over both king and Church. The property-owners who were represented in Parliament considered this to be a great liberation. Hence, by 1700, church courts were becoming ineffective for they were unable to compel churchwardens to present offenders, and disputes heard in the consistory became increasingly concerned with tithes, pews, faculties, and matrimony.

Prior to the Civil War, the Chester consistory was beginning to hear fewer causes concerning working on the Sabbath and holy days, and after 1660 the court ceased dealing with them completely. One pre-Civil-War cause came from Tarvin, where John and Ralph Wright were cited for following their secular work on Sundays and festivals.[14] Ten alebrewers in Chester were cited in 1613 for 'making malt, brewing and carrying ale on the feasts of the Ascension, St John the Baptist, St Peter, St James, St Bartholomew, St Matthew, St Luke, Sts Simon & Jude and on All Saints and not attending church on these days'.[15] Even Alderman Richard Partington, tailor, was cited for employing his servants and apprentices at secular work on Sundays.[16] At Rochdale three men were cited: Michael Butterworth for opening his alehouse in time of divine service and cutting his timber in church; Charles Stott who spent Sunday mending his barn doors; and Ralph Holt for 'mending his cloth and heeling his stockings or hose on Sundays'.[17]

The court could not imprison offenders, though prior to 1640 it had the support of the prerogative courts in this matter, so excommunication, or imposition of a public penance or correction, were the chief weapons. Originally, excommunication was the exclusion of an offending individual from any participation in the rites and ceremonies which bound the community together, a very ancient practice, which according to R. Hill predates Christianity.[18]

There were two degrees of excommunication, major and minor. Minor excommunication involved exclusion from the Eucharist, marriage, and attending divine service. The sentence of minor excommunication was passed against those who were contumacious – those who refused to appear in court following a citation of 'viis et modis' (ways and means). Major excommunication was reserved for cases of assaults in church or churchyard, for marriages in private houses or taverns, and for such irreligious acts as brawling over seats or fighting in church. These cases were regarded by the church as far more offensive than they appeared to the layman. Those who were convicted were placed under severe legal and social disabilities, for they were unable to conduct suits in secular courts, or be buried in consecrated ground, and in theory were excluded from all contact with the faithful.

An illustration of attitudes towards excommunication is revealed in a case from Manfield in 1667. The vicar had refused to admit the Cockerell family to communion on the grounds that 'they were open and notorious evil livers'. None of the family had communicated at Easter and the court requested information as to why they were refused communion. In his reply, the vicar stated that

> they are known to be open and notorious ill livers, full of
> malice & hatred both towards me and many of their
> neighbours & are persons who Seldome come to church,
> never give in their names before communion . . . and are
> grown obstinate in their naughtyness.[19]

Upon further appearance in court they were given a public penance to perform in their parish church in January 1668. This had little effect, for they were cited to appear in 1675 for the same offence, and having ignored the citation, were excommunicated.[20]

According to the third rubric in the Order for Holy Communion it is stated that if the curate refuses to admit any person to Holy Communion he is obliged to give an account to the bishop within fourteen days, and the bishop 'shall proceed against the offending person according to the Canon'. The Richmond consistory, as the bishop's court, was entitled to request details as to their exclusion.

A study of the court act books reveals that excommunications must have flown round the diocese like sparks from a catherine wheel. It is easy to condemn the church courts for using the weapon of excommunication indiscriminately, which in the long term brought discredit to the Church, and in time seriously weakened the respect of the laity for their parish clergy.[21]

The only alternative to excommunication was the imposition of a penance as a standard method of punishment. In Essex thousands performed penances over the years, as they did in York and Chester dioceses.[22] Others were allowed to compurgate or purge their offence. In the earlier part of the seventeenth century, money fines were also imposed at the same time as the penance. In 1609, compurgation was used in a fornication cause from Forcet in Richmond,[23] as well as in causes involving defamation, brawling, and irregular attendance at church. Scorn has been poured upon this form of penance on the grounds that it was only too easy for a man to obtain a group of neighbours to swear to his innocence. The following causes show the opposite to be true.

The first citation is: '1610 *Aysgarth* Wednesday 23rd May. The Office contra Thomas Spence a slanderous person, a slacke comer to the Church & will not send his servants to be catechized'. He appeared and denied the charge whereupon the judge ordered him 'to compurgate under the hands of four honest men'. Spence failed to get any of his neighbours to testify to his innocence, either on the grounds that he was unpopular or his reputation was bad. Accordingly Spence made a second appearance on 10 June whence the following took place: '1610 *Aysgarth* Office against Thomas Spence of Bishopdale a slanderous person, a slack comer to the Church'. He submitted himself to the correction of the court whence the judge assigned him a declaratory penance in the presence of the churchwardens and minister, 'and to pay iis.vid to the poor of Aysgarth parish and to certify the distribution of the same under the hands of the minister and churchwardens'.[25]

The monetary fine attached to a penance was used for the relief of the poor, a practice that was in accordance with Elizabethan and later policy on the relief of the poor, to relieve the burden upon the parish poor rates. Compurgation was also used in the case of drunkenness upon three occasions at Melsonby. In this instance the judge increased the number of compurgators because he disbelieved the statements of the accused.[26] At Bowden in 1612, when Thomas Barker cited Ellen Ryland for saying he was the father of her bastard child, several of her compurgators refused to swear on oath that the accusations were true.[27]

The method of performing public penances was for the accused to stand at the entrance to the church and request members of the congregation to pray for the offender as he or she entered the church. It was normally the custom for the penance to be performed in the parish church of one or both parties on Sunday, and occasionally in one or more churches as specified in the sentence of the court. The penance was usually performed between the first and second lesson at mattins. At Catton, in 1702, the penance was ordered to be performed after the reading of the Gospel, between the hours of nine and eleven.[28] Afterwards the certificate of performance had to be signed by the minister and churchwardens. At Grinton, Anthony Freer was sentenced to a public penance for fishing on Sunday. He was to 'stand in the market place at Askrigg with an angling Rode and a fish on it and a vessell on his breast . . . on Thursday in Whitsun weke and to certify'.[29]

A list of penances imposed at Chester in 1625 on offenders from the deanery of Malpas includes fourteen persons for fornication; five for carrying salt on Sundays; Henry Hutton of Malpas, 'mynstrell for travelling on the Sabbath to play on greens'; and Grace Wood of Hanmer, for 'casting down mooldywarp hillocks [molehills] on the feast of the Annunciation 1624'.[30]

The serving of citations and orders to perform penance was undertaken by the apparitors who were the court messengers. It was no doubt a demanding task, for these apparitors had to face the hardship and dangers of crossing the Pennines and traversing the trackless parts of Cumbria, as well as the dangerous crossing over the sands of Morecambe Bay. In addition they had to face opposition from those on whom they served citations. On 10 July 1679, Richard Heptenstall, when served with a citation for non-attendance at church and not communicating, insulted the apparitor: 'I did take the mandate from the hands of John Watson and did dropp the same into my breeches and did then affirme that I would wipe my arse with the same and did refuse to redeliver'.[31]

Sometimes it was difficult to find the person or persons cited to appear, while others moved outside the diocesan jurisdiction into one of the peculiars. That apparitors were not over-scrupulous is noted in a letter addressed to Sagar, one of the Richmond apparitors by the deputy registrar in which he is instructed 'to keep it clean'.[32] Apparitors also had the power to collect petitions for private penances[33] and were able to certify commutation of penances, as the certificates from William Robson indicate: 'These are to inform you that Ann daughter of George Fryer of Whastow has commuted or changed the order of penance enjoined her for the crime of Fornication to a pecuniary Fine, a sum received by the hands of William Robson.' Occasionally, they would act as informers, as when they reported the dilapidations in the vicarage of Marton-cum-Grafton and the exhumation of the body of Mary Jefferson by the parish clerk at Hudswell.[34]

The arduous duties attached to the office gave rise to the temptation to make the task of earning a living somewhat easier by accepting bribes to keep quiet about an indictable offence or to make excessive charges when serving a process.[35] During his visitation of 1698, Bishop Stratford recorded a note from the vicar of Grasmere against apparitors, 'who did not serve the citation in person but send them by the common carriers'.[36] Some, like Edward Rothwell, were not above exercising the office of apparitor, as he was doing in Warrington deanery, 'without a patent under seal and citing persons to appear before John Gee dean rural for clandestine marriages, adultery, recusancy and nonconformity'.[37]

Another who attempted to make a 'bit on the side' was Samuel Wilson, apparitor for the Manchester deanery. He was cited on the grounds that he had suppressed the names of many delinquents in the deanery. Some of the parties concerned confessed that he 'had agreed and compounded with them to excuse them from penance and punishment at least from trouble and appearance in this Court'. He had also compounded and agreed with many for fees which they paid and he then put them into his pocket. Fourteen people named in the schedule had paid him fees ranging in value from 2s. to 20s.[38] In his defence he attempted in vain to prove that the fees he had received were those which he and the court were entitled to have.

The practice of commuting penances into pecuniary payment

was one that called for constant rebuke from authority, but despite rebuke the practice continued from time to time. The commutation of penances, according to Hale, was common to all dioceses and arose from the desire to increase the revenue to meet expenses.[39]

It was a great temptation for court officers to commute a penance placed on wealthy persons, who were only too willing to pay large fines rather than stand up to perform a public penance: a practice that brought excommunication into disrepute. When in 1694 Bishop Stratford visited his archdeaconry of Richmond, he discovered that the commissary claimed to have the right to commute penances, but on further enquiry found that the proctors of the court were most vague concerning the whole matter.[40] An excellent example occurs in a letter from the Commissary of Richmond's registrar to his opposite number at York: 'some proposals will shortly be made of a commutation of penance for fornication and the parties may be prevailed upon to advance seven or eight guineas rather than perform a penance'.[41] When the Commissary of the peculiar jurisdiction of Masham agreed to commute a penance incurred by Thomas Wintersgill for adultery, he assessed the fine at £12; the matter was taken before the chancery court at York on appeal.[42]

The court records reveal how some defendants openly despised church courts. Some information comes from formal accusation of contempt of court and some from open disputes between the parties in court. According to Emmison, such events took place in the Essex courts.[43] James Gerrard of Brindle was cited by the churchwardens for 'a loiterer and irregular attender at church'. It was alleged that he came to the court at Chorley Church and threatened the judge, Robert Fogg, with a bow to shoot him. In his defence he stated that he, 'was excommunicated and molested and defamed although he was a frequent attender at church'. The sentence against him, unfortunately, is lost.[44]

The most interesting case of a dispute in open court was recorded by Henry Prescott in his diary for 1705, at Wigan:

August 1. . . . Next enters Mrs Pilkington who claims a right to sit in the Seat belonging to the house sold to Mr. Herle, hee allows that hee gave her leave till she disturb'd his servants good as she is. Shee in a passion returns, villifies the servants, scorns to sit with 'em. . . . As Mr. Walmisley & my cozen Holt interpose, shee indevors to represse 'em, the most malitious words and reflections are used. Mr. Herle saies her Father used to call her Brandy Whore, and adds he knew her to sell potts of ale. Shee replies she never sold pins, Inckle &c. tells him of a whore hee had and mencions him as of the brood of the rebellion. Mr. Walmisley shee calls of yesterday & reminds him of being clerk to Henry Rowe &c.

Eventually she was made to understand by the chancellor that she could sit in the servants pew by Mr Herle's permission, so long as she behaved herself.[45]

Clearly there was opposition in many communities to the sentence of excommunication and penance for members of that community. Peter Foster of Distrington, who was presented at Kendal for getting a bastard child on Lydia Sheppard, was supported by two men from the community, William Fletcher and Ralph Cuthbert. Both men certified that Fisher was a man of good character, and that Lydia Sheppard was a 'verie naughtie woman having had a bastard child three years since . . . also when this child should have been gott Peter Foster was under the Phisicians hands and troubled with vomiting of blood'. Therefore they requested that the case be dismissed, which was granted.[46]

According to Emmison, the clergy, by canon law, were not supposed to be penanced, yet in the northern province there are several instances where this occurred. In 1700, John Bland, vicar of Ripon, was penanced and ordered to appear in the collegiate church, 'dressed in mourning apparell to make his penance for fornication with Marion Hoope at the lectern. She is to wait until the communicants are settled and make her penance at the communion rails for fornication with John Bland'. The penances of both parties were to be heard by the Dean of Ripon.[47]

When Thomas Slinger, vicar of Helmsley, was suspended for 'solemnising clandestine marriages, reading of prayers disorderly and also services', the parishioners presented a petition for his restoration to his benefice.[48] Arthur Hickson of Leeds was accused by Rebecca Dawson of being the father of her child and was cited to court for the offence. The vicar of Leeds, J. Killingbeck, the churchwardens, and a number of parishioners, petitioned that Hickson, who had lived in Leeds for fourteen years, was a good honest man and that Dawson was a

> very ill woman of a Scandalous life and Impudent behaviour
> and is a Strowler about the County. . . . We believe that
> Arthur Hickson is very much wrong'd by her evill Reports
> and false which are false malitious and groundless and
> believe him not guilty of the Crime.

As a result, Hickson was absolved from any connection with the crime.[49]

At Bradford, in 1693 a penance for a clandestine marriage was arranged to be performed in church, not in the presence of the normal congregation, but acknowledged in the presence of the parents of both parties and witnesses chosen by the parents. Nathaniel and Mary Webster were to make a declaration before Mr and Mrs Waterhouse and one other person, in addition to the parents, that the couple had been married by Thomas Harrison, vicar of Otley.[50]

By the late seventeenth century, it had become customary for many persons to pay for a penance to be performed privately. In 1684 at Ripon, Edward Kirkby had to perform his penance for adultery in the vestry of the collegiate church before five witnesses. At Thorp Arch, penance was to be performed in the private house of Richard Connett on the afternoon of Saturday 23 June by Hannah Dickinson for calling Katherine Wright a strumpet. A penance was performed in the vicarage of Bishopthorpe, York, on Monday 30 October 1699, by Robert Dunmore for saying that 'Bess Lowther was with child by Joseph Danish gott in the Green Bed at Bishopthorpe Palace and he paid her money to lay it on Ned Carter'.[51]

In Somerset there appears to have been little evidence of puritan morality amongst the lower orders and the same is correct concerning many parts of Chester diocese. However, there do seem to have existed double standards of morality in which male adventurers were permitted to operate, and female virginity before marriage came to be highly prized.[52] It is clear, however, that by the late seventeenth century there was increasing concern about the morality of the masses by those in authority. The second half of the seventeenth century saw a massive increase in causes that involved bastardy and sexual immorality in Chester diocese. It seems a possibility that concern over sexual matters, especially amongst those who are usually referred to as 'the middling sort' and the stable but respectable poor of Stuart England, indicates a strong desire to demonstrate that their conduct was in no way comparable with that of the ungodly and disorderly poor whom the magistrates watched with care.

The problem that confronted northern society in these matters arose from the fact that the geographical and climatic conditions made life hard. Whereas in many sections of society women could often be protected from male predators, in the north, where survival meant that women had to work alongside men, this protection was not available. Northern agriculture demanded the hands of men and women so there was little opportunity of 'protection'. Working under such conditions and in close proximity meant that harvest field fornication, with resulting bastardy, was a reality, as it was at the annual fair time, so gossip thrived.

Indeed, when a detailed examination of the evidence in the cause papers concerning sexual slander is undertaken, it is clear that sexual reputation was important to married women, for the majority of causes concern married women rather than spinsters. Many causes arose from words spoken in anger rather than the result of a longstanding slander of a good name, implying that there existed those who were anxious to identify themselves as distinct from the increasing body of fornicators, adulterers, and bastard-getters. However, overall there appears to have been a fear the church courts were becoming increasingly unable to detect and punish sexual offenders.

Chapter Fourteen

THE DECLINE
OF THE COURTS

The Restoration of Charles II saw at the same time the restoration of the Church as it was organized in 1640. Though the church courts were restored, the prerogative courts of High Commission and Star Chamber were not. This meant that the coercive power which had upheld and enforced the sentences imposed by the church courts was missing. Therefore sabbath breaking, profanity, and debauchery could only be punished by penance and excommunication.

F.S. Hockaday in his study of the consistory courts of Gloucester states that 'the most prominent feature of the decline of the ecclesiastical courts lies in the failure to employ the aid of the temporal powers, as legally they might do'. Indeed the civil power was there to support the Church if requested by means of a Significavit calling for the sheriff to arrest the party named in the writ, but the church courts were reluctant to request state support. Basically this reluctance was a feature of the long-standing rivalry between civil and ecclesiastical lawyers.[1]

Hence by 1678 there was much concern for the need to purge the vices of the lower classes and reform their morals. Englishmen began to realize that London was one of the most disorderly and dissipated cities in Europe. Restoration drama was the most obscene of its kind and the author of a pamphlet on the need to reform manners wrote: 'A thick gloominess hath overspread our horizon and our light looks like the evening of the world'.[2]

The religious policy of James II had aroused a national reaction against him that led to his fall. This and the popular interpretation of the 1689 Act of Toleration saw a rapid decline in *ex officio* causes (those promoted directly by the court), not only in Chester diocese but also in other English dioceses.[3] The number of causes coming before the Chester consistory declined from an average of 120 per annum in the first half of the century to an average of 40 in the 1680s, and to 20 or less by 1730. These figures do not include the testamentary causes which are filed separately from the general run of papers. At Chester the decline in morality and defamation causes was replaced by an increase in those involving private pews and faculty disputes which figure prominently in the eighteenth century.

The increase in the issue of prohibitions for transfer of the cause from the church to the secular courts led to a rapid fall in the number of tithe disputes heard at York between 1660 and 1696.[4] In Chester the decline was not so marked, and in the remoter parts of Richmond archdeaconry they continued well into the eighteenth century.[5] The provision by Parliament for recovering small tithes before two Justices of Peace provided a quicker and cheaper method of recovery. The consistory's far slower procedures, which meant that some cases could take up to four years to complete and involved high costs and the clumsy use of excommunication, made them unable to compete. A further feature that led to the courts' decline was the introduction in 1712 of stamp duty on official documents. This duty had to be paid on each document, and with as many as thirty documents involved in some causes the cost mounted enormously.[6]

Parliament began to interfere increasingly with matters that were strictly within the areas of canon law. Edmund Gibson stressed this point when he informed William Wake that statutes against Sabbath-breaking and drunkenness, which were designed to shorten the court process and increase punishment, meant that in the long term both clergy and people came to believe that these offences could be punished nowhere except in the secular courts.[7]

Parliament weakened the sentence of excommunication by its measures. The sentence of minor excommunication was becoming increasingly ignored by the close of the century. That of major excommunication, with the legal disabilities attached to it, became a source of annoyance to those who owned property or substance and who had political or social ambitions. In this field, also, Parliament interfered by enacting a series of general pardons by which penances and excommunications were annulled from time to time. If, then, Parliament was periodically to enact general pardons, then church courts would find it extremely difficult to retain any spiritual significance for excommunication.[8] In 1708 the churchwardens of Kendal, of whom there were twelve, refused to present Henry Wilson on an allegation of fornication with Hannah Bateman, his servant, on the grounds that 'not having heard any such fame from any persons of credit & affirming that they did believe him innocent of the said pretended crime', they believed the case unfounded.[9] The acts of general pardon had the same effect as prohibitions, for they encouraged offenders to delay and defy the church courts in expectation of a future pardon which would relieve them from the need to submit. In 1709, Thomas Lumley of Pickhall, stated that when cited to appear before the court, that 'he denied his faith and defied the Court to compel him to come to Church'. This was doubtless a shock to the court offices who were so suspicious that they instructed the church-wardens to observe and report upon his movements and actions in three months' time.[10]

The decline of the church courts, though arguments were brought forward to defend them, and the willingness of Parliament to legislate in areas formerly believed to belong to the courts spiritual, encouraged some persons to find an alternative solution to the problems. Since the church courts were unable or reluctant to enforce standards of morality, then responsible citizens began to form religious societies to encourage self-help in spiritual matters and encourage charity and mutual self-help. In 1691 the officers and more prosperous inhabitants of Tower Hamlets, London, formed an association to suppress immorality which led to the founding of a London Society for the Reformation of Manners. The movement had a degree of success and was supported by Archbishop Tennison and later by Queen Anne. Although the movement made a good start in London and other parts, especially Durham, there was a serious problem in that universal support from persons in authority was lacking.[11] The desire to foster religion is clearly evident in the founding of the Society for Promoting Christian Knowledge in 1698 to counter the prevalent national sinfulness.

An excellent illustration of the problems dealing with ecclesiasti-cal discipline is found in the records of the Archbishop of York's peculiar jurisdiction of Hexham between 1705 and 1733, which highlights the difficulties of enforcing canon law at this period.[12]

One characteristic of these reforming societies was the way in which Anglicans and Dissenters co-operated. Thousands and thousands of tracts were printed against drunkenness, swearing, indecency, and Sunday trading. It is not known what success attended the distribution of the tract 'Kind caution against Swearing', which was distributed to London's hackney coachmen, nor the one, 'Kind cautions to Watermen', which was issued to bargees in the west of England.[13] Far more effective were the prosecutions before magistrates who were shamed into enforcing laws regarded by some as obsolete.

Naturally, activities in this field by the secular authorities roused the opposition of churchmen. Dr Sacheverell called for excommunication, 'the ancient discipline of the Church', to be enforced to suppress vice, immorality, heresy, and schism, instead of the Society for Reformation of Manners, which permitted laymen and Dissenters to take part. Some persons, such as Archbishop John Sharp of York and Mr Justice Holt, feared that in the long term these reforming societies could lead to ill-feeling and corruption. During the reign of Queen Anne debauchery became less fashionable, though in the northern deaneries of Chester diocese, sexual immorality and bastardy tended to increase for the first thirty years of the following century.[14]

What had commenced as an attempt to penalize tippling, Sabbath-breaking and vice among the lower orders in London expanded into a nationwide reformation that created an atmosphere of pietism and restraint that later in the eighteenth century ensured the success of the Evangelical and Wesleyan movements, which encouraged public opinion to exert political pressure to remove the deep-seated evils in our civilization.

This study concludes at the time when great changes were about to influence English life. The expansion of industry, the improvements in travel, the industrial and agrarian revolutions with all that they involved for people, were to highlight the inability of the Church to cope with a sudden expansion in population. The consistory causes in the eighteenth century reveal the failure of clergy to nurture their parishioners, with the result that the Church of England became a middle- and upper-class stronghold. Though the consistory records after 1700 reveal a steady flow of defamation causes, nevertheless economic change is reflected in the tithe disputes and demand for private pews in churches.

214

However, there are problems when one attempts to enter the world of the middling sort and the poor of Stuart England during a century of continuity and change. A detailed study of these court files over a number of dioceses may help us to understand our own times better, by understanding the past. For, as Christopher Hill states, 'We ourselves are shaped by the past: but from our vantage point in the present we are continually reshaping the past which shapes us'.[15]

NOTES

1 THE STRUCTURE OF THE DIOCESE

1 J. Addy, 'Two eighteenth-century bishops and their diocese of Chester 1771–1787', unpubl. Ph.D. thesis, University of Leeds, 1972.
2 F. Walker, 'Historical geography of south-west Lancashire before the Industrial Revolution', *Chetham Society*, vol. 103 n.s., 1939.
3 R.H. Morris, *Chester Diocesan History*, London, 1895, 105.
4 C.M.L. Bouch and G.P. Jones, *A Short Social and Economic History of the Lake Counties 1500–1880*, Manchester, 1962, 245ff.
5 Cheshire Record Office (CRO), Articles Preparatory to Visitation EDV.7/2.
6 Bouch and Jones, op. cit., 175–88.
7 J. Addy (ed.), *The Diary of Henry Prescott*, vol. 1: *1704–1710*, Lancashire and Cheshire Record Society, no. 127, 1987.
8 Lancashire Record Office (LRO), Silverdale Parish Papers DR.Ch.37.

2 THE ADMINISTRATION OF THE DIOCESE

1 R.M.T. Hill (ed.), *Register of William Melton 1317–1340*, Canterbury and York Society, vol. 1, no. 147, 1976.
2 *Letters and Papers of Henry VIII*, XVI, 535–6.
3 ibid., XVI, 535. Thomas Cromwell had proposed a new diocese based on Fountains Abbey and Richmond Archdeaconry but it was not implemented.
4 Cheshire Record Office (CRO), Precedent Book EDR/1, 103.
5 W.F. Irvine, 'Church discipline after the Restoration', *Transactions of the Historic Society of Lancashire and Cheshire*, vol. lxiv, 1912, 43.
6 Leeds District Archives (LDA), Probate Act Book RD/PB/8, 146.
7 CRO, Precedent Book EDR.6, 57–60, 75–7.
8 CRO, Bishop's Register EDA. 2/7, unfoliated section at the end of the volume.

9 Lancashire Record Office (LRO), Consistory Court Act Book ARR/12, 152.

10 LDA, Faculty Book RD/RF/D, 14.

11 LDA, Masham Peculiar Records MP/29; J. Fisher, *History of Masham*, London, 1865, *passim*.

12 W. Atthill (ed.) *Documents Relating to the Church of Middleham*, o.s., vol. xxxviii, Camden Society, 1847.

13 LRO, Kirby Ireleth Parish Papers DR.Ch.37; Borthwick Institute of Historical Research (BIHR), Bishopthorpe Papers R.Bp. 6B.

14 W. Brown (ed.), *Register of Thomas Corbridge*, Surtees Society, vol. 138, 1925.

15 A. Warne, *Church and Society in Eighteenth-Century Devon*, Newton Abbot, 1969, 19.

16 J. Addy, *The Archdeacon and Ecclesiastical Discipline in Yorkshire 1559–1714*, York, 1963, 6–12.

17 LDA, Commissary's Act Books RD/A.4–6; CRO, Correction Court Books EDV1/13–38.

18 CRO, Precedent Book EDR/6; Thomas Oughton, *Ordo Iudiciorum*, London, 1738; F.S. Hockaday, 'The consistory courts of the diocese of Gloucester', *Transactions of the Bristol and Gloucester Archaeological Society*, vol. 16, 1924; A.T. Thacker, 'The Chester Diocesan Records and the local historian', *Transactions of the Historic Society of Lancashire and Cheshire*, vol. 130, 1981.

19 A.E.O. Whiteman, 'The re-establishment of the Church of England 1660–1662', *Transactions of the Royal Historical Society*, 5th series, vol. 5, 1955, 111–51.

20 LDA, Richmond Comperta Books RD/C/1–15; LRO, Richmond Comperta Books (Western Deaneries) ARR/37. The records at Leeds cover the three eastern deaneries while those at Preston cover the five western deaneries.

21 BIHR, High Commission Act Books 1561–1640, vols 17–19.

22 The writ requested the sheriff to whom it was addressed to arrest the person named in the writ and detain him in prison until required to appear in court.

23 G.F.A. Best, *Temporal Pillars*, Cambridge, 1964, 43.

24 C.A. Richie, *The Ecclesiastical Courts of York*, Arbroath, 1953, *passim*.

3 INTRODUCTION

1 J. Addy, 'The archdeacon and ecclesiastical discipline in the County of York 1559–1714', unpubl. M.A. thesis, University of Leeds, 1960, 42.

2 H.D. Hazeltine, 'Roman and canon law in the Middle Ages', *Cambridge Medieval History*, vol. 5, ch. 21.

3 Addy, op. cit., 46.

4 Society for Promoting Christian Knowledge, *Canons and Homilies 1604*, London, 1871; nos 92–137 deal with ecclesiastical courts.

5 C. Hill, *Puritanism and Society in Pre-Revolutionary England*, London, 1964, 315.

6 Hill, op. cit., 315.

7 Hill, op. cit., 320.

8 C. Hill, 'Puritans and the dark corners of the land', *Transactions of the Royal Historical Society*, 5th series, vol. 13, 1963, 77–102.

9 Hill, *Puritanism and Society*, 306.

10 Leeds District Archives (LDA), Richmond Comperta Book RD/C/3 1668. Borthwick Institute of Historical Research (BIHR), Archdeacon's Court Book Y/V 1613.

11 R. Houlbrook, 'Decline of ecclesiastical jurisdiction', in R. O'Day and F. Heal, *Continuity and Change*, Leicester, 1976, 239ff.

12 J. Addy (ed.), *The Diary of Henry Prescott*, vol. 1: *1704–1710*, Lancashire and Cheshire Record Society, no. 127, 1987.

13 *Randolph's Poems*, London, 1646.

14 C.E. Whiting, *Studies in English Puritanism*, London, 1931, 445.

15 ibid., 274.

16 P. Stubbs, *Anatomie of Abuses*, London, 1583, reprint 1870, ed. J. Connor.

4 SIN AND THE CLERGY

1 A.G. Dickens, 'The first stages of Romanist recusancy in Yorkshire 1560–1590', *Yorkshire Archaeological Society Journal*, no. 35, 1948, 159.

2 C. Haigh, *Reformation and Resistance in Tudor Lancashire*, Cambridge, 1975, 231.

3 J. Addy, 'Two eighteenth-century bishops and their diocese of Chester 1771–1787', unpubl. Ph.D. thesis, University of Leeds, 1972, 65.

4 Haigh, op. cit., 237–8.

5 Lancashire Record Office (LRO), Returns of Poor Livings to Queen Anne's Bounty 1711, Wythop Chapel WD/1A.

6 S.L. Ollard and P.C. Walker (eds), *Archbishop Herring's Visitation Returns 1743*, Yorkshire Archaeological Society Record Series, vol. 73, 1929.

7 Addy, op. cit., 62.

8 G. Ormsby, *Correspondence of John Cosin*, vol. 52, Surtees Society, 82.

9 Borthwick Institute of Historical Research (BIHR) High Commission Act Book HCAB 19, 106–10.

10 Leeds District Archives (LDA), Richmond Comperta Book RD/C/3, 16.

11 ibid., 18.

12 ibid., 8v.

13 ibid., RD/C/5, 35.

14 LDA Richmondshire Wills, 28 March 1685.

15 Cheshire Record Office (CRO) Consistory Court Causes EDC.5 (1663), no. 30 Blackburn.
16 BIHR, High Commission Act Book 19, 110–11.
17 ibid., 135, 140.
18 CRO, EDC.5 (1674), no. 17, Coppenhall.
19 BIHR, Cause Paper CP.G.1817.
20 A. Tindal Hart, *Country Clergy in Elizabethan and Stuart Times*, London, 1958, 79.
21 BIHR, Cause Paper CP.G.1817.
22 CRO, EDC.5 (1674), no. 44 Burton in Kendal.
23 CRO, EDC.5 (1613), no. 52 Doddleston.
24 CRO, EDC.5 (1638), no. 31 Alford.
25 CRO, EDC.5 (1638), no. 49 Witton.
26 CRO, EDC.5 (1663), no. 56 Prestwich.
27 CRO, EDC.5 (1640), no. 42 Blackburn.
28 CRO, EDC.5 (1666), no. 44 Chester.
29 CRO, EDC.5 (1616), no. 19 Goostrey.
30 CRO, EDC.5 (1628), no. 20 Whalley.
31 CRO, EDC.5 (1640), no. 71 Crosthwaite.
32 BIHR, Archdeacon of York's Court Book Y/V.1664–1670, *passim*.
33 BIHR, Visitation Court Book, V.1579, 108.
34 CRO, EDC.5 (1614), no. 7 Ribchester.
35 CRO, EDC.5 (1628), no. 59 Christleton.
36 CRO, EDC.5 (1626), no. 58 Wilmslow.
37 CRO, EDC.5 (1634), no. 104 Tarvin.
38 CRO, EDC.5 (1634), no. 100 St Bees.
39 LDA, Consistory Court Cases RD/AC/1–6, no. 25.
40 CRO, EDC.5 (1640), no. 24 Haslingden.
41 CRO, EDC.5 (1676), no. 4 Over.
42 CRO, EDC.5 (1678), no. 14 and (1681), no. 17 Thurstaston.
43 CRO, EDC.5 (1604), no. 61 Macclesfield.
44 CRO, EDC.5 (1626), no. 51 Bunbury.
45 CRO, EDC.5 (1638), no. 13, and (1638), no. 88 Over Kellett.
46 CRO, EDC.5 (1703), no. 12 Maghull; J. Addy (ed.), *The Diary of Henry Prescott*, vol. 1: *1704–1710*, 7, Lancashire and Cheshire Record Society, no. 127, 1987.
47 CRO, EDC.5 (1704), no. 5 Maghull.
48 CRO, EDC.5 (1733) unsorted; LRO, ARR.13/4, no. 131 Ulverstone 1830.
49 CRO, EDC.5 (1704), no. 4 Cartmel.
50 CRO, EDC.5 (1705), no. 6 Cartmel; Addy, *The Diary of Henry Prescott*, 25, 69, 72.
51 CRO, EDC.5 (1697), no. 14, and (1698), no. 10 Doddleston.
52 BIHR, Visitation Court Book V.1578, 99, 101.
53 BIHR, Visitation Court Book V.1595, 4.
54 LDA, Commissary's Act Book, RD/A/6, 20.
55 CRO, EDC.5 (1638), no. 14 Kirkham.

56 CRO, EDC.5 (1638), no. 14 Kirkham, deposition.
57 CRO, EDC.5 (1615), no. 17 Shotwick.
58 CRO, EDC.5 (1631), no. 24 Pilling.
59 CRO, EDC.5 (1604), no. 24 Manchester.
60 CRO, EDC.5 (1638), no. 113 Manchester.
61 CRO, EDC.5 (1637), no. 16 Ormskirk.
62 CRO, EDC.5 (1683), no. 9 Childwall.
63 CRO, EDC.5 (1639), no. 83 Colton.
64 CRO, EDC.5 (1637), no. 32 Plemondstall.
65 CRO, EDC.5 (1631), no. 29 Harthill.
66 CRO, EDC.5 (1638), no. 112 Manchester.
67 CRO, EDC.5 (1637), no. 9 Archolme.
68 CRO, EDC.5 (1638), no. 1 Eriholme.
69 CRO, EDC.5 (1635), no. 111 Stockport.
70 CRO, EDC.5 (1640), no. 67 Chester.
71 BIHR, Visitation Court Book, V.1632–3, 11, 18, 36.
72 T.A. Bainbridge, 'Wesley's travels in Westmorland and Lancashire', *Transactions of the Cumberland and Westmorland Archaeological Society*, vol. 52, 1952, 106.
73 CRO, EDC.5 (1663), no. 71 Eccles.
74 CRO, EDC.5 (1665), no. 42 Walton.
75 BIHR, High Commission Act Book 1582–1591, HCAB.11, 164.
76 LRO, Furness Deanery Comperta Book 1666, ARR/37, 14; Lonsdale Comperta Book 1668, ARR/37, 4.
77 CRO, Articles Preparatory to Visitation EDV.7/2, no. 350.
78 T.S. Eliot, *Murder in the Cathedral*, London, 1936.

5 SIN AND THE CHURCHWARDENS

1 J. Addy, *The Archdeacon and Ecclesiastical Discipline 1559–1714*, York, 1963, 20.
2 H.E. Salter, *Medieval Oxford*, Oxford Historical Society, vol. 100, 1936, 12.
3 Borthwick Institute of Historical Research (BIHR), Archbishop Grindal's Register, R.30, 157.
4 Addy, op. cit., 21.
5 Society for Promoting Christian Knowledge, *Canons and Homilies 1604*, London, 1871, Canon 89.
6 W.E. Tate, *The Parish Chest*, Cambridge, 1969, 18ff.
7 J.S. Purvis, *Introduction to Ecclesiastical Records*, York, 1955, 47.
8 *Statutes and the Realm*, 5, Henry VII, c 6: 32, Henry VIII c 40: 7 and 8, William III, c 21: 10 and 11, William III, c 23: 1, Anne, c 11.
9 Leeds District Archives (LDA), Richmond Comperta Books RD/C/2, 33; RD/C/8, 16.
10 ibid., RD/C/5, 25, 27, 28, 30, 40, 50, East Witton, Muker,

Startforth, Barton Cuthberts, Coverham, Forcett; RD/C/5, ff. 36, 40, Kirby Ravensworth, Marrick, Muker.

11 BIHR, Visitation Court Book, V/1632–3, St Bees, Hugil, Workington; Cheshire Record Office (CRO), EDC.5 (1685), no. 3 Blackburn.

12 CRO, EDC.5 (1702), no. 5 Over.

13 LDA Richmond Comperta Book, RD/C/2, 46 Smeaton.

14 BIHR, Visitation Court Book, V/1684.

15 CRO, EDC.5 (1635), no. 120 Lawton.

16 CRO, EDC.5 (1635), no. 29 Manchester.

17 CRO, EDC.5 (1636), nos 68, 110 Prescott.

18 CRO, EDC.5 (1636), no. 65 Chorley.

19 CRO, EDC.5 (1636), nos 86, 39, 50, 81 Chorley, Bolton, Colne, Astbury.

20 CRO, EDC.5 (1635), no. 90 Prescott.

21 CRO, EDC.5 (1639), no. 28 St Bees.

22 LDA, Mandates and Commissions, RD/RA.

23 H. Prideaux, *Directions to Churchwardens*, London, 1692, 111ff.

24 BIHR, Visitation Court Book, V. 1578, 78v.

25 CRO, EDC.5 (1638), no. 142 Ashton-under-Lyne.

26 CRO, EDC.5 (1631), no. 15 Warrington.

27 CRO, EDC.5 (1640), no. 60 Chester.

28 CRO, EDC.5 (1672), no. 29 Ormskirk.

29 CRO, EDC.5 (1678), no. 9 Ormskirk.

30 CRO, EDC.5 (1677), no. 9 Ormskirk.

31 CRO, EDC.5 (1695), no. 8 Christleton.

32 A detailed study of pew disputes that were heard in the consistory court would reveal a substantial amount of information on the interior arrangement of churches and the structure of society in the parish; *Statutes of the Realm*, 5, Edward VI, C 4: 1551.

33 LDA, Churchwardens' Presentments, RD/CB/8/1 Askrigg; LDA Commissary's Act Book 1609 RD/A/6, 6 East Cowton.

34 BIHR, Precedent Papers RVIII/PL No. 113 Bolton.

35 BIHR, Cause Papers R/AS.21B/96 Middleham.

36 CRO, EDC.5 (1687), no. 10 Marbury.

37 CRO, EDC.5 (1631), no. 37 Stockport.

38 CRO, EDC.5 (1631), no. 10 Holt.

39 CRO, EDC.5 (1684), no. 5 Saddleworth.

40 CRO, EDC.5 (1681), no. 30 Doddleston.

41 CRO, EDC.5 (1632), no. 30 Guilden Sutton.

42 CRO, EDC.5 (1639), no. 56 Daresbury.

43 CRO, EDC.5 (1638), no. 103 Wrenbury.

44 CRO, EDC.5 (1636), no. 94 Liverpool.

45 CRO, EDC.5 (1636), no. 12 Wybunbury.

46 CRO, EDC.5 (1632), no. 34 Liverpool.

47 CRO, EDC.5 (1697), no. 1 Christleton.

48 CRO, EDC.5 (1640), no. 77 Crosthwaite Chapel (Heversham).

49 BIHR, Cause Papers CP.H.1431.
50 LDA, Consistory Court Causes RD/AC/1/1, no. 20 Whixley; LDA Depositions RD/AC/5/1, no. 8
51 BIHR, Cause Paper, CP.H.427 Whixley.
52 CRO, EDC.5 (1618), no. 48 Saddleworth.
53 BIHR, HCAB.18, 189v.
54 BIHR, HCAB.18, 204.
55 Cumbria Record Office, Kendal Parish Papers.
56 C. Hill, *The World Turned Upside Down*, London, 1972, 233ff.
57 F. Proctor and W.H. Frere, *A New History of the Book of Common Prayer*, London, 1901, *passim*.
58 W.C. Costin and J.S. Watson, *The Law & Working of the Constitution*, vol. 1, London, 1967, 20–8.
59 CRO, EDC.5 1661, 1662, 1663.
60 Typical parishes were Bolton, 'the Geneva of the north', Rochdale, Bury, Ratcliffe in Lancashire, Halifax, Bradford, Wakefield, and Leeds in York diocese.
61 A.E.O. Whiteman, 'The re-establishment of the Church of England, 1660–1662', *Transactions of the Royal Historical Society*, 5th series, vol. 5, 1955, 121ff.
62 BIHR, Visitation Court Book V.1662/3; LDA Comperta Book RD/C/1–6; CRO, Correction Court Books, EDV1/34, 35.
63 CRO, EDC.5 (1662), no. 4 Walton.
64 CRO, EDC.5 (1661), no. 64 Oldham.
65 CRO, EDC.5 (1662), no. 2 Manchester.
66 A.T. Thacker, 'The Chester Diocesan Records and the local historian', *Transactions of the Historic Society of Lancashire and Cheshire*, vol. 130, 1981.
67 CRO, EDC.5 (1662), no. 5 Marple.
68 J.P. Earwaker, *East Cheshire*, vol. 2, London, 1877, 57.
69 CRO, EDC.5 (1662), no. 4 Altham.
70 J. Horsfall Turner (ed.) *The Diaries of Oliver Heywood*, Brighouse, 1881, *passim*.
71 CRO, EDC.5 (1662), no. 5 Depositions of John Angier.
72 LRO, Richmond Comperta Book ARR/15, 1668, 11. The Consistory Act book for this period 1662–8 is defective and there is no record of the case being heard.
73 LRO Western Deaneries Cause Papers, ARR/13/11.
74 *Statutes of the Realm 1*, Elizabeth I, c.2: vol. IV, 355.8.
75 LDA, Churchwardens' Presentments, RD/CB/8/6, no. 84.
76 BIHR, Visitation Court Book, V.1632, vol. 2 Chester, 12, 19, 81, 92, 93, 96, 109, 124 and 170.
77 CRO, EDC.5 (1681), no. 22, (1682), nos 6, 7, 8, 9, 10.
78 CRO, EDC.5 (1682), no. 17 Liverpool.
79 CRO, EDC.5 (1683), no. 6 Leigh.
80 LRO, Richmond Comperta Books ARR/37 (Furness and Copeland Deaneries).

81 Prideaux, op. cit., 73.
82 Lynwood, *Provinciale*, Bk. III, Tit. xxviii, ch. 4.
83 House of Lords MSS. vol. 1, n.s. (1900).
84 CRO, EDC.5 (1638), no. 157 Mobberley.
85 CRO, EDC.5 (1631), nos 42, 91 Woodchurch.
86 CRO, EDC.5 (1634), no. 122 Thurstaston.
87 CRO, EDC.5 (1635), nos 27, 28 Manchester.
88 CRO, EDC.5 (1635), no. 20 Stockport.
89 CRO, EDC.5 (1635), no. 126 Christleton.
90 CRO, EDC.5 (1636), nos 110, 68 Prescot, Chorley; BIHR, HC.CP.1634/5, 9, 17, 18.
91 CRO, EDC.5 (1636), no. 39 Colne.
92 CRO, EDC.5 (1636), no. 81 Astbury.
93 CRO, EDC.5 (1635), no. 2, (1637), no. 23 Bolton.
94 CRO, EDC.5 (1635), no. 108 Broughton.
95 CRO, EDC.5 (1641), no. 25 Haslingden.
96 CRO, EDC.5 (1664), no. 62 Shotwick.
97 CRO, EDC.5 (1684), no. 22 Chester.
98 CRO, EDC.5 (1684), no. 12 Sefton.
99 CRO, EDC.5 (1685), no. 14 Leigh.
100 CRO, EDC.5 (1700), no. 1 Manchester.
101 CRO, EDC.5 (1635), no. 30 Doddleston.
102 BIHR, Visitation Court Book, V.1595, 95.
103 LDA, Citations RD/AB/2/1, no. 37 Marrick.
104 CRO, EDC.5 (1631), no. 23 Great Harwood.
105 CRO, EDC.5 (1631), no. 63 Upholland.
106 CRO, EDC.5 (1694), no. 26 Chester.
107 CRO, EDC.5 (1637), no. 26 Rostherne.
108 LRO, Comperta Books, ARR/15 (1707), f.11v Cockermouth.
109 LRO, Richmond Comperta Books, ARR/15 (1710), 5 Troutbeck.
110 C.M.L. Bouch, *Prelates and People of Lake Counties*, Kendal, 1948, 334 ff.
111 CRO, EDC.5 (1690), no. 18 Aughton, (1691), no. 22 Halsall, (1699), no. 12 Culceth.
112 CRO, EDC.5 (1633), no. 52 Cheadle.
113 CRO, EDC.5 (1673), no. 14 Warrington.
114 CRO, EDC.5 (1683), no. 31 Warmington.
115 West Yorkshire Record Office, Cawthorne Churchwardens' Accounts.
116 CRO, EDC.5 (1632), no. 4 Kirkham.
117 CRO, EDC.5 (1608), nos 69, 70 Doddleston.
118 BIHR, Archdeacon of York's Court Book Y/V1691; BIHR Visitation Court Book V.1637.
119 CRO, EDC.5 (1630), no. 30 Bury.
120 BIHR, Visitation Court Book V.1632.
121 *North Riding Sessions Records*, vol. 1, 1884, 22, 46, 71, 128, 240.
122 CRO, EDC.5 (1639), no. 101 Prestbury.

123 LRO, Richmond Comperta Books ARR/15 (1689), 2.
124 CRO, EDC.5 (1700), no. 2 Little Budworth.
125 LDA, Commissary's Act Book, RD/A/6, 23 Wath.
126 LDA, Churchwardens' Presentments RD/CB/8/7, no. 46 Eriholme.

6 SIN AND THE SCHOOLMASTERS AND READERS

1 J. Mansi, *Acta Conciliorum*, Venice, 1798, vol. vii, 30.
2 39 Elizabeth I repealed by 43 Elizabeth I c.9 and replaced by 45 Elizabeth I c.6.
3 J. Strype, *Life of Grindal*, London, 1821, 378.
4 Society for Promoting Christian Knowledge, *Canons and Homilies 1604*, London, 1871.
5 3 James I c.4, and 7 James I c.6.
6 25 Charles II, c.1.
7 Borthwick Institute of Historical Research (BIHR), HCAB, 1580–1585, 90.
8 ibid., 98.
9 ibid., 106.
10 Lancashire Record Office (LRO), Urswick Parish Papers DRCh/37.
11 Cheshire Record Office (CRO), EDC.5 (1621), no. 16 Urswick.
12 CRO, EDC.5 (1628), no. 12 Urswick.
13 CRO, EDC.5 (1689), no. 4 West Kirby.
14 CRO, EDC.5 (1626), no. 15 Crosthwaite.
15 CRO, EDC.5 (1634), no. 3 Whalley.
16 CRO, EDC.5 (1636), no. 52 Whalley.
17 CRO, EDC.5 (1636), no. 44 Congleton.
18 CRO, EDC.5 (1636), no. 58 Thornton-le-Moors. This document contains a wealth of detail on education in the parish but is too fragile to handle.
19 Leeds District Archives (LDA), Commissary's Act Book RD/A/4, 7 Ainderby Steeple.
20 LDA, Churchwardens' Presentments, RD/CB/8/5, no. 47; RD/CB/8/1, nos. 76, 89, 130.
21 BIHR, Visitation Court Book, V.1632/3, 98, 181, 199, 203, 206, 217, 232, 312.
22 CRO, EDC.5 (1606), no. 33 Weaverham.
23 W.A.L. Vincent, *The State and School Education 1640–1660*, London, 1950, 94–108.
24 14 Charles II c.4.
25 CRO, EDC.5 (1663), no. 10 Northwich.
26 CRO, EDC.5 (1663), no. 26 Walton.
27 CRO, EDC.5 (1667), no. 42 Ringley.
28 CRO, EDC.5 (1663), no. 14 Farnworth.
29 25 Charles II C.1.

30 CRO, EDC.5 (1689), no. 4 West Kirby; LDA, CD/PB/2 Bedale Parish Papers.

31 CRO, EDC.5 (1668), no. 32 Hargreave.

32 CRO, EDC.5 (1698), no. 9 Frodsham.

33 Proverbs 13:24.

34 CRO, EDC.5 (1636), no. 103 Malpas.

35 CRO, EDC.5 (1696), no. 3 Blackrod.

36 CRO, EDC.5 (1701), no. 13 Blackrod. The Latin grammar prescribed by Henry VIII was *Lyly's Latin Grammar* which was revised by Benjamin Kennedy in 1868 as *Kennedy's Latin Primer.*

37 CRO, EDC.5 (1702), no. 3 Blackrod; J. Addy (ed.), *The Diary of Henry Prescott*, vol. 1: *1704–1710*, Lancashire and Cheshire Record Society, no. 127, 1987, 42, 104, 105; M.M. Kay, *History of Rivington and Blackrod Grammar School*, Manchester, 1966, 124ff.

38 CRO, EDC.5 (1704), no. 6 Rainford.

39 CRO, EDC.5 (1706), no. 6 Rainford.

40 CRO, EDC.5 (1706), no. 5 Goostry.

41 W.K. Jordan, *The Charities of Rural England*, London, 1961, 315.

42 CRO, EDC.5 (1700), no. 11 Kirby Ravensworth; BIHR, Transmissions on Appeal, Trans. CP.1700/1; LDA, Parish Papers CD/PB/3.

43 CRO, EDC.5 (1691), no. 3 Burton-in-Kendal.

44 LDA Consistory Court Causes RD/AC/1–7, no. 20 Bowes; Parish Papers CD/PB/2, no. 4 Bowes.

45 BIHR, Cause Papers CP.H.4378, Kirkheaton.

46 BIHR, Cause Papers CP.I.360, Holme. King's Evil was the term given to the disease scrofula. Monarchs were supposed to possess power to heal by 'touching'. The last English monarch to practise this art of touching was Queen Anne.

47 BIHR, Cause Papers CP.H.1319, Cawthorne.

48 CRO, EDC.5 (1637), no. 108 Wybunbury.

49 LRO, Valuation of Livings 1714, WD/B/1 (Temporary reference).

50 W. Nicholson, *Miscellany Accounts of the Diocese of Carlisle*, ed. R.S. Fergusson, Cumberland and Westmorland Archaeological Society, extra series, vol. 1, 98.

51 C.M.L. Bouch and G.P. Jones, *A Short Social and Economic History of the Lake Counties 1500–1600*, Manchester, 1962, 186.

52 ibid., 186–7.

53 Addy, op. cit., 60–3.

54 CRO, EDC.5 (1628), no. 14 Old Hutton.

55 CRO, EDC.5 (1627), no. 42 Lowick.

7 DRUNKENNESS

1 W. Brown (ed.), *Yorkshire Star Chamber Cases*, Yorkshire Archaeological Society Record Series, vols 41, 45, 51, and 70, 1909, 1911, 1914, and 1916; R. Steward Brown (ed.), *Lancashire*

and Cheshire Star Chamber Cases, Lancashire and Cheshire Record Society, vol. 71, 1916.

2 W.E. Tate and P. Wallis, 'A register of old Yorkshire grammar schools', *Journal of Educational Studies*, Leeds, 1958; P. Wallis, 'A register of old schools in Lancashire and Cheshire', *Transactions of the Historic Society of Lancashire and Cheshire*, vol. 120, 1968.

3 H. Perkins, 'The Social Causes of the Industrial Revolution', *Transactions of the Royal Historical Society*, vol. 18, 1968, 123–41.

4 C. Hill, *Puritanism and society in Pre-Revolutionary England*, London, 1964.

5 ibid., 175.

6 J. Harland (ed.), *Lancashire Lieutenancy under the Tudors and Stuarts*, Chetham Society, vol. 2, 1859, 218.

7 Hill, op. cit., 195.

8 Bodleian Library, Tanner MSS 144, 25.

9 *Calendar, State Papers and Domestic*, Elizabeth I, vol. ccxl, 158–9.

10 Borthwick Institute of Historical Research (BIHR), High Commission Act Book, 1585–1591, HCAB.11, 164.

11 Cheshire Record Office (CRO), Articles Preparatory to Visitation EDV.7/1 Middleton.

12 CRO, EDC.5 (1640), no. 67 Chester.

13 J. Addy (ed.), *The Diary of Henry Prescott*, vol.1: *1704–1710*, Lancashire and Cheshire Record Society, no. 127, 1987, 224.

14 Leeds District Archives (LDA), Commissary's Act Book, RD/A/6, 60 Kirby Fleetham.

15 BIHR, Visitation Court Book, V.1595 n.f.

16 LDA, Consistory Court Causes RD/AC/1/4, no. 38 Askrigg.

17 CRO, EDC.5 (1626), no. 86 Winwick.

18 BIHR, Visitation Court Book V.1627.

19 CRO, EDC.5 (1663), no. 68 Manchester.

20 CRO, EDC.5 (1632), no. 17 Broughton.

21 CRO, EDC.5 (1635), no. 8 Ashton.

22 CRO, EDC.5 (1637), no. 79 Wigan.

23 CRO, EDC.5 (1678), no. 4 Sephton.

24 CRO, EDC.5 (1719), no. 4 West Derby.

25 CRO, EDC.5 (1630), no. 45 Runcorn.

26 CRO, EDC.5 (1664), no. 4 Clayton-le-Moors.

27 CRO, EDC.5 (1666), no. 3 Warrington.

28 CRO, EDC.5 (1665), no. 36 Christleton.

29 CRO, EDC.5 (1636), no. 28 Lower Peover.

30 CRO, EDC.5 (1612), no. 7 Chester.

31 CRO, EDC.5 (1670), no. 3 Grappenhall.

8 DEFAMATION AND SEXUAL SLANDER

1 H. Consett, *Practice of the Spiritual Courts*, London, 1708, 335.

2 F.G. Emmison, *Elizabethan Life, Morals and the Church Courts*, Chelmsford, 1963, 48.

3 J.A. Sharpe, *Defamation and Sexual Slander in Early Modern England*, Borthwick Paper no. 58, York.

4 ibid., 2.

5 Borthwick Institute of Historical Research (BIHR), Cause Paper CP.H.4499.

6 Cheshire Record Office (CRO), EDC.5 (1605), no. 14 Warrington.

7 CRO, EDC.5 (1616), no. 12 Chester.

8 CRO, EDC.5 (1616), nos 35, 39 Lower Peover, Middlewich.

9 Lancashire Record Office (LRO), Western deaneries Cause Papers ARR.13/4, no. 138 Lancaster.

10 LRO, Western Deaneries Cause Papers ARR.13/4, no. 142 Caton.

11 CRO, EDC.5 (1603), no. 37 Manchester.

12 CRO, EDC.5 (1631), no. 12 Tattenhall.

13 CRO, EDC.5 (1691), no. 93 Stockport.

14 CRO, EDC.5 (1634), no. 6 Shotwick.

15 CRO, EDC.5 (1631), no. 107 Malpas.

16 CRO, EDC.5 (1617), no. 7 Chester.

17 CRO, EDC.5 (1601), no. 12 Chester.

18 CRO, EDC.5 (1618), no. 10 Chester.

19 CRO, EDC.5 (1672), no. 26 Chester.

20 CRO, EDC.5 (1673), no. 19 Manchester.

21 CRO, EDC.5 (1686), no. 7 Chester.

22 S. Hughes, 'Church and society in seventeenth-century Halifax', unpubl. B.Ed. dissertation, St John's College, York, 1974.

23 CRO, EDC.5 (1694), no. 12 Congleton.

24 CRO, EDC.5 (1694), no. 7 Davenham.

25 CRO, EDC.5 (1677), no. 15 Chester.

26 CRO, EDC.5 (1676), no. 20 Aughton.

27 CRO, EDC.5 (1684), no. 16 Aldford.

28 CRO, EDC.5 (1637), no. 37 Halsall.

29 CRO, EDC.5 (1621), no. 3 Chester.

30 CRO, EDC.5 (1607), no. 26 Manchester.

31 CRO, EDC.5 (1640), no. 1 Halton.

32 CRO, EDC.5 (1668), no. 19 Chester.

33 CRO, EDC.5 (1622), no. 13 Harthill.

34 CRO, EDC.5 (1697), no. 6 Middlewich.

35 CRO, EDC.5 (1711), no. 79 Heversham.

36 CRO, EDC.5 (1634), nos 75, 77 Rochdale.

37 CRO, EDC.5 (1694), no. 24 Chester.

38 CRO, EDC.5 (1663), no. 41 Chester.

39 CRO, EDC.5 (1664), no. 25 Chester.

40 CRO, EDC.5 (1634), no. 77 Rochdale.

41 CRO, EDC.5 (1636), nos 45, 46 Chester.

42 *Statutes of the Realm*, 39, 40 Elizabeth I c.4.

43 CRO, EDC.5 (1613), no. 70 Tarvin.

44 LRO, Western Deaneries Cause Papers ARR.13/4 (1698), no. 58 Bentham.

45 CRO, EDC.5 (1697), no. 59 Bolton-le-Sands.
46 CRO, EDC.5 (1672), no. 18 Woodchurch.
47 CRO, EDC.5 (1603), no. 48 Rochdale.
48 CRO, EDC.5 (1628), no. 27 Rochdale.
49 CRO, EDC.5 (1639), no. 45 Warrington.
50 CRO, EDC.5 (1669), no. 29 Manchester (Blakeley).
51 CRO, EDC.5 (1663), no. 40 Blackburn.
52 CRO, EDC.5 (1640), no. 16 Prestbury.
53 CRO, EDC.5 (1632), no. 25 Manchester.
54 CRO, EDC.5 (1623), no. 47 Winwick.
55 CRO, EDC.5 (1636), no. 38 Budworth Magna.
56 CRO, EDC.5 (1627), no. 10 Congleton.
57 K. Thomas, *Religion and the Decline of Magic*, London, 1971, 502–12.
58 J.A. Sharpe, *Crime in Early Modern England 1550–1750*, London, 1984, 87–8.
59 CRO, EDC.5 (1601), no. 28 Tattenhall.
60 CRO, EDC.5 (1603), no. 27 Stockport.
61 CRO, EDC.5 (1632), no. 32 Egremond.
62 CRO, EDC.5 (1631), no. 34 Chester.
63 CRO, EDC.5 (1625), no. 7 Chester.
64 CRO, EDC.5 (1631), no. 110 Plemondstall.
65 CRO, EDC.5 (1607), no. 25 Clitheroe.
66 CRO, EDC.5 (1608), no. 25 Clitheroe.
67 CRO, EDC.5 (1633), no. 48 Grappenhall.
68 G.B. Harrison, *The Trial of Lancashire Witches*, London, 1929; A. Macfarlane, *Witchcraft in Tudor and Stuart England*, London, 1970.
69 CRO, EDC.5 (1662), no. 63 Nantwich.
70 P. Tyler, 'York witchcraft persecutions 1567–1640', *Northern History*, vol. 4, 1969, 107–8.
71 I. Hulland, 'The Lancashire witch cult', unpubl. B.Ed. dissertation, St John's College, York, 1975.
72 CRO, EDC.5 (1672), no. 40 Hankelow.
73 CRO, EDC.5 (1692), no. 7 Sutton-in-Wirral.

9 FORNICATION, ADULTERY, AND BASTARDY

1 *Letters and Papers*, Henry VII, vol. IV.
2 *Statutes of the Realm*, 3, Elizabeth I c.4.
3 S. Hughes, 'Church and society in seventeenth-century Halifax', unpubl. B.Ed. dissertation, St John's College, York, 1974.
4 M. Spufford, *Contrasting Communities*, London, 1974, 253.
5 Cheshire Record Office (CRO), EDC.5 (1638), no. 7 Lamplugh.
6 C. Hill, *The World Turned Upside Down*, London, 1972, 247.
7 J. Addy, 'Two eighteenth-century bishops and their diocese of Chester 1771–1787', unpubl. Ph.D. thesis, University of Leeds, 1972, 15.

8 CRO, EDC.5 (1633), no. 10 Broughton.
9 Lancashire Record Office (LRO), Western Deaneries Cause Papers ARR.13/4, no. 2 Dalton.
10 G.R. Quaife, *Wanton Wenches and Wayward Wives*, Guildford, 1979, 165.
11 CRO, EDC.5 (1606), no. 35 Coddington.
12 CRO, EDC.5 (1606), no. 63 Rochdale.
13 CRO, EDC.5 (1609), no. 35 Witton.
14 CRO, EDC.5 (1628), no. 28 Manchester.
15 CRO, EDC.5 (1636), no. 42 Manchester.
16 CRO, EDC.5 (1637), no. 111 Eccleston.
17 CRO, EDC.5 (1664), no. 79 Warrington.
18 CRO, EDC.5 (1667), no. 45 Pendleton.
19 CRO, EDC.5 (1676), no. 1 Hale.
20 CRO, EDC.5 (1681), no. 20 Chester (St Mary); kissing is a term used in Chester for sexual intercourse.
21 CRO, EDC.5 (1697), no. 10 Walton.
22 CRO, EDC.5 (1704), no. 3 Bowden.
23 CRO, EDC.5 (1691), no. 18 Whitefield.
24 CRO, EDC.5 (1680), no. 12 Ormskirk.
25 CRO, EDC.5 (1672), no. 5 Budworth; EDC.5 (1671), no. 34 Stoake.
26 CRO, EDC.5 (1677), no. 17 Bunbury.
27 CRO, EDC.5 (1694), no. 4 Wigan.
28 CRO, EDC.5 (1663), no. 50 Macclesfield.
29 CRO, EDC.5 (1666), no. 45 Woolton.
30 CRO, EDC.5 (1672), no. 1 Holt.
31 CRO, EDC.5 (1677), no. 26 Childwall.
32 CRO, EDC.5 (1683), no. 27 Leighton.
33 CRO, EDC.5 (1664), no. 17 Runcorn.
34 CRO, EDC.5 (1607), no. 32 Bowden.
35 CRO, EDC.5 (1671), no. 38 Macclesfield.
36 CRO, EDC.5 (1704), no. 13 Dean.
37 CRO, EDC.5 (1697), no. 14 Doddleston.
38 CRO, EDC.5 (1664), no. 1 Wrenbury.
39 CRO, EDC.5 (1703), no. 11 Newchurch.
40 CRO, EDC.5 (1635), no. 16 Rochdale.
41 CRO, EDC.5 (1663), no. 17 Bredbury.
42 CRO, EDC.5 (1663), no. 49 Sandbach.
43 CRO, EDC.5 (1670), no. 53 Cheadle Heath.
44 CRO, EDC.5 (1611), no. 32 Malpas.
45 CRO, EDC.5 (1631), no. 72 Nantwich.
46 CRO, EDC.5 (1636), no. 128 Warrington.
47 CRO, EDC.5 (1639), no. 118 Over.
48 CRO, EDC.5 (1672), no. 14 Wrenbury.
49 CRO, EDC.5 (1633), no. 7 Blackrod.
50 CRO, EDC.5 (1674), no. 3 Northenden.

51 Quaife, op. cit., 118.
52 CRO, EDC.5 (1667), no. 13 Holt.
53 CRO, EDC.5 (1632), no. 11 Bury.
54 CRO, EDC.5 (1612), no. 4 Chester.
55 Quaife, op. cit., 118–19.
56 CRO, EDC.5 (1630), no. 14 Knutsford.
57 CRO, EDC.5 (1613), no. 7 Stockport.
58 CRO, EDC.5 (1631), no. 33 Budworth.
59 CRO, EDC.5 (1627), no. 36 Liverpool.
60 CRO, EDC.5 (1627). no. 31 Barrow.
61 CRO, EDC.5 (1664), no. 29 Leyland.
62 CRO, EDC.5 (1615), no. 15 Tattenhall.
63 CRO, EDC.5 (1686), no. 10 Nantwich.
64 CRO, EDC.5 (1639), no. 91 Wigan.
65 CRO, EDC.5 (1637), no. 90 Ashton-under-Lyne.
66 CRO, EDC.5 (1607), no. 43 Wigan.
67 CRO, EDC.5 (1623), no. 46 Malpas.
68 CRO, EDC.5 (1631), no. 106 Prescot. (It has not been possible to find what the local measurement was.)
69 CRO, EDC.5 (1712), no. 11 Whitegate.
70 CRO, EDC.5 (1713), no. 5 Chester.
71 CRO, EDC.5 (1703), no. 14 Frodsham.
72 CRO, EDC.5 (1615), no. 37 Marbury.
73 CRO, EDC.5 (1699), no. 2 Whalley.
74 CRO, EDC.5 (1699), no. 11 Chester.
75 CRO, EDC.5 (1635), no. 135 Chester.
76 CRO, EDC.5 (1713), no. 6 Davenham.
77 CRO, EDC.5 (1632), no. 45 Chester.
78 CRO, EDC.5 (1634), nos 24–5, Prestbury.
79 LRO, Western Deaneries Cause Papers, ARR.13/4, no. 65 Woodplumpton.
80 CRO, EDC.5 (1616), no. 6 Chester.
81 CRO, EDC.5 (1633), no. 54 Macclesfield.
82 CRO, EDC.5 (1609), no. 17 Blackburn.
83 CRO, EDC.5 (1634), no. 18 Chester.
84 CRO, EDC.5 (1637), no. 80 Wigan.
85 F.G. Emmison, *Elizabethan Life, Morals and the Church Courts*, Chelmsford, 1963, 31–6.
86 W. Shakespeare, *Timon of Athens*, IV. iii.86; *Comedy of Errors*, IV. iii.58.
87 G. de Chauliac, *Chirugia Magna 1363*, Early English Text Society, no. 265, 1971.
88 CRO, EDC.5 (1604), no. 59 Nantwich.
89 CRO, EDC.5 (1604), no. 8 Chester.
90 CRO, EDC.5 (1608), no. 13 Audlem.
91 CRO, EDC.5 (1637), no. 87 Macclesfield.
92 CRO, EDC.5 (1604), no. 4 Chester.

93 CRO, EDC.5 (1638), no. 23 Backford.
94 CRO, EDC.5 (1664), no. 24 Chester.
95 CRO, EDC.5 (1698), no. 16 Ditton.
96 CRO, EDC.5 (1693), no. 17 Barthomley.
97 CRO, EDC.5 (1639), no. 21 Whalley.
98 CRO, EDC.5 (1608), no. 67 Rochdale.
99 CRO, EDC.5 (1608), no. 66 Rochdale.
100 CRO, EDC.5 (1704), no. 7 Winwick.
101 CRO, EDC.5 (1679), no. 6 Tarporley.
102 CRO, EDC.5 (1638), no. 128 Chester.
103 CRO, EDC.5 (1639), no. 10 Chester.
104 CRO, EDC.5 (1635), no. 114 Wybunbury.
105 CRO, EDC.5 (1635), no. 72 Rochdale.
106 CRO, EDC.5 (1638), no. 60 Barrow.
107 CRO, EDC.5 (1604), no. 52 Malpas.
108 Borthwick Institute of Historical Research (BIHR), Cause Papers CP.I.342 Giggleswick.
109 LRO, Richmond Comperta Books, 1665–1699, ARR/37.
110 CRO, EDC.5 (1683), no. 22 Chester.
111 CRO, EDC.5 (1624), no. 23 Marbury.
112 CRO, EDC.5 (1630), no. 69 Stockport.
113 CRO, EDC.5 (1638), no. 4 Clapham.
114 CRO, EDC.5 (1624), no. 23 Bunbury.
115 CRO, EDC.5 (1633), no. 38 Waverton.

10 CHILD MARRIAGES

1 J.R.H. Moorman, *Church Life in England in the Thirteenth Century*, Cambridge 1946, 85–6.
2 L.A. Smith, *Church and State in the Middle Ages*, London, 1913, 61.
3 J. Addy, 'The archdeacon and ecclesiastical discipline in the County of York 1559–1714', unpubl. M.A. thesis, University of Leeds, 1960, 109.
4 Borthwick Institute of Historical Research (BIHR), Cause Papers CP.H.1319.
5 Statutes of the Realm, Lord Hardwicke's Marriage Act 1752.
6 Leeds District Archives (LDA), Archdeacon of Richmond v Dean of Middleham RDA/6, 655ff.
7 *Report on the Canon Law of the Church of England*, London, 1947, 125–53.
8 G.R. Quaife, *Wanton Wenches and Wayward Wives*, Guildford, 1979, 38–41.
9 C. Hill, *The World Turned Upside Down*, London, 1972, 248.
10 Addy, op. cit., 96.
11 Hill, op. cit., ch.15, *passim*.
12 C. Haigh, *Reformation and Resistance in Tudor Lancashire*, Cambridge, 1975, 47–50.

13 F.J. Furnival, *Child Marriages, Divorce and Ratification in Chester Diocese*, Early English Text Society, 1897.
14 P. Laslett, *The World We Have Lost*, London, 1983, 83–6.
15 Cheshire Record Office (CRO), EDC.5 (1600–1700), classified by year.
16 CRO, EDC.5 (1663), no. 38 Christleton.
17 CRO, EDC.5 (1680), no. 17 Stidd.
18 CRO, EDC.5 (1667), no. 16 Doddleston.
19 CRO, EDC.5 (1673), no. 15 Tottington.
20 CRO, EDC.5 (1628), no. 48 Prescot.
21 CRO, EDC.5 (1626), no. 16 Cartmel.
22 CRO, EDC.5 (1615), no. 27 Preston.
23 CRO, EDC.5 (1610), no. 15 Woodchurch.
24 CRO, EDC.5 (1634), no. 14 Doddleston.

11 MATRIMONIAL CONTRACTS AND DISPUTES

1 Leeds District Archives, Consistory Court Causes RD/AC/1/2, no. 66 East Witton.
2 Cheshire Record Office (CRO), EDC.5 (1623), no. 14 Manchester.
3 CRO, EDC.5 (1623), no. 14 Manchester.
4 CRO, EDC.5 (1608), no. 23, Middlewich.
5 CRO, EDC.5 (1625), no. 10 Colne.
6 CRO, EDC.5 (1600), no. 12 Holt.
7 CRO, EDC.5 (1672), no. 4 Adlington.
8 CRO, EDC.5 (1668), no. 17 Broughton.
9 S. Hughes, 'Church and society in seventeenth-century Halifax', unpubl. B.Ed. dissertation, St John's College, York, 1974, 67.
10 ibid., 68.
11 ibid.

12 CLANDESTINE MARRIAGES AND DIVORCE

1 W. Atthill, *Documents Relating to the Church of Middleham*, Camden Society, o.s., vol. 38, 1847.
2 Leeds District Archives (LDA), RD/C/6, 15: RD/C/10, 20.
3 LDA, RD/C/2, 10.
4 LDA, RD/C/2, 42.
5 LDA, Consistory Court Causes RD/AC/1/4, no. 34 Thornton Steward.
6 Cheshire Record Office (CRO), EDC.5 (1690), no. 2 Warrington.
7 CRO, EDC.5 (1638), no. 4 Clapham.
8 CRO, EDC.5 (1628), no. 6 Tarvin.
9 CRO, EDC.5 (1637), no. 78 Wigan.
10 CRO, EDC.5 (1669), no. 3 Christleton.
11 CRO, EDC.5 (1613), no. 46 Macclesfield; EDC.5 (1669), no. 3 Christleton.

12 CRO, EDC.5 (1671), no. 15 Sephton.
13 CRO, EDC.5 (1690), no. 5 Winwick.
14 F.G. Emmison, *Elizabethan Life, Morals and the Church Courts*, Chelmsford, 1963, 36.
15 CRO, EDC.5 (1692), no. 8 Leyland.
16 CRO, EDC.5 (1692), no. 19, (1693), no. 14 Accrington.
17 CRO, EDC.5 (1669), no. 18 Whitegate.
18 CRO, EDC.5 (1603), no. 11 Chester.
19 CRO, EDC.5 (1703), no. 6 Manchester.
20 CRO, EDC.5 (1638), no. 125 Rochdale.
21 CRO, EDC.5 (1675), no. 15 Dunham.
22 CRO, EDC.5 (1617), no. 23 Sandbach.
23 CRO, EDC.5 (1632), no. 77 Sandbach.
24 CRO, EDC.5 (1639), no. 65 Mobberley.
25 CRO, EDC.5 (1634), no. 39 Runcorn.
26 CRO, EDC.5 (1632), no. 85 Tattenhall.
27 CRO, EDC.5 (1633), no. 18 Prescot.
28 CRO, EDC.5 (1636), no. 10 Nantwich.
29 CRO, EDC.5 (1640), no. 80 Marbury.
30 CRO, EDC.5 (1601), no. 49 Winwick.
31 CRO, EDC.5 (1604), no. 72 Leigh.
32 CRO, EDC.5 (1623), no. 40 Walton.
33 CRO, EDC.5 (1681), no. 13 Upholland.
34 J. Addy, 'The archdeacon and ecclesiastical discipline in the County of York 1559–1714', unpubl. M.A. Thesis, University of Leeds, 1960. Shovel board or shove groat was one of the games prohibited by the Statute of 33, Henry VIII. A shove groat shilling is mentioned in Shakespeare's *2 Henry IV*. The shove groat is supposed to have consisted of a piece of polished metal used in the game of shovel board which was popular in alehouses and taverns.
35 CRO, EDC.5 (1625), no. 8 Chester.

13 THE ATTITUDES OF SOCIETY

1 C. Hill, *Puritanism and Society in Pre-Revolutionary England*, London, 1964, 309.
2 J.R.H. Moorman, *Church Life in England in the Thirteenth Century*, Cambridge, 1946, 206–10.
3 J.A. Sharpe, *Crime in Early Modern England 1550–1750*, London, 1984, 65ff.
4 P. Tyler, *The Ecclesiastical Commission 1560–1600*, Wakefield, 1966; Borthwick Institute of Historical Research (BIHR), High Commission Act Book, HCAB.19 f.189V.
5 W.H.D. Longstaffe (ed.), *Acts of the High Commission in Durham*, Surtees Society, vol. 34, 1858, 62–4.
6 Hill, op. cit., 323.
7 C.A. Richie, *The Ecclesiastical Courts of York*, Arbroath, 1953.

8 R.A. Marchant, *Puritans and the Church Courts 1560–1640*, London, 1960, 93, 106.

9 C. Hill, *Economic Problems of the Church*, Oxford, 1956; J. Addy, 'Tithe disputes in north Lancashire', *Lancashire Local Historian*, 1983, 26.

10 C. Hill, *Puritanism and Society*, 331 n.2.

11 C. Hill, ibid., 342.

12 C. Hill, ibid., 343.

13 Statutes of the Realm 14 Charles II c.4.

14 Cheshire Record Office (CRO), EDC.5 (1628), no. 48 Tarvin.

15 CRO, EDC.5 (1613), no. 4 Chester.

16 CRO, EDC.5 (1609), no. 2 Chester.

17 CRO, EDC.5 (1631), no. 13 Rochdale.

18 R. Hill, 'Theory and practice of excommunication in medieval England', *History*, no.144, 1941, 1–8.

19 Leeds District Archives (LDA), Commissary's Act Book RD/A/5 n.f. 1668–74.

20 LDA, Richmond Comperta Book RD/C/5 f.38.

21 F.G. Emmison, *Elizabethan Life, Morals and the Church Courts*, Chelmsford, 1963, 305.

22 Emmison, op. cit., 281–91.

23 LDA, Consistory Court Causes RD/AC/1/7 Forcett.

24 LDA, Commissary's Act Book RD/A/6 f.21. 1610.

25 LDA, Commissary's Act Book RD/A/6 f.21v; the Latin of the court order has been translated.

26 LDA Commissary's Act Book RD/A/6 f.21.

27 CRO, EDC.5 (1612), no. 49 Bowden.

28 BIHR, Churchwardens' Presentments and Letters Y/V Misc.

29 LDA Commissary's Act Book RD/A/4 f.4; Absolutions RD/AB/10; Excommunications RD/CB/9.

30 Lancashire Record Office (LRO), Penances RD/WD/1c (temporary reference); CRO, EDC.5 (1625), no. 67.

31 BIHR, Churchwardens' Presentments and Letters Y/V Misc.

32 LDA, Apparitors' Letters RD/C/1 no. 15.

33 LDA, Apparitors' Letters RD/C/1 nos 6, 7.

34 LDA, Apparitors' Letters RD/C/1 nos 25, 26.

35 *North Riding Sessions Records*, vol. 2, 1884, 171.

36 CRO, EDC.5 (1698), n.f. Visitation Court Book.

37 CRO, EDC.5 (1621), no. 66 Winwick.

38 CRO, EDC.5 (1633), no. 56 Manchester.

39 T. Hale, 'Elizabethan penances in the Diocese of Ely', *Transactions of the Royal Historical Society*, 3rd series, vol. 1, 263–9.

40 Bodleian Library, Tanner MSS 152, f. 62 ff.

41 BIHR, Precedent Papers PN.21.

42 BIHR, Cause Papers CP.H.3587.

43 Emmison, op. cit., 307–13.

44 CRO, EDC.5 (1633), no. 2 Brindle.

45 J. Addy (ed.), *The Diary of Henry Prescott*, vol. 1: *1704–1710*, Lancashire and Cheshire Record Society, no. 127, 1987, 65.

46 BIHR, Churchwardens' Presentments and Letters Y/V Misc. (1690).

47 ibid. (1700).

48 ibid. (1684).

49 ibid. (1705) Leeds.

50 ibid. (1693) Bradford.

51 ibid. (1684, 1690, 1699).

52 G.R. Quaife, *Wanton Wenches and Wayward Wives*, Guildford, 1979, 245.

14 THE DECLINE OF THE COURTS

1 F.S. Hockaday, 'The consistory courts of the Diocese of Gloucester', *Transactions of Bristol and Gloucester Archaeological Society*, vol. xvi, 1924, 195–287.

2 *Proposals for a National Reformation of Manners*, Bodleian Library, Firth E.25, no. 8.

3 M.G. Smith, 'Administration of the Diocese of Exeter 1689–1707', unpubl. Oxford B.D. thesis, 1980, 84–90.

4 B.D. Till, 'The ecclesiastical courts at York 1660–1693: a study in decline', unpubl. typescript at Borthwick Institute, 68–9.

5 Lancashire Record Office (LRO), Western Deaneries Cause Papers ARR.13/10 Tithe Causes.

6 Stamp Act 10 Anne.

7 Wake Manuscripts, Christ Church Library, Oxford, vol. xvii, f.239.

8 S.L. Ollard and P.C. Walker (eds), *Archbishop Herring's Visitation Returns 1743*, vols iii and iv, Yorkshire Archaeological Society Record Series, vols 75 and 77, 1929, 1930.

9 LRO, Kendal Comperta Book ARR/37/1708 (Old Hutton Chapel).

10 Leeds District Archives (LDA), Richmond Comperta Book RD/C/18, 5 (Pickhill).

11 J.A. Sharpe, *Crime in Early Modern England 1550–1750*, London, 1984, 154ff.

12 Borthwick Institute of Historical Research (BIHR), Hexham Peculiar Records HEX2.

13 G.M.Trevelyan, *Blenheim*, London, 1936, 6.

14 LRO, Richmond Comperta Books ARR/37 1707–1734 *passim*.

15 C. Hill, *Change and Continuity in Seventeenth-Century England*, London, 1974, 284.

BIBLIOGRAPHY

UNPUBLISHED SOURCES

Bodleian Library, Oxford

Firth E.25 No. 8
Tanner MSS 144, 152

Borthwick Institute of Historical Research, York

Archbishop Grindal's Register R.30
Archdeacon of York's Court Book Y/V1613, Y/V1691, Y/V1664–1670
Bishopthorpe Papers RBp.6B
Cause Papers CP.G.1817, CP.H.427, CP.H.1431, CP.H.1319,
    CP.H.3587, CP.H.4378, CP.H.4499, CP.I.342, CP.I.360,
    HC.CP.1634/5
Cause Papers R/AS.21B/96
Churchwardens' Presentments and Letters Y/V.Miscellaneous
Hexham Peculiar Records HEX2
High Commission Act Books HCAB.17, 18, 19
Precedent Papers PN.21, PL.113
Transmissions on Appeal CP.1700/1
Visitation Court Books V.1578, V.1579, V.1595, V.1627, V.1632–3,
    V.1637, V.1662–3, V.1684

Cheshire Record Office

Articles Preparatory to Visitation EDV.7/2
Bishop's Register EDA.2/7
Consistory Court Act Books EDC.1–100
Consistory Court Causes EDC.5 1600–1720
Correction Court Books EDV1/13–38
Precedent Books EDR/1, EDR/2, EDR/6

BIBLIOGRAPHY

Cumbria Record Office

Parish Papers CDR.10

Lancashire Record Office

Consistory Court Act Book ARR/12
Parish Papers DR.Ch.37
Penances RD/WD/1c (temporary reference)
Return of Poor Livings to Queen Anne's Bounty 1711 WD/1A
    (temporary reference)
Richmond Comperta Books (Western Deaneries) ARR/15, ARR/37
Valuation of Livings 1714 WD/B/1 (temporary reference)
Western Deaneries Cause Papers ARR.13/4, ARR.13/10, ARR.13/11

Leeds District Archives

Absolutions RD/AB/10
Apparitors' Letters RD/C/1
Archdeacon of Richmond v Dean of Middleham RDA/6
Churchwardens' Presentments RD/CB/8
Citations RD/AB/2/1
Commissary's Act Books RD/A/1-6
Consistory Court Causes RD/AC/1-7
Depositions RD/AC/5
Excommunications RD/CB/9
Faculty Book RD/RF/D
Mandates and Commissions RD/RA
Masham Peculiar Records MP.29
Parish Papers CD/PB/1-9
Probate Act Book RD/PB/8
Richmond Comperta Books RD/C/1-18
Richmondshire Wills

West Yorkshire Record Office

Cawthorne Churchwardens Accounts

OTHER REFERENCES

Addy, J., 'The archdeacon and ecclesiastical discipline in the county of
    York 1559–1714', unpubl. M.A. thesis, University of Leeds,
    1960.
Addy, J., *The Archdeacon and Ecclesiastical Discipline 1559–1714*, York,
    1963.
Addy, J., 'Two eighteenth-century bishops and their diocese of Chester
    1771–1787', unpubl. Ph.D. thesis, University of Leeds, 1972.

Addy, J., 'Tithe disputes in north Lancashire', *Lancashire Local Historian*, 1983.

Addy, J. (ed.), *The Diary of Henry Prescott*, vol. 1: *1704–1710*, Lancashire and Cheshire Record Society, no. 127, 1987.

Atkinson, J.C. (ed.), *North Riding Quarter Sessions Records*, vols 1–2, 1884–6.

Atthill, W., *Documents Relating to the Church of Middleham*, Camden Society, o.s., vol. 38, 1847.

Bainbridge, T.A., 'Wesley's travels in Westmorland and Lancashire', *Transactions of the Cumberland and Westmorland Archaeological Society*, vol. 52, 1952.

Best, G.F.A., *Temporal Pillars*, Cambridge, 1964.

Bouch, C.M.L., *Prelates and People of the Lake Counties*, Kendal, 1948.

Bouch, C.M.L. and Jones, G.P., *A Short Social and Economic History of the Lake Counties 1500–1600*, Manchester, 1962.

Brown, R. Steward (ed.), *Lancashire and Cheshire Star Chamber Cases*, Lancashire and Cheshire Record Society, vol. 71, 1916.

Brown, W. (ed.), *Register of Thomas Corbridge*, Surtees Society, vol. 138, 1925.

Brown, W. (ed.), *Yorkshire Star Chamber Cases*, Yorkshire Archaeological Society Record Series, vols 41, 45, 51, 70, 1909, 1911, 1914, 1916.

Calendar, State Papers and Domestic, Elizabeth I, vol. 240.

Chauliac, G de, *Chirugia Magna 1363*, Early English Text Society, no. 265, 1971.

Clark, P.A., *The English Alehouse*, Leicester, 1983.

Consett, H., *Practice of the Spiritual Courts*, London, 1708.

Costin, W.C. and Watson, J.S., *The Law and Working of the Constitution*, vol. 1, London, 1967.

Dickens, A.G., 'The first stages of Romanist recusancy in Yorkshire 1560–1590', *Yorkshire Archaeological Society Journal*, no. 35, 1943.

Earwaker, J.P., *East Cheshire*, London, 1877.

Eliot, T.S., *Murder in the Cathedral*, London, 1936.

Emmison, F.G., *Elizabethan Life, Morals and the Church Courts*, Chelmsford, 1963.

Fisher, J., *History of Masham*, London, 1865.

Furnival, F.J., *Child Marriages, Divorce and Ratification in Chester Diocese*, Early English Text Society, 1897.

Green, I.M., *The Re-Establishment of the Church of England 1660–1662*, Oxford, 1978.

Haigh, C., *Reformation and Resistance in Tudor Lancashire*, Cambridge, 1975.

Hair, P., *Before the Bawdy Courts*, London, 1972.

Hale, T., 'Elizabethan penances in the Diocese of Ely', *Transactions of the Royal Historical Society*, 3rd series, vol. 1, 1907.

Harland, J. (ed.), *Lancashire Lieutenancy under the Tudors and Stuarts*, Chetham Society, vol. 2, 1859.

Harrison, G.B., *The Trial of Lancashire Witches*, London, 1929.

Hart, A. Tindal, *Country Clergy in Elizabethan and Stuart Times*, London, 1958.

Hazeltine, H.D., 'Roman and canon law in the Middle Ages', *Cambridge Medieval History*, vol. 5, ch.21, 1966.

Hill, C., *Economic Problems of the Church*, Oxford, 1956.

Hill, C., *Puritanism and Society in Pre-Revolutionary England*, London, 1964.

Hill, C., *The World Turned Upside Down*, London, 1972.

Hill, C., *Change and Continuity in Seventeenth-Century England*, London, 1974.

Hill, C., 'Puritans and the dark corners of the land', *Transactions of the Royal Historical Society*, 5th series, vol. 13, 1963, 77–102.

Hill, R., 'Theory and practice of excommunication in medieval England', *History*, no. 144, 1941.

Hill, R.M.T., *Register of William Melton 1317–1340*, Canterbury and York Society, vol. 1, no. 147, 1976.

Hockaday, F.S., 'The consistory courts of the Diocese of Gloucester', *Transactions of Bristol and Gloucester Archaeological Society*, vol. 16, 1924, 194–287.

Houlbrook, R., 'Decline of ecclesiastical jurisdiction', in R. O'Day and F. Heal (eds.), *Continuity and Change*, Leicester, 1976.

Hughes, S., 'Church and society in seventeenth-century Halifax', unpubl. B.Ed. dissertation, St John's College, York. (Copy in Calderdale Central Library, Halifax.)

Hulland, I., 'The Lancashire witch cult', unpubl. B.Ed. dissertation, St John's College, York, 1975.

Irvine, W.F., 'Church discipline after the Restoration', *Transactions of the Historic Society of Lancashire and Cheshire*, vol. 64, 1912.

Jordan, W.K., *The Charities of Rural England*, London, 1961.

Kay, M.M., *History of Rivington and Blackrod Grammar School*, Manchester, 1966.

Laslett, P., *The World We Have Lost*, London, 1983.

Longstaffe, W.H.D (ed.), *Acts of the High Commission in Durham*, Surtees Society, vol. 34, 1858.

Lynwood, *Provinciale*, Book III Tit,xxviii, 1912.

Macfarlane, A., *Witchcraft in Tudor and Stuart England*, London, 1970.

Mansi, J., *Acta Conciliorum*, Venice, 1798, vol. vii.

Marchant, R.A., *Puritans and the Church Courts 1560–1640*, London, 1960.

Moorman, J.R.H., *Church Life in England in the Thirteenth Century*, Cambridge, 1946.

Morris, R.H., *Chester Diocesan History*, London, 1895.

Nicholson, W., *Miscellany Accounts of the Diocese of Carlisle*, ed. R.S. Fergusson, Cumberland and Westmorland Archaeological Society, extra series, vol. 1, 1877.

Ollard, S.L. and Walker, P.C. (eds), *Archbishop Herring's Visitation*

Returns 1743, Yorkshire Archaeological Society Record Series, vols. 75, 77, 1929, 1930.

Ormsby, G., *Correspondence of John Cosin*, Surtees Society, vols 52, 55, 1869, 1872.

Oughton, T., *Ordo Iudiciorum*, London, 1738.

Perkins, H., 'The social causes of the Industrial Revolution', *Transactions of the Royal Historical Society*, 5th series, vol. 18, 1968, 123–41.

Prideaux, H., *Directions to Churchwardens*, London, 1692.

Proctor, F. and Frere, W.H., *A New History of the Book of Common Prayer*, London, 1901.

Purvis, J.S., *Introduction to Ecclesiastical Records*, York, 1955.

Quaife, G.R., *Wanton Wenches and Wayward Wives*, Guildford, 1979.

Randolph's Poems, London, 1646.

Report on the Canon Law of the Church of England, London, 1947.

Richie, C.A., *The Ecclesiastical Courts of York*, Arbroath, 1953.

Salter, H.E., *Medieval Oxford*, Oxford Historical Society, vol. 100, 1936.

Sharpe, J.A., *Crime in Early Modern England 1550–1750*, London, 1984.

Sharpe, J.A., *Defamation and Sexual Slander in Early Modern England*, Borthwick Paper no. 58, York, 1982.

Smith, L.A., *Church and State in the Middle Ages*, London, 1913.

Smith, M.G., *Pastoral Discipline and the Church Courts: the Hexham Court 1680–1730*, York, 1982.

Smith, M.G., 'Administration of the Diocese of Exeter 1689–1707', unpubl. Oxford B.D. thesis, 1975.

Society for Promoting Christian Knowledge, *Canons and Homilies 1604*, London, 1871.

Spufford, M., *Contrasting Communities*, London, 1974.

Strype, J., *Life of Grindal*, London, 1821.

Stubbs, P., *Anatomie of Abuses*, London, 1583, reprint 1870, ed. J. Connor.

Tate, W.E., *The Parish Chest*, Cambridge, 1969.

Tate, W.E. and Wallis, P., 'A register of old Yorkshire grammar schools', *Researches and Studies*, vol. 13, Leeds University, 1956.

Thacker, A.T., 'The Chester Diocesan Records and the local historian', *Transactions of the Historic Society of Lancashire and Cheshire*, vol. 130, 1981.

Thomas, K., *Religion and the Decline of Magic*, London, 1971.

Till, B.D., 'The ecclesiastical courts at York 1660–1693: a study in decline', unpubl. typescript at Borthwick Institute, 1963.

Trevelyan, G.M., *Blenheim*, London, 1936.

Turner, J. Horsfall (ed.), *Diaries of Oliver Heywood*, Brighouse, 1881.

Tyler, P., *The Ecclesiastical Commission 1560–1600*, Wakefield, 1966.

Tyler, P., 'York witchcraft persecutions 1567–1640', *Northern History*, vol. 4, 1969.

Vincent, W.A.L., *The State and School Education 1640–1660*, London, 1950.

Walker, F., 'Historical geography of south-west Lancashire before the Industrial Revolution', *Chetham Society*, n.s., vol. 103, 1939.

Wallis, P., 'A register of old schools in Lancashire and Cheshire', *Transactions of the Historic Society of Lancashire and Cheshire*, vol. 120, 1968.

Warne, A., *Church and Society in Eighteenth-Century Devon*, Newton Abbot, 1969.

Whiteman, A.E.O., 'The re-establishment of the Church of England 1660–1662', *Transactions of the Royal Historical Society*, 5th series, vol. 5, 1955, 111–51.

Whiting, C.E., *Studies in English Puritanism*, London, 1931.

INDEX

243